Vespers

*I know the night is near
at hand:*

*The mists lie low on hill
and bay,*

*The autumn sheanes are
dewless, dry:*

But I have had the day.

*Yes, I have had, dear Lord,
the day:*

*When at Thy call I have
the night,*

*Brief be the twilight
as I pass*

*From light to dark
to light.*

Joe Kotcka

284E

DESIGN COPR. 1955 DEVOTIONAL PUBLISHING CO. LITHO IN U.S.A.

BEHIND THE RAPE OF HUNGARY

Behind the
RAPE OF HUNGARY

by

FRANÇOIS FEJTÖ

Foreword by

JEAN-PAUL SARTRE

David McKay Company, Inc.

New York

FOREWORD

I AM happy to write these few lines for the first page of your book: you are giving me the opportunity of restating, as so many Frenchmen have done before me, our deep feelings of solidarity with your nation, our respect for its sufferings, and our admiration for its courage. But it would be pointless to introduce you to a public already familiar with your *Histoire des Démocraties Populaires:* this book is justly esteemed as being the only true source of light on those countries so close to us, and yet so mysterious for the last ten years. In the name of all of us who have been impressed by your profound insight into social problems, and who, thanks to you, have for the first time understood the economic contradictions against which these new societies are struggling, may I tell you that your most precious quality is the objectivity of your approach? This objectivity is the result of your perspicacity and knowledge, but it is also a mark of your self-control. It is difficult, almost impossible, for an exile to be impartial. Yet you have decided to be impartial, and you have succeeded. How lucky we have been to find your book in the midst of so many works variously motivated, but all equally suspect, some celebrating the Eastern regimes, and others condemning them. This time you speak to us only about Hungary, and yet, despite everything you have felt since October 23, 1956, you have preserved the same distance—which is not aloofness, but an ardent wish to understand and to inform. Before having your manuscript in hand, I read in periodicals several of your studies and articles which give a foretaste of this book. Despite your constant effort to

v

tell the truth without unnecessary pathos, they moved me deeply because they gave expression to your hopes—as did the remarkable article you wrote on the Writers' Union and the Petofi Society—and a little later, to your anxieties. I experienced with you, and thanks to you, the tragedy of your people; the readers of the present book will be able to re-experience it in its entirety. Thanks to you they will understand the daily struggle and the courage of these workers and these intellectuals, many of whom are dead today. The long chain of events, which on two occasions, in 1953 and in 1956, might have terminated with the emergence of the Hungarian people from the night of oppression, and which has led this people back into blood, mud, and darkness, will seem to them like a terrible fate. But all this is not in vain, all this blood that has been shed will not be wasted: we see emerging from the ruins a new proletariat, hardened, conscious of its strength, possessing its organs of self-defense, and compelling Kadar to negotiate with it. These new men, whose existence you had the merit of announcing in your first book, will resume the struggle by other means, under different forms; they will not permit the process of democratization to be halted; and thanks to you we shall follow their efforts. In this sense your present book seems to me particularly valuable: it informs, hence it brings us closer to the events. In this age of confusion, lies, and violence, what we need above all is what you give us about Hungary—the truth.

JEAN-PAUL SARTRE

CONTENTS

vii

Chronology of Principal Events in Hungary from Liberation to 1956

1944

Dec. 22   Provisional government is formed under General Bela Miklos.
Hungary declares war on Germany.

1945

Jan. 20   Delegates of provisional government sign armistice in Moscow.

Jan. 30   Matyas Rakosi arrives from Moscow.

Feb. 13   Budapest is liberated.

March 15   Agrarian reform becomes operative.

Apr. 4   Liberation of Hungary is completed.

Aug. 4   National minorities are granted equal rights.

Nov. 4   General elections (Smallholders party obtains 57.5 per cent of all votes).

Nov. 15   First coalition government is formed. Rakosi appointed vice-premier.

Dec. 6   Nationalization of mines.

1946

Feb. 1   Hungary is proclaimed a republic.

Mar. 1   The pastor Zoltan Tildy is elected first President of the Republic.

May to July   Inflation assumes catastrophic proportions.

Aug. 1   Creation of new currency (the florin).

Nov. 25   Nationalization of heavy industry.

1947

Feb. 10	Peace treaty is signed.
Mar. 7	The Communists open drive for power.
	Formation of bloc of left, which includes Communists, Social Democrats, peasant nationalists, and trade-unions.
	Workers and peasants multiply demonstrations.
May 28	Nationalization of banks.
	Bela Kovacs, secretary of Smallholders party, former member of anti-German underground, is arrested by the Soviet police, after Hungarian police refuse to proceed against him.
May 30	Ferenc Nagy, president of Smallholders party, is charged with conspiracy and forced to resign. His place is taken by Lajos Dinnyes, who adopts a policy of close co-operation with Communists.
July 22	Dissolution of Sulyok's extreme-right party.
July 29	Formation of new extreme-right party under Pfeiffer.
Aug. 1	Three-Year Plan drawn up by Erno Gero becomes operative.
Aug. 31	General elections (Communists obtain 22.4 per cent of votes).
Sept. 15	Peace treaty is ratified. Last meeting of Allied Control Commission.
Nov. 4	Discovery of alleged plot hatched by reactionaries and right-wing Socialists—Pfeiffer, Sulyok, Peyer.
Nov. 28	Nationalization of aluminum industry.
Dec. 8	Treaty of friendship and mutual assistance concluded with Yugoslavia.

1948

Jan. 24	Treaty of friendship and mutual assistance with Romania.

Feb. 18	Treaty of friendship and mutual assistance between Hungary and Soviet Union is signed in Moscow.
Mar. 2	Purge of Social Democratic party.
Mar. 25	Nationalization of enterprises employing more than one hundred workers.
June 11	Nationalization of religious schools.
June 13	Merger of Communist and Social Democratic parties.
June 18	Treaty of friendship and mutual assistance with Poland is signed in Warsaw.
July 6	Treaty of friendship and mutual assistance with Bulgaria is signed in Sofia.
July 30	President Tildy, compromised by his son-in-law, Victor Chornoky, Hungarian envoy in Cairo, resigns.
Aug. 3	Arpad Szakasits (leftist Socialist) is elected President.
Nov. 26	Maort (branch of Standard Oil) is put on trial.
Dec. 4	Miklos Nyarady, minister of finance (member of the Smallholders party), on trip abroad goes over to *émigré* camp.
Dec. 7	Execution of Victor Chornoky, convicted of espionage.
Dec. 9	Premier Lajos Dinnyes resigns as a result of the Nyarady affair.
Dec. 10	Istvan Dobi, leader of left wing of Smallholders, is appointed new premier.
Dec. 26	Cardinal Mindszenty is arrested.

1949

Feb. 9	Mindszenty is sentenced to life imprisonment.
Apr. 16	Treaty of friendship and mutual assistance with Czechoslovakia.
May 15	General elections (single list of coalition parties).
June 11	Dobi government is reshuffled; Ladislas Rajk, foreign minister, disappears, and is replaced by Gyula Kallai.

June 18	Ladislas Rajk is arrested.
Aug. 20	New constitution becomes operative.
Aug. 23	Election of Presidium. Arpad Szakasits becomes chairman of Presidium.
Sept. 16 to 24	Rajk trial.
Oct. 15	Rajk is executed.
Dec. 10	Parliament approves Five-Year Plan.
Dec. 28	Nationalization of factories employing more than ten workers or belonging to foreigners.
Dec. 31	Three-Year Plan is completed five months ahead of schedule.

1950

Jan. 1	Five-Year Plan becomes operative.
Feb. 17 to 21	Trials of Vogeler and Sanders.
Apr. 24	Arpad Szakasits resigns and is arrested.
May 8	Sandor Ronai is elected new chairman of Presidium.
June 12	Dissolution of Free Mason lodges.
Aug. 30	Agreement between government and Catholic Church.
Sept. 7	Dissolution of religious orders.

1951

Jan. 19	Travel restrictions are imposed on foreign diplomats in Budapest.
Apr. 15	Bread is rationed.
Apr. 17	Duties of janitors in surveillance of tenants are specified in decree.
May 17	Five-Year Plan is revised, investments are increased from 50 to 85 billion florins.
June 1 to 15	Part of Budapest population deported.
June 22	Trial of Groesz, deputy primate of Hungary.
July 7	Decree on protection of state secrets.
July 21	Episcopate swears allegiance to republic and constitution.
Dec. 1	Rationing is abolished, prices are raised.

Dec. 6   Government publishes White Book on American hostile activities against Hungary.

Dec. 16   Statue of Stalin, eight meters high, is unveiled at Budapest.

1952

Feb. 19   Nationalization of apartment houses.

June 28   Note to Yugoslavia charges Yugoslav army with fifty-five violations committed in three months.

Aug. 14   Matyas Rakosi is appointed premier. Istvan Dobi is elected chairman of Presidium.

Dec. 30   Hungary leaves UNESCO.

1953

Jan. 20   Last installment of war debts is paid by Hungary to Russia.

May 17   Legislative elections (single list of Popular Front).

June 28   Workers' [Communist] party is reorganized; secretary general is replaced by three-man secretariat, Rakosi becomes first secretary.

July 2   Rakosi government resigns.

July 4   Formation of Imre Nagy government, which announces inauguration of new policy.

July 26   Amnesty, abolition of internment camps and deportation orders.

Aug. 28   Agreement with Yugoslavia concerning the settlement of border incidents.

Sept. 14   Cabinet reduces heavy industry investments and increases light industry investments. Subsidies to food industries are increased by 50 per cent.

December   Series of measures aimed at remedying inadequacy of food deliveries.

1954

Jan. 23   In a speech before Parliament Imre Nagy advocates higher standards of living and economic relations with capitalist countries.

Mar. 12   Gabor Peter, former chief of people's police, is sentenced to life imprisonment.

May 29   Formation of new Popular Front.

Oct. 14   Istvan Kovacs, first secretary of Budapest Communist party organization, announces rehabilitation of "those unjustly convicted."

Nov. 29   Matyas Rakosi returns to Budapest after two months in U.S.S.R.

1955

Jan. 25   Rakosi insists on need for industrialization.

February   Political turn in favor of Rakosi.

Mar. 2 to 4   Meeting of Central Committee of Workers' party.

Mar. 9   Publication of Central Committee resolutions charging Imre Nagy with rightist deviationism and anti-Marxist opportunism; describing the decisions of June, 1953, as correct, but as having been distorted; and declaring that welfare of the people can be achieved only by giving priority to heavy industry.

Apr. 3   Large-scale amnesty for political refugees.

Apr. 18   Imre Nagy is expelled from Politburo and party. Andras Hegedus replaces him as premier.

June 14   *Szabad Nep,* party organ, comes out against the neutrality of the people's democracies.

July 16   Communiqué announces release of Mindszenty, but release does not take place.

Oct. 14   Msgr. Groesz is released from prison.

Dec. 14   Revolt of Communist writers against the party; several members resign from executive board of Writers' Union. Hungary admitted to UN.

1956

Jan. 21   Border agreement with Yugoslavia.

Jan. 22   Hungarian government grants passports to refugees wishing to stay abroad.

Feb. 25	Release of nine codefendants of Mindszenty.
Mar. 15	Rakosi condemns personality cult.
Mar. 29	Rakosi announces rehabilitation of Rajk.
April	Former Socialists, Zoltan Tildy and Bela Kovacs are released from prison.
May 12	Msgr. Groesz restored to office of president of Bishops Council.
May 18	Auto-criticism of Rakosi.
June 16	Popular Front is reorganized.
June 19	Meeting of journalists demands restoration of freedom of press.
July 8	Writers Dery and Tardos are expelled from the party. Large-scale amnesty and rehabilitations.
July 18	Rakosi resigns from Politburo. Erno Gero is appointed first party secretary. Politburo is reshuffled.
July 22	General Farkas is expelled from the party and demoted.
July 23	Arpad Szakasits and General Palffy, codefendants of Rajk, are rehabilitated.
Aug. 1	Rehabilitation of a number of Communist party officials.
Aug. 11	Rehabilitation of Msgr. Lajos Ordass, head of Hungarian Lutheran Church.
Sept. 11	Writers demand complete freedom.
Oct. 6	State funeral of Rajk and codefendants.
Oct. 13	General Farkas is arrested.
Oct. 14	Imre Nagy readmitted to the party.
Oct. 15	Government delegation headed by Gero leaves for Belgrade.
Oct. 20	Writers demand convocation of special party congress.
Oct. 23	Students demonstrate. Revolution begins.

Part One

HUNGARY FROM 1945 TO 1956

1

BIRTH OF A PEOPLE'S DEMOCRACY

A Product of Victory

ONE of the most widespread myths of the postwar period charges Franklin D. Roosevelt with full responsibility for Russia's domination of central Europe. This charge cannot withstand a scrupulous examination of the facts. Indeed, in the light of the published memoirs of Winston Churchill, Sumner Welles, Edward Stettinius, James Byrnes, and Charles de Gaulle it is possible to establish the truth, which is complex and cannot be reduced to the action, deliberate or not, of a few individuals. The fate of the so-called people's democracies after 1945 was determined by the international forces that confronted one another at the end of the hostilities, and, later, in the cold war.

It was only after the victory of Stalingrad and the westward advance of the Red army that the Allies considered an extension of the security zone in Europe. This policy did not originate with Roosevelt. With a candor that does him credit, Churchill himself has helped to dispel the legend which tended to make him a hero of anti-Soviet resistance against an imaginary Roosevelt given to idyllic anticipations. For it was Churchill who in March, and in October, 1943, showed himself willing to divide central and eastern Europe with Soviet Russia. The rather cynical clauses of the agreement concluded between the British statesman and Stalin are well known:

Soviet influence was to be preponderant in Romania, Bulgaria, and Hungary; Great Britain and the U.S.S.R. were to divide Yugoslavia equally between them; while Greece was to be entirely in the British zone. As for Poland, the negotiators could not reconcile their views. Churchill regarded the restoration of Polish independence as a matter of prestige; while Stalin, who knew that Polish nationalism was anti-Russian and anti-Soviet, wanted to liquidate it once and for all.

The Churchill-Stalin agreement met with a hostile reception in Washington. Roosevelt refused to recognize even the incorporation of the Baltic states into the Soviet Union. Actually, if American diplomacy is partly responsible for the postwar developments in Europe (it shares this responsibility with British diplomacy), it is primarily because the Western powers refused to define their war aims immediately after concluding their alliance with the Soviets, without waiting for the end of the hostilities. The Russians, anxious to learn what their allies had in mind, made several proposals to this effect, all of which were rejected. Now, it is certain that in 1941, when German might was at its apogee, Soviet Russia would have been satisfied with a far smaller share of the spoils than in 1943 or 1944. The second mistake of the Western powers was their insistence that Germany must surrender unconditionally. This absurd demand enabled Hitler and the Nazis to appear as the sole possible guarantors of the Reich's survival; it implied the future division of Germany, and hence the present division of Europe. The anti-Nazi war was thus transformed into a war of succession, which could end only with a *de facto*, if not a *de jure*, division of all German-occupied countries between the West and the East. The principle of unconditional surrender did away with the European balance of power, which is impossible without the existence of at least one great sovereign nation in the center of the continent.

The records of the negotiations conducted by the Soviets

with the Western powers in 1938 and 1939, with the Nazis in 1939-1941, and with the Western Allies in 1941-1945 confirm our thesis. They give us a glimpse of the strategic conceptions that inspired Soviet diplomacy and show that these were determined by the part the Germans played in the European balance of power. When the Russians were faced with a strong and threatening Germany, they asked the Western powers for bases in Finland and in the Baltic states, and for the right to send troops to Poland and Romania in the event of hostilities. After the failure of this policy, which is associated with the name of Litvinov, the Soviets sought to protect themselves by an agreement with Nazi Germany. This was intended to delimit their zone of strategic interests in relation to Germany and, in some measure, to England.

At that time Stalin did not intend to spread communism by force of arms. He and his advisers acted as traditional diplomats rather than as revolutionaries: their purpose was to avoid war and to strengthen Russia's strategic positions, which were very vulnerable on the Baltic and the Black Seas. The partition of Poland between Russia and Germany, the improvement of the defenses of Leningrad, the annexation of Bessarabia, and the establishment of zones of influence in Bugaria, Romania, and Hungary were part of that conception, which also implied German recognition of Soviet interests in the Danube and the Straits. On the other hand, out of consideration for Germany and Italy, the Soviets at that time took no further interest in Czechoslovakia and Yugoslavia.

Finally, in 1943-1944, as the destruction of Nazi Germany's military power became increasingly probable, the Soviets began to think in terms of a division of all German-dominated Europe between the East and the West. The so-called German assets, the spoils of war that the U.S.S.R. was preparing to share with the Allies, were not merely the German economic resources, but also Germany itself, and with Germany, that

Europe of 1939 whose fragility had been revealed by Hitler's blitzkrieg. Under the Churchill-Stalin agreement of 1944, western Europe was to go to the Anglo-Saxons, and eastern and southeastern Europe to the Soviet Union, except for Greece which was to to be a British protectorate, and Turkey, in which the British and Soviet interests were to be balanced, just as they were in Iran. To be sure, the ways and means of implementing Soviet hegemony were not specified. The negotiators contented themselves with vague formulas inspired by the Atlantic Charter—democracy, free elections, restoration of sovereignty. This sovereignty was, however, restricted by the provision that the future governments of the countries liberated from the Third Reich were to be "friendly." Incidentally, Churchill was the first to show to what extent concern for democracy was subordinated, even by those Allies who could not be suspected of totalitarianism, to strategic considerations: he declared at Yalta that in his opinion it was "very doubtful whether a representative government could be set up in Greece, for the parties there hated one another too much." Alas, Greece was not the only country whose parties fought one another with implacable hatred. And yet it was Great Britain that by her armed intervention in the domestic affairs of Greece started that wave of interventionism which after World War II obstructed parliamentary and democratic action in Europe, and from which the Soviets and the Communist parties of eastern and central Europe profited most heavily.

The continual alternation of foreign interventions and genuine struggles between parties which instinctively placed themselves under the protection of one or the other of the great world powers is a crucial characteristic of postwar Europe. But nothing justifies the contention that, as early as 1944 or 1945, the Russians had planned to Sovietize the countries they occupied or in which they had predominant influence as a result of the relative strength of communism. The postwar people's democracies had historical precedents. As early as 1924, the Soviets helped the Mongolian Communists to set up the People's Republic of Mongolia, which made it possible for the Russians to control this country without annexing or actually Sovietizing it. Similarly, in 1939, during the war against Finland, the Soviets set up a puppet government presided over by the Communist Otto Kuusinen and called "the People's Government of the Democratic Republic of Finland." After the war the Soviets made use of the same formula, which was part of their stock in trade of political accessories, as a means of consolidating their political and economic positions in eastern and southeastern Europe without offending their allies. This accounts for the flagrant contradictions of their policies in Eastern Europe between 1944 and 1947, which were marked on the one hand by brutal interventions in the domestic affairs of their neighbors, and on the other by declarations such as the one made by Molotov on April 2, 1945, asserting that the Soviet government "seeks in no way to change the social order prevailing in Romania." Similarly, in 1946, Stalin told Ferenc Nagy, premier of Hungary: "We should disavow our ideology, we should disorganize the ranks of our party, if we did not respect the small nations, if we did not respect their rights, their independence, if we planned to intervene in their domestic affairs." (Quoted in *Szabad Nep,* August 28, 1951.)

It is not surprising, then, that with regard to economic and social issues Soviet spokesmen and Communist leaders at that time displayed a moderation that even moderate Socialists often found excessive. After the collapse of the Horthy regime in Hungary no one would have protested against the immediate nationalization of all industries—just as no one had protested against the radical agrarian reform decreed by the provisional government at the explicit request of the Soviet occupation authorities. Instead, big industrialists were brought out from their hiding places and ordered to resume management of their plants.

Only with the onset of the cold war did the Communists proclaim that the people's democracy was a specific form of the dictatorship of the proletariat, whose first embodiment was the so-called Soviet democracy. The function of this dictator- ship was defined as that of building socialism—a process which implied the carrying out of long-range programs for industri- alization and collectivization of agriculture in the Russian style.

At this point, however, we must examine the economic and political evolution of Hungary from 1945 to 1948, when the country was brought to heel.

Democratic Prelude

The economic ruin, political disorganization, and moral confusion in Hungary at the moment of Liberation are easy to imagine. For five months, the country had been ruled by the Arrow Cross terrorists, who exterminated over half a million Jews and thousands of intellectuals, Socialists, Communists, and liberals; and then it had been the scene of ferocious battles between Soviet and German armies. Between 1945 and 1948, the Communist leaders gave evidence of a political realism and organizational talents that even their most implacable enemies cannot deny. They had indeed to act with great cau- tion, considering the insignificant number of their followers in 1939 or 1944—party members and fellow travelers totaled fewer than 12,000!

The 1945 elections gave a large majority to the Smallholders party, which combined the votes of the peasants and those of the middle class, and secured very strong positions for the Social Democrats, to which the most advanced workers had remained faithful. Under these circumstances, the greatest danger threatening the Communist party was the possibility of an agrarian-Socialist coalition on the Finnish model, which would exclude it from the government, and above all deprive it of the ministry of the interior, then held by Ladislas Rajk. Thanks primarily to Rajk's energy, the Communists averted this danger, first by disorganizing the Smallholders party through the discovery of an alleged plot to restore "capitalist fascism," in which several leaders of this party, including Premier Ferenc Nagy, were implicated, and then by forcing the Socialists after the 1947 elections to expel their so-called rightist leaders, such as Peyer, Anna Kethly, Anton Ban, and Szelig. The latter had dared to serve as spokesmen for the workers' protests against the anti-democratic terrorism exercised by the Communists—indeed, many of these were former Nazis who had only recently joined the Communist party.

From 1945 on, the policy of the Hungarian Communists was entirely inspired by the principle of *divide et impera.* Shortly before the 1947 elections, they authorized the formation of several opposition parties for the sole purpose of splitting up the Smallholders party, their chief enemy. The maneuver was successful. To consolidate their hold on the government the Communists forced all their partners in the coalition to purge their ranks. In the course of this process, the masses lost all confidence in their non-Communist representatives, or, more accurately, became so intimidated that they no longer dared to appeal to them. The merger of the two workers' parties (June, 1948), the Mindszenty trial (January, 1949), organized for the sole purpose of breaking the resistance of the Church—the last hope of the opposition groups, which were not anti-democratic, but which had been deprived of all other means of voicing their disapproval of the rapid Sovietization of the country—and finally the elections of May, 1949, from which opposition parties were excluded, marked the principal stages of this political development.

The Mindszenty trial and the 1949 elections took place in an atmosphere of tension, terror, and propaganda very different from the atmosphere which had prevailed in Hungary until June, 1948. "We have taken a crucial step toward the complete liquidation of the political heritage of reaction, and toward the political founding of the new people's republic," wrote Marton Horvath, Cominform journalist, shortly after the 1949 elections (*Tarsadalmi Szemle,* June-July, 1949). In this sentence the most important words are "complete" and "new." For after June, 1948, when the workers' parties merged, the Communist party was in actual control of the political situation, holding all the key positions, social, economic, and political. The opposition parties were reduced to impotence. The clergy and the intellectuals could manifest their hostility to the regime only platonically: these scattered forces, kept under constant supervision, seemed to represent no threat to the government, which had solid administrative and economic roots. On the contrary, it was possible to believe—and the Hungarian Communist leaders themselves believed—that after the political revolution had been carried out, and this under very favorable conditions, without any bloodshed, the people's democracy, a slightly disguised and mild form of proletarian dictatorship, would evolve undisturbed toward socialism. The pace of this development, it might have been thought, would ultimately depend only on the potentialities inherent in the economic and social structures of Hungary, and on the ideological progress of a population which, consisting of a majority of peasants and handicraftsmen, was still to be won over to Socialist ideas.

The rulers of Hungary seemed to realize that it was in their interest to preserve the liberal and democratic façade they had given themselves after the Liberation. The relative freedom enjoyed by the opposition before 1948 aroused sympathy abroad: it served to prove to the world that communism was not necessarily intolerant and terroristic. But when, in the spring of 1948—an important date—the political evolution of

Soviet Russia was imposed as a model to be followed, a *new* policy, securing for the party *complete* power, had to be adopted. This power was to be complete both in form and in substance.

This new and complete policy made its appearance in Hungarian life very spectacularly with the Rajk trial. This trial took only a few days. But in the course of these few days the country underwent a true mutation, or, to use Marxist terms, a "qualitative change."

The situation in Hungary before the trial was in broad outline as follows:

Industry. After the stabilization of the currency (1946)— this operation was carried out with a masterful and brutal energy—the government set for itself several objectives, including reconstruction of damaged plants, gradual nationalization of the industries, and the carrying out of a Three-Year Plan which was to lay the foundation of a thorough industrialization of the country. The authors of this plan believed that Hungary could replace Germany in the Balkan markets by developing primarily her machine-tool industries. Nor did they lose sight of the fact that Hungarian economy could be redeemed only in co-operation with other Danubian countries, particularly Yugoslavia, whose economic structure is actually complementary to Hungary's.

In June, 1948, shortly before the publication of the Cominform resolution condemning Tito, Yugoslavia held first place in Hungarian imports with 20.6 per cent, Russia coming second with 17.7 per cent. In the same month 17.1 per cent of Hungarian exports went to Yugoslavia, as against 22.5 per cent to Russia; this also gave Yugoslavia first place, considering that the deliveries to Russia included reparations payments. We may add that in 1946 a special ten-year agreement had been concluded betwen Yugoslavia and Hungary, providing for close co-operation, and enabling Hungary, which is rich in bauxite but poor in electricity, to exploit these resources by processing part of its bauxite production in Yugoslavia, and by processing another part of it in Hungary itself thanks to electric current supplied by Yugoslavia.

This pre-1948 economic policy, formulated and carried out with great skill, enabled Hungary to rebuild itself with a speed that amazed the world. However, various difficulties impeded this industrial progress. For example, Soviet Russia, which in 1945 and 1946 had not shown more consideration for Hungary than for other countries occupied by her armies, had proceeded, despite the protests of Hungarian leaders, including Communists, to dismantle a number of major industrial installations. Then Russia demanded reparations amounting to two hundred million dollars. It is true that late in 1948, at the request of the Hungarian government, the U.S.S.R., in a spectacular gesture, reduced these reparations to a total of 134.3 millions, of which 68.6 had been paid. But the economic significance of this concession is considerably diminished in the light of the fact that the deliveries made by Hungary on account of the reparations payments were always calculated on the basis of the 1938 world prices, or about half their actual prices. Moreover, Russia had instituted a system of fines payable in the event of late deliveries, and the quality of all deliveries was severely checked over by ever-present and vigilant Russian commissions. Finally, under the peace treaty Russia had acquired a great number of Hungarian mines and plants, which were regarded as German assets, even though most of them had fallen into German hands as a result of the illegal eviction of their former Jewish owners; and the mixed Hungarian-Soviet companies exploiting river transports, air transports, oil wells, etc., exceeded by far, in number and importance, similar companies formed in Yugoslavia.

However, despite the magnitude of this tribute paid to the great ally—it must also be noted that Hungary was compelled to pay for all her imports from Russia at prices about 20 per cent above the world prices, and to supply her own products to Russia at 20 per cent below the world prices—the organized and persistent efforts of the Hungarian workers had wrought miracles.

Agriculture. Before the summer of 1948, the Hungarian Communist party's attitude toward the peasants was characterized by great caution, which was quite justified. There was no wish to arouse the resentment of the peasants; everyone knew how deeply they were attached to their individual holdings and that they feared collectivization more than the devil. (Memories of Bela Kun haunted the Hungarian peasants like bad dreams.) Their individualism was strengthened by the agrarian reform of 1945, which created about 400,000 new smallholders, and consolidated the material existence of some 200,000 peasants who were granted additional plots of land. The agrarian reform revolutionized Hungary: it corrected a thousand-year-old evil, and it should not be forgotten that one of its most deserving architects was the Communist Imre Nagy, even though he was inspired by tactical considerations. Thus a system of feudal exploitation which had lasted for centuries was ended; an era of democracy based on the alliance of peasants, workers, and intellectuals was in prospect.

Needless to say, the economic advances of the country required (and this was not overlooked by the Hungarian government) that the agrarian reform be followed by a number of measures encouraging the formation of co-operatives, with a view to the progressive mechanization of agricultural labor. To achieve this goal the authorities counted on time, the example of model co-operatives, the establishment of tractor stations, and a skillful mixture of education and propaganda.

Social gains. In this field, too, Hungary achieved important advances between 1945 and 1948. The standard of living of workers and intellectuals reached and sometimes even exceeded the levels of 1938; nurseries, kindergartens, new primary, secondary, and technical schools were founded; the system of paid vacations and social insurance was expanded and consolidated. Plant committees were given an increasingly important function in industry. They participated in the management, contributed to giving the workers a sense of dignity and responsibility, and opened for them the joyous prospect of an age of industrial democracy.

The new policy cut short this development. It inaugurated a managerial age, an age of Stakhanovism, with all that it implies of intransigence, continuous propaganda, and coercive measures, following the difficult but promising beginning of industrial democracy. Beginning with the summer of 1948, the Hungarian press and radio never ceased to urge the workers to engage in collective as well as individual emulation. True enough, a Socialist society must use means different from those used in a capitalist society to increase industrial productivity. But to all those familiar with the character of Hungarian workers—most of whom are attached to their trades and proud of their status—it was clear that the unremitting pressure was bound to arouse their resentment. Moreover, seductive appeals were accompanied by threats of reprisals and severe sanctions in the event of failure to fulfil work quotas (which were continually increased) as a result of absenteeism; and the working day (from eight to ten hours) was considerably extended by various meetings (party cells, trade-unions, cultural groups, youth, women, street committees, security committees, labor brigades, etc.) which the workers were more or less officially obliged to attend. Nor must we forget that all these obligations extended to holidays. Here, too, the authorities faithfully toed the Russian line, and the work done was "new" and "complete."

The new policy was also applied to the administrative and technological intelligentsia. In the fall of 1948, the Hungarian Communist party began in all haste to eliminate not only the former, so-called bourgeois officials, but also the Communist or near-Communist intellectuals of middle-class or lower middle-class origin who had been appointed by the new regime. The latter, however docile they had shown themselves to be, were replaced by workers who, though honest and trustworthy by Cominform standards, had no professional training. The purpose was to strengthen the working-class character of the regime. The result, both economically and culturally, was disquieting.

It was Matyas Rakosi himself who, in a burst of seemingly Leninist self-criticism (unlike Lenin, and for good reasons, he took good care not to raise fundamental issues), sounded the alarm. "Thousands of workers have been placed at the head of plants," he declared. "Now we must supervise our selection. ... Those who are incapable of preserving discipline, who strive to be popular with the backward sections of the working class, with those wage earners who have not class consciousness, and who are under enemy influence ... will be removed and held accountable for their management." In other words, the purgers themselves were to be purged! In the same speech, made in 1949, Rakosi pointed out that "the intellectuals evidence less and less interest in the building of socialism." "We have heard an engineer say," he added, "that he would not send his son to the Polytechnic School but would make him work as an unskilled laborer, for in this way he would have a better chance of becoming plant manager. ... Thus the intellectuals are uninterested in socialism not only because they are not treated in the proper way, but also because they see that poor management of the plants results in the relaxation of work discipline." What, then, was to be done? "The intellectuals must be given better treatment." But how could they, since all those of bourgeois origin had been eliminated? Rakosi evaded answering this question, and confined himself to inviting worker-managers to get themselves trained by the engineers who were their subordinates.

Culture. In 1945, the Communists introduced themselves to the public as the most consistent champions of progressive ideas, anxious to resume the best democratic and national traditions. During the first years after Liberation, their major concern was to overcome the distrust with which they had been received, and to show themselves in a favorable light to the intellectuals of all schools, except Fascists and implacable anti-Communists. They extended a friendly hand to Catholics, nationalists, Social Democrats, and to intellectuals of peasant extraction. They even displayed great tolerance with regard to writers, artists, scientists, and teachers whose conduct in the preceding years had not always been irreproachable from a national and democratic standpoint. For instance, they defended against the Socialists a number of writers and poets who, like Laszlo Nemeth and Lawrence Szabo, had flirted with nazism.

That was the heyday of the Marxist philosopher, Gyorgy Lukacs. His aim was to make the Communist party the patron and protector of all cultural activities, to use it as a rallying center with a view to carrying out great reforms. Education was to be democratized and modernized, the popular basis of culture was to be broadened, minds were to be emancipated. That was the time of pluralism and of "the dialogue." Socialist culture was portrayed as the end result of a long development, a goal that each nation was to achieve in its own way and on the basis of its own traditions.

2

SOVIETIZATION OF HUNGARY

The Rajk Trial

THE Soviet break with Tito spelled the end of the climate of relative tolerance that prevailed in Hungary between 1945 and 1948. In the spring and the exceptionally glorious summer of 1949 discontent and fear dominated the scene. The peasants dreaded collectivization; the workers grumbled against Stakhanovism and the speed up of production; the middle classes thought only of emigration; the Jews apprehended new pogroms; the intellectuals did not know where to turn. Confusion spread to the party machine: some of the best-known Communist militants were vocal in their criticism of the new line.

It was to silence the intra-party opposition and to terrorize the country into complete submission to Moscow that Matyas Rakosi staged the Rajk trial. By compelling the leading critic of the new line to "confess" that he was motivated by a desire to enslave his country to Tito, Rakosi rid himself of a dangerous rival and at the same time served notice that from now on any disagreement with the decisions of the leader would be treated as heresy punishable by death. Everything was done to make the trial a sensational, unique event, and to present Rajk as an inhuman monster. Actually, there was nothing new or unique about the trial, which slavishly followed the pattern of the infamous Russian show trials of the 1930's.

It all began in September 11, 1949, with the publication of

17

the indictment in all Hungarian newspapers. Among Rajk's codefendants were such prominent national figures as General Palffy-Oesterreicher, inspector general of the army; Tibor Szonyi, chief of the party personnel department; Andras Szalai, leader of the Communist youth organization; and Pal Justus, Socialist deputy. "Rajk and his gang," as the indictment referred to the defendants, were charged with plotting to destroy Hungarian independence, to restore the capitalist regime, "to make Hungary a colony of Tito and his gang, who have deserted the camp of socialism and gone over to the camp of foreign capitalism and reaction," etc., etc. Except for the names and dates, the charges repeated the one made against Bukharin, Zinoviev, Kamenev, and many others. And just as in the Russian trials of the 1930's, the chief villain was beyond the reach of Communist justice: then it had been Trotsky, the agent of Nazi Germany and Japan; now it was Tito, the agent of the United States.

In line with the standard procedure in such cases, publication of the indictment was the signal for a gigantic propaganda campaign. Throughout the country meetings were held, and the laboring masses were told to express their spontaneous indignation at "the murderers in the pay of imperialism," and to demand "the gallows for Rajk and his accomplices." The Communist press throughout the world dutifully echoed the abuse, and joined in the clamor for blood.

The trial opened on September 16. The courtroom was filled with model workers who had been summoned from all over the country, to enable them to report on the proceedings to their towns and villages. Many of the spectators were army officers, high government officials, and writers. So sure of themselves were the organizers of the trial that they had also invited a large number of diplomats, from the West and the East, and thirty-three foreign correspondents to witness the spectacle.

Everything went according to schedule. Just like the protagonists of the Russian trials before him, Rajk, to the amaze-
ment of all students of psychology, calmly announced, in a
somewhat hollow voice, that he was guilty of all the crimes
with which he had been charged. More than that, he went out
of his way to portray himself as a degenerate criminal, and did
not forget to compliment his persecutors for their superior
wisdom which had enabled them to foil his treacherous plans.
The former minister of the interior attributed to himself the
most ignoble motives, and invented for the occasion an imaginary autobiography, in which he described himself as an
ordinary stool pigeon. The court did not bother to analyze
Rajk's testimony or to confront it with the actual facts of his
career, and chose to take his confessions, no matter how im-
plausible, at their face value. He and three of his codefendants
were sentenced to death, and the others to life imprisonment.

Today, there is no need to analyze these confessions and to
prove the absurdity of the charges: for seven years after the
trial, Matyas Rakosi himself admitted that it had been a vast
frame-up, and Rajk and his codefendants were rehabilitated.
(In this respect, incidentally, the Rajk trial *is* unique. Khrushchev, although he has denounced Stalin's crimes, so far has
not taken the trouble to rehabilitate the victims of Stalin's
frame-ups.) Nor are we today entirely reduced to conjecture in
trying to account for the mysterious behavior of the accused.
Thanks to the disclosures made by the survivors of the trial,
we know by what methods they were made to confess their
imaginary crimes.

Among these methods, physical torture played an important
part. An approximate idea of the treatment to which the defendants were subjected is provided in the following account
by the Hungarian journalist Dezso Kozak of a visit to the
political police (the AVO) offices in Budapest, which were

thrown open to the public after the insurgents had stormed them in October, 1956:

"We were first taken to a large soundproof room where the defendants were questioned. The floor was covered with rubber, and in one corner there was an impressive battery of searchlights. Our guide told us that the police officer who did the questioning was seated behind his desk, while the victim was politely invited to occupy a chair opposite him, his face exposed to the glare of the reflectors.

"At a given point the police officer pressed a button, which opened a trap under the defendant's chair, sending him to a room below. There a special team of torturers was waiting for him. . . . I noticed a kind of press one surface of which was hollowed out in the form of two hands. In an adjoining room was a kind of dentist's chair equipped with solid leather straps to hold the victim in place. A glass case held a number of instruments that looked like a surgeon's outfit—pliers, wrenches, etc. Another glass case held injection needles and syringes."

In addition to physical torture, the defendants were subjected to other types of pressure. For instance, Rajk was told that unless he confessed his wife and little boy—then only a few months old—who had been arrested at the same time as himself, would be killed. Such threats were often followed by promises: the prisoners were told that the sentences against them would not be carried out, and that they would be released and allowed to live incognito in a remote village.

The main weapon, however, was ideological and psychological torture, of the kind so brilliantly described in Arthur Koestler's novels. The inquisitors took advantage of the defendants' loyalty to the party in order to persuade them that once they had failed to follow the party line they had become "objectively" criminals and traitors, and that they could atone for their fatal deviations by confessing to heinous crimes, thus helping the party leaders to save the party's unity, homogeneity, and prestige. For this purpose, the men whose only real crime was to oppose the party line were to portray themselves to their own supporters as degenerates who deserved neither respect nor pity. All the defendants in the Rajk trial did precisely that, some with a display of repentance, like Palffy-Oesterreicher and Justus, and others, like Rajk, with contemptuous calm.

Rajk succumbed to this Stalinist logic all the more easily because he was in full agreement with the goals of the new policy, opposing only the methods. His rebellion against the Russification of Hungary was sentimental rather than ideological in origin; he did not doubt Stalin's authority and essential wisdom. He went to the gallows, I was told, crying, "Long live the party! Long live Stalin!" Tibor Szonyi, who was hanged next, murmured: "This can't be true. It's impossible. I was promised. . . ." But it was not impossible; it was true. Under the Stalinist regime of Rakosi more Communists were executed in Hungary than under the White terror of Admiral Horthy.

Matyas Rakosi

For Soviet propaganda, the myth of Rajk's treason was primarily "a lesson of vigilance." For the Kremlin, it was a pretext for seizing full control of the Communist party machines of all satellite countries, including Hungary. All party officials were summoned to track down and crush every manifestation of anti-Soviet sentiment. Everyone was to demonstrate his devotion to Stalin's party by undertaking to increase industrial output, to raise work quotas, to lower production costs. The collective energy released by the myth was to be directly converted into political and economic energy. "The deep hatred for the battalion of imperialist agents led by Tito must be the driving force of the Hungarian people's struggle for peace," said the official Communist newspaper, *Szabad Nep*. The myth was used as a stimulant; and at the same time it supplied a substitute for certain aspirations of a religious character, which are always present in the hearts of men terrorized and seduced by power and haunted by the Absolute.

The Rajk trial served to dramatize the new line. With it began a reconditioning of minds, which was carried out by a tremendous propaganda machine. This propaganda enveloped all the people's democracies in an artificial fog, and under its cover the "purging" of the Communist parties advanced by leaps and bounds. The Rajk trial, however, also served important political purposes: Soviet Russia used it to increase the tension in the Balkans, and thus to relieve American pressure on the other fronts of the cold war.

In a note addressed to the Budapest government shortly after the trial, Tito branded it as "an incitement to war." Indeed, the charges again Rajk could have been used as an excuse for preventive measures directed against Yugoslavia. But Stalin did not wish to go that far. He confined himself to threats. Soviet Russia was to display less self-control in 1956, no doubt because of the weakness of and the dissensions among Stalin's successors, who are far from equal to their task.

After the Rajk trial, the economic blockade of Yugoslavia was tightened. Following on the heels of Soviet Russia, Hungary abrogated her treaty of mutual assistance with Yugoslavia. There was a notable increase of border incidents.

This economic, diplomatic, and military pressure, kept up by a flood of rumors about troop concentrations and other warlike measures, was supplemented by a continuous propaganda campaign. The press and the radio of the people's democracies, and above all those of Hungary, were mobilized for that purpose. Only the French Communist press surpassed in virulence the campaign of hatred conducted in Hungary.

At a meeting held in November, 1949, the Cominform adopted a resolution on Yugoslavia, which was based on Rajk's confessions. According to this resolution, the Yugoslav Communist party was a nationalist bourgeois clique that had gone over to fascism and "directly betrayed the national interests of Yugoslavia." Belgrade, it said, had become "an American center of espionage and anti-Communist propaganda," and Tito had transformed "his regime into an anti-Communist police state of the Fascist type." In consequence of this, the Cominform denied the Yugoslav party the right to call itself Communist, and declared that all Communist parties and workers had "the international duty" to struggle against Tito and "to come to the assistance of the workers and toiling peasants of Yugoslavia," who, according to the resolution, "had been compelled to adopt the same methods of struggle for communism and Communists of countries in which they are reduced to illegality." This was an appeal to civil war—a civil war, however, that did not take place. Among those who applied this resolution, Matyas Rakosi and Erno Gero distinguished themselves by the fervor of their servility.

Their servility was not dictated by sectarian or dogmatic considerations. Rakosi was perhaps the least dogmatic and the most opportunistic of all the Cominform leaders. He was also the subtlest and the most ruthless. The character of this bald, thickset, bull-necked man had been formed by three experiences —the Bela Kun revolution in which he took part as a young man; his years of exile in Soviet Russia where he witnessed the irresistible rise of Stalin; and his long imprisonment in the Szeged penitentiary where he had sufficient leisure to ponder his fate.

The Bela Kun revolution of 1919 taught Rakosi some useful lessons. Bela Kun had attempted to solve the centuries-old agrarian problem in Hungary in a hurry, by nationalizing the big estates. This aroused against him all the Hungarian peasants, who were starved for land and demanded not nationalization but division. In 1945, Rakosi did not press for the collectivization of agriculture and supported Imre Nagy who distributed land to the peasants. In this way he neutralized them, and launched the battle for collectivization only after the party had seized full political control of Hungary. Rakosi's ferocious hatred of the Social Democrats also dates from 1919, when they deserted Bela Kun. In 1950, he sent thousands of Socialists and trade-unionists to prisons and concentration camps.

Stalin was his ideal of the statesman. It is from Stalin that Rakosi borrowed his conception of the party as a supreme god, incarnated in the person of the secretary-general. Like Stalin, Rakosi regarded the party as a kind of army or secular order, which must observe an iron discipline. The party is everything; the party and its leader are one—these are the basic tenets of Rakosi's religion. The leader must know everything, control everything, direct everything. He is bound to be infallible. It is again from Stalin that Rakosi learned the secret of how never to deviate, while letting others, the blunderers and dupes, commit deviations. "In our political and ideological struggle we must never make left or right turns: we must always move straight ahead, following the correct line charted by our resolutions." All Rakosi is in this sentence from an article he published in *Szabad Nep* of March 10, 1955, after his victory over Imre Nagy. Stalin, too, was always careful to take a centrist position—his position of supreme arbiter.

By studying the career of Stalin, Rakosi groomed himself for the dangerous and exalted role of a Communist ruler. He realized that to become a totalitarian leader he had to divest himself of all sentimentality and scruples, and that he had to preserve a benign appearance while acting with the utmost ruthlessness; that he must never compromise himself, and always be right; and that he must fool everyone, without ever fooling himself. It is this philosophy that he brought with him when he returned to Hungary in a Red army wagon. By then he was an accomplished politician. During his first, demagogic period, following the Liberation, Rakosi became a tribune of the people. He was the best public speaker in Hungary. This son of a Jewish haberdasher was as skillful in the use of Hungarian as Churchill, the descendant of Marlborough, was in the use of English. He knew how to speak to peasants, to workers, to intellectuals; he seduced, he overpowered all of them. With his typically Stalinian joviality, his caustic and cultivated mind, he impressed all his listeners, Hungarian and foreign.

In 1948, when Stalin began to take a "tough" line against the West, Rakosi the man of the world and the tribune suddenly changed into Rakosi the man of iron, the terrorist dictator. After bribing or crushing his non-Communist enemies he turned against his adversaries within the party, his possible rivals. In Gabor Peter, chief of the security police, he had a high-class executioner always ready to serve him. He sent Rajk to the gallows, and imprisoned hundreds of left-wing and right-wing Communists, including many of his former fellow prisoners and exiles. Fully aware of the hatred he inspired, he gave himself the title of "Beloved Leader of the People."

As for Erno Gero, Rakosi's chief assistant, he is a typical Comintern bureaucrat. His first important mission dates from 1925, when he was sent to Paris to keep an eye on the Communist militants active in various *émigré* organizations. After his expulsion from France he continued to do this work for the G.P.U. In 1932, he was in Barcelona, where he was little known but more powerful than the important Communists he supervised. In 1936, he emerged to the surface, acting as one of the Kremlin's principal agents along with Antonov-Ovseenko, Russian consul in Barcelona. In 1940, he returned to Moscow where he became one of Manuilsky's closest associates in the Comintern offices. After the war, he was appointed to the government as a representative of the party, and displayed a great deal of energy in reorganizing the transportation services and in rebuilding bridges. While Rakosi's model was

Stalin, Gero's was Kaganovich, the gray eminence of the Kremlin. It was Gero who launched the slogan to transform agricultural Hungary into a country of "iron and steel" and who made productivity a Moloch to which everything had to be sacrificed.

The New Political Structure

After the Rajk trial, the Soviet theoreticians redefined the concept of the people's democracy, bringing it into conformity with the new political line. A people's democracy, they now declared, was nothing but a "specific form" of proletarian dictatorship, established with the help of the Soviet Union; its primary function was, as Dmitrov put it in a report to the Fifth Congress of his party (December, 1948), "to secure the transition to socialism." Dmitrov particularly stressed the need for people's democracies to co-operate with the Soviet Union: "Any attempt to hinder that co-operation is directed against the vital nerve of the people's domocracy." This clearly implied that Yugoslavia had no right to call herself a people's republic after her break with Russia. The tendency to emphasize the similarities and to overlook the differences between the new regimes and Soviet Russia asserted itself more and more strongly. "After the victory of the Soviet Union, there is no need to prove that the principles of Bolshevism are fully applicable not only within the borders of former Russia, but also the world over," wrote Matyas Rakosi in *Szabad Nep* of November 7, 1951. And in a study published in the party's theoretical review, *Tarsadalmi Szemle* (February-March, 1952, p. 143), the same author distinguished two stages in the establishment of a people's democracy: "The primary function of the first stage is to achieve the objectives of the bourgeois democratic revolution, and that of the second to set up the dictatorship of the proletariat and to proceed to the building of socialism." But he stressed the fact that certain features of the dictatorship of the proletariat "were present from the outset of the new era," and that it was thanks to Soviet protection that the Rubicon between the two stages had been crossed at the end of 1947 without violent upheavals. At about the same time the *Annals of the Soviet Academy of Sciences* (Historical and Philosophical Series, No. 1, 1952) said that the people's democracies of the Far East (China, Mongolia, North Korea, and Vietnam) differed from those of Europe, and that their sole task in the present period was to complete the anti-feudal and national revolution, "without performing the functions of the dictatorship of the proletariat."

In Hungary, the dictatorship of the proletariat was established within a constitutional framework. The new Hungarian constitution, promulgated in 1949, was a copy of the Russian model. It proclaimed that all power originates in the people, i.e., "the workers of the cities and villages," and that the leading force is "the working class, which is in turn led by its vanguard, and supported by the democratic union of the people in its entirety" (a corresponding article of the Soviet constitution proclaims the leading role of the vanguard of the proletariat, the Communist party). The power of the people is indivisible; it is expressed through direct elections on the basis of universal suffrage and secret ballot. All men and women aged eighteen or over are voters; at twenty-one they are eligible to office. The elected representatives of the people are responsible to their constituents and can be recalled before the expiration of their mandates. In actual fact, since 1949 the elections have been each time large-scale propagandistic manifestations similar to plebiscites. Since there were no opposition parties, freedom of elections was merely a phrase. The secrecy of the ballot was not always respected, and even when it was, few citizens ever dared to cast a negative vote. The lists of candidates were drawn up by the Communist party in collaboration with other parties and mass organizations grouped in the so-called Popular Front of Independence, which was the Hungarian counterpart of the Soviet "bloc of Communists and people belonging to no party." The elected deputies had no real power; nevertheless, their posts were not supposed to be sinecures. They were expected to keep permanently in touch with their constituencies, in order to promote government measures and supervise their enactment. But in most cases these activities were purely formal in character.

The powers usually held by the President of the Republic were vested in a Supreme Presidium elected by the National Assembly. The Presidium calls elections, issues decrees that have the force of law, appoints and recalls diplomatic representatives, receives the credentials of foreign diplomats, ratifies and abrogates treaties, awards decorations, and has the right to pardon. When the Assembly is not in session the Presidium also has the right to declare war if Hungary is attacked.

The first chairman of the Presidium was a renegade Social Democrat, Sandor Ronai; the second was a renegade Smallholder, Istvan Dobi. Neither had any influence whatever. On the other hand, the vice-chairmen, the secretary, and other members of the Presidium were important members or deputy members of the Politburo and Central Committee of the Communist party. In other words, the Presidium served to bridge the gap between the democratic façade of the government and the dictatorship of the Communist Politburo: though formally elected by the National Assembly, it was in fact appointed by the Politburo. Similarly, the Cabinet was theoretically appointed by the Presidium, but in practice it was chosen by the Communist leadership. The state machinery was the reflection and servant of the party machine.

The structure of the local administrative bodies was also modified along Soviet lines. Municipal and provincial people's councils were elected on the basis of universal suffrage; these in turn appointed executive committees that carried out the administrative work—collection of taxes in kind and in currency, organization of collections of foodstuffs, and execution of various government decrees. The overwhelming majority of the presidents of these executive committees were Communists or crypto-Communists, who were distrusted by their fellow countrymen, and whose election was dictated by the party. During the insurrection of 1956, most of them were dismissed by the revolutionary committees that took the place of the so-called people's councils.

On paper the new constitution was a veritable anthology of democratic and liberal principles, corrected and supplemented by Socialist principles. It guaranteed individual freedom, freedom of speech, conscience, religion; it guaranteed everyone's right to work, to education, and complete equality of women. Within the boundaries defined by law it recognized the right to individual property and to inheritance. It provided for the protection of national minorities, which was a considerable progress over the laws in effect before the war. The constitution prohibited incitement to racial, national, or religious hatred; and special laws promulgated after 1949 banned all war propaganda. But the fragility of the new system of tolerance was revealed after the break between the Cominform and Yugoslavia. All of a sudden, the Yugoslav minorities in southern Hungary found themselves in a precarious situation. In December, 1951, Djilas, speaking at the United Nations, complained about the persecutions and even deportations to which a large section of these minorities was subjected.

The new criminal code was inspired by eminently progressive principles, and aimed at the simplification and acceleration of the judicial process. Under this new code, the people's assessors to the professional magistrates in the courts had the same rights and duties as the professional magistrates themselves. The authorities had the right to restrict the individual freedom of citizens only in cases explicitly provided for by law.

The new code asserted the principle of publicity of judicial trials, which, in the words of one of the architects of the new procedure, Istvan Timar (cf. *Parallele 50,* June 28, 1951), "is an instrument of education, and an effective guarantee of the working people's right to control, which must be exercised everywhere." The code also guaranteed the rights of defense counsels. In short, the principles invoked by the new code more than met all requirements of humanity and justice; their application, however, was in the hands of officials over whom the people could exercise no control. There were public trials that served "to educate the working people," and these were broadcast and fully commented on in the press; but far greater was the number of trials *in camera*. Thousands, tens of thousands of persons were arrested and interned by administrative decree, and many of them vanished without a trace. In 1953, when Imre Nagy took over the government, the Hungarian internment camps held 150,000 persons—Communists, Titoists, Socialists, trade-unionists, members of opposition parties, former functionaries, etc.

This Hungarian people's democracy with its model constitution and ultra-progressive criminal code was ravaged by a disease that was commonly referred to as "doorbell-itis." A citizen who heard his doorbell ring in the morning could never tell whether this was the milkman or a security police agent. In fact, the constitution itself contained loopholes that gave the government discretionary powers.[1] So-called class enemies, i.e., members of the dispossessed classes, such as aristocrats, well-

[1] Article 41 of this constitution specifies that the courts "punish the enemies of the working people, protect and secure the state," etc.; and between 1949 and 1951 all the satellites, including Hungary, enacted laws concerning "state secrets." Now, the terms "enemies of the people," "Fascists," "state secrets" were given a very broad interpretation, making it possible for the police to proceed against any citizen considered dangerous by the party. Not only specific actions prohibited by law were punished with or without a show of legality, but also presumed intentions. There was no clear demarcation line between suspicion and actual guilt.

to-do peasants, professionals, shopkeepers, former officials, were subject to decrees of expulsion, deportation, and internment even if they abstained from any form of political activity.

The police was controlled by the party. In addition to the political police proper (the AVO), it included Frontier Guard units equipped with tanks and light artillery. In 1956, these formidable "forces of the interior" numbered 90,000 men and 10,000 officers. In Budapest alone, the AVO represented 1 per cent of the total population—an index of the authoritarian pressure exerted upon the country at large.

Another pillar (or rather supposed pillar) of the regime was the army. The infiltration of the army was one of the most arduous tasks confronting the Communist leaders between 1945 and 1948. They began by making ideological concessions to the traditional nationalism of the officers who agreed to serve the new government. The inspector general of the army, Palffy-Oesterreicher, and his successor, General Ladislas Solyom, were representative of officers of this type, Communists or fellow travelers who attempted to create a new spirit in the army by appealing to the patriotic instincts and the revolutionary sentiment of their colleagues.

The year 1949 marked a turning point in the development of the armies as well as the other institutions of the East European countries. Mihaly Farkas, a Communist of the Moscow team, who had been appointed minister of defense as early as 1947, and Rakosi's Number One policeman, Gabor Peter, were entrusted with the job of Sovietizing the Hungarian army. General Palffy-Oesterreicher, a Communist, was tried, sentenced, and executed at the same time as Rajk. General Ladislas Solyom and his close collaborator, General Kuthy, were in turn arrested in 1950; the same fate befell eighty other officers (among them a number of Communists) charged with plotting a Titoist *coup d'état*. Major General Istvan Bata, a Hungarian by birth who had served in the Soviet army, was appointed chief of staff. He was dismissed only *in extremis,* in October, 1956. In 1951, the army was subjected to a third purge, aimed at technicians of bourgeois extraction. One of its victims was General Bela Kiraly, commander in chief of the infantry, and later head of the Military Academy. He was released a few weeks before the insurrection of 1956.

While combating nationalism directed against the Soviet Union, the Communists strove to revive the national traditions of the Hungarian army. For this reason they exalted the revolutionary forces of 1848-1849, which inflicted a number of defeats on the numerically superior Austrians. At the same time they did their best to propagate the myth of the invincibility of the Red army.

The new army constituted a kind of state within a state. It was a people's army, as a result of the methods of recruiting and the origin of its officers' corps; and it was subject to a conditioning far more intensive than that imposed on the rest of the population. It was endowed with ample material resources. The army had its own newspapers, illustrated magazines, motion-picture houses, a theater, sports teams. Writers and poets, such as Gabor Devecseri, donned the uniform to devote themselves entirely to propaganda in the armed forces. Military training, moreover, began in adolescence, through the paramilitary sports organization, "Ready for Work and Combat." It was in this way that the Hungarian youth was trained for— the uprising of 1956! The Communist leaders harvested what they had sown when they militarized the youth.

Military service was compulsory. In 1950, the period of service was extended to two years in the land forces, and three years in the air force. At the same time the draft age was lowered from twenty-one to twenty. The regulations were copied from those of the Soviet army. A large number of Soviet instructors assisted the native officers in their tasks of indoctrination and training, and many Hungarian officers were sent to complete their studies in Soviet military schools.

An ever-increasing part of the budget was appropriated for military expenditures, and in 1950 the investments program was changed in favor of armaments production. Hungary produced primarily light armaments, but also tanks.

As for the effectives, they amounted to between 150,000 and 200,000 men, even though the peace treaties allowed Hungary an army of no more than 70,000 men. Under the Warsaw Pact, this army was put at the disposal of the Eastern counterpart of NATO, with Marshal Konev as commander in chief. But, as was clearly demonstrated by the events of October, and November, 1956, the Sovietization of the Hungarian army had barely scratched its surface. Privates and officers, originating from among the people, remained faithful to the people; and all the artifices of propaganda never convinced them that Hungarian and Soviet interests were identical. In the eyes of the Hungarian military, the alliance with the Soviet Union was contrary to the interests of Hungary, which was traditionally oriented toward the West, and therefore attracted by the idea of a Central European federation in which it would play a role worthy of its historic tradition. In October, 1956, even before the insurrection, the army had begun to rid itself of its Stalinist fetters, and obtained the rehabilitation of its martyrs of 1949-1952. On October 23, it went over to the side of the insurgents, thus illustrating the total failure of eight years of Stalinist indoctrination and training. Only the high-ranking officers, who had been carefully picked from among the most zealous Communists, and who associated closely with the security police, remained faithful to the regime. They succeeded in disarming and neutralizing a number of units. In most cases, the rank and file fought without leaders: the case of Colonel Pal Maleter is one of the rare exceptions.

Super-Industrialization and Anarchic Planning

"It becomes ever more evident that the great achievement of the revolution is a planned economy. Socialism is planning," a lucid observer of Soviet life wrote in 1938 (Yvon, *L'U.R.S.S. telle qu'elle est*. Preface by André Gide. Paris: 1938). Along with its conception of dictatorship, the U.S.S.R. passed on to the Communist leaders, if not to the nations, of Eastern Europe its methods of industrialization, its religion of planning, its faith in the supreme virtues of mechanization, electrification, and construction. The party dictatorship considered itself the indispensable means of mobilizing national energies, with a view to increasing productivity and creating modern industrial societies. It was asserted that in order to catch up with the advanced countries in the face of a hostile capitalist world, the backward Eastern countries, several decades behind in development, must declare war on laziness, routine, and stagnation. And it was the Communist state that had the task of organizing the great battles of production: the supreme justification of this state lay in the results it achieved in this field. But that is precisely where it failed most signally.

However seductive the idea of industrialization and planning may be, it is a historical fact that the Soviets did, not fully embrace it from the outset. Charles Bettelheim, in the first edition of his great work on Soviet planning (*La planification soviétique*, Paris: 1939, pp. 15–26), shows that from 1923 to 1929 the Soviet government consistently fought against "the super-industrialists, partisans of planning." The Fifteenth Congress of the Bolshevik party still insisted on the danger of "investing too much capital in large-scale industrial construction." At that time, Stalin and his partisans believed that progress toward socialism would be, as Molotov said in 1928, "necessarily slow," and that private enterprise would continue for a long time, particularly in agriculture.

Nevertheless, in November, 1929, the Soviet state embarked upon the collectivization of agriculture and large-scale industrialization and planning—the very measures Trotsky had advocated in 1921. This crucial change was accounted for by the economic failure of the New Economic Policy (N.E.P.), the failure of the policy of "concessions" as well as that of what Soviet economists called "primitive Socialist accumulation" (i.e., accumulation by the state of material resources primarily created by the nonsocialized sectors of the economy). The about-face of 1929 was probably due to a number of factors—the natural tendency of nationalized industry toward expansion; the workers' resentment against the so-called N.E.P. profiteers; theoretical and sentimental motives, such as admiration for American technology; military requirements; and, finally, the necessity for the party to go ahead, for it could not continue to mark time without being exposed to the danger of "bourgeois degeneration." After conquering the absolute state of the Czar, the Communist party became in a sense the prisoner of its conquest. Between 1923 and 1929, the Bolsheviks gradually abandoned the language of revolution in favor of the language of statesmanship. Their concern for the oppressed working class yielded to their concern for the state, which was now regarded as the instrument of the proletariat. The contradiction between a strongly organized political superstructure and a disorganized, chaotic economy, which was developing in accordance with capitalist laws, seemed intolerable. And so it came about that the state concentrated all its energies on the economic front, unleashing a second civil war that was no less violent than the first and organizing a new "war communism" on a higher economic and political level. The Soviet state had been born in the midst of the dramatic vicissitudes of a bitter struggle in which the totalitarian regime came to grips with an economic life governed by capitalist laws. Lenin's disciples thus had to carry on not only the political task of czarism, but also that of the pioneers of Russian capitalism—they had to bring new land into cultivation, to colonize, to build. *Stalinism was primarily a technique, a doctrine, a weapon of what might be called the "auto-colonization" of Soviet Russia.*

But what about the other countries of Eastern Europe? For them, too, even independently of their political situation, industrialization was an imperious need. On this point all the left-wing elements of those countries were agreed as early as 1945. Opinions differed only with regard to the methods and the pace of industrialization.

The first plans for industrial development in Czechoslovakia, Poland, and Hungary were based on the hope of obtaining credits and supplies from the United States. The American ban on shipments of strategic materials to those countries, following their refusal to participate in the Marshall Plan, and the unexpected refusal on the part of the International Bank to grant them loans, increased Hungary's and the other satellites' dependence on the Soviet Union, and reduced these countries to a quasi-colonial status. But unlike highly industrialized nations, which get raw materials at low prices from colonial or semi-colonial countries, Russia, a great power relatively undeveloped, found herself in a position of dominance with regard to a country whose industrial potential could supplement her own. Too weak to meet her own economic and military requirements, Russia, far from preventing Hungary from building up her heavy industry, encouraged her to do so, even though Hungary had no adequate economic foundations for such a development. Thus the super-industrialization of the period of 1950–1953 was out of all proportion with the national requirements, and served only Soviet interests, to which the chiefs of Hungarian economic life, namely, Gero and Berei, were devoted body and soul.

Zoltan Vas, head of the planning commission, was dismissed because he warned against the dangers of super-industrialization. A few years later, in 1954, after Imre Nagy appointed him a member of his economic brain trust, he clearly explained what had happened. In an article published in *Szabad Nep* (October 10, 1954), he said, referring to the increased heavy industry investments that the party had decreed in 1951 (probably in connection with the Korean crisis):

"Our splendid achievements intoxicated our party leadership. Under the slogan of 'a country of iron and steel' we entered the road of disproportionate and excessive industrialization. Today we see the nefarious consequences of such a policy.

"What are the consequences of that serious error?

"Our party strove to raise the standard of living; the Second Party Congress defined this as the goal to be pursued. But the policy of super-industrialization implied so many sacrifices on the part of the population that in the end the revised Five-Year Plan was bound to come into conflict with the party's main political objective—a prosperous and flourishing Hungary.

"The original Five-Year Plan provided for the reinvestment of 20 per cent of the national income. Under the revised Five-Year Plan, this ratio was continually increased. The share absorbed by state organizations and administrative departments increased even more rapidly: it almost tripled, accounting for 24 to 26 per cent of the national income. Thus more than half our national income was absorbed by new investments and state expenditures; and despite the steady increase in production, since 1951 the share reserved for the consumption of our laboring population has grown continually smaller. In other words, excessive investments and inadmissibly large expenditures of our state organizations cut down the amount of consumer goods needed to increase living standards. Because we forced the pace of our industrial development, we could not get increased amounts of clothes, shoes, foodstuffs;

and we failed to develop agricultural production, the main source of all these consumer goods.

"Needless to say, it is not the principle of industrialization that is to be blamed. We went astray when we misinterpreted the policy of Socialist industrialization. We could have done without the rapid growth of Stalinvaros [new industrial center near Dunapentele, which was to be the backbone of the Five-Year Plan]. We could have done without some other industrial investments for which we lacked the needed raw materials. Already at the end of 1951 it was obvious that our Five-Year Plan had no realistic basis."

It was only after the death of Stalin that the majority of the Central Committee, yielding to the pressure of facts and the arguments of Imre Nagy, who was seconded by Vas, recognized their errors. We shall return to this later. But Gero and his team never acknowledged their blunders, and did their utmost to sabotage the Nagy program.

The Working Class

In 1951, Hungary, which before the war had been over-populated, began to suffer from a shortage of manpower—not only of skilled workers who are always in demand, but of manpower pure and simple. The population had remained almost stationary since 1939: in 1956, it was 9,600,000 as against 9,000,000 in 1939.

During the first years after Liberation there were still many unemployed in Hungary: the agrarian reform had not completely absorbed the surplus population in the villages. But the reserves of industrial manpower were progressively dwindling. The Five-Year Plan of 1949 provided for a 20 to 40 per cent increase of employment. The industrial population, which numbered 450,000 in 1945, reached 1,060,000 in 1951 (93.2 per cent of these workers were employed in large plants). The share of industry in the national income had risen to 45 per cent, while that of agriculture had dropped to 23.9 per cent. Under the revised plan, 600,000 to 650,000 new workers were to be hired, instead of the 480,000 under the original plan.

Now, in 1951, the manpower reserves in the villages were virtually exhausted. A large part of the abundant crop of cereals was lost that summer because the agricultural co-operatives could not find additional hands. As in some Western countries which had achieved full employment, there arose the need for a more rational use of available manpower. Late in 1951, the government proceeded to transfer workers from nonessential industries and clerks from the hypertrophied administrative offices to key industries, particularly mining and metallurgy. At the same time, large numbers of women were recruited for industrial work. In 1951, plans were made for hiring 300,000 new female workers. New nurseries and children's homes operating night and day were hastily created to enable mothers to devote themselves entirely to factory work. Following complaints by workers, the authorities made special arrangements to enable married couples to work in the same locality.

The recruitment of hundreds of thousands of young peasants, and men and women from various social milieus raised problems of housing, sanitation, food, and leadership. The new workers did not easily adjust to the unfamiliar conditions of life, and they became an element of disorder, a potential source of unrest. They were dissatisfied with their wages, their improvised, overcrowded quarters, their inadequate food. Ever-increasing numbers of them ignored the prohibition against leaving their plants. They could always easily find new jobs, for the high production quotas compelled most enterprises continually to hire new personnel. The labor exchanges were snowed under by requests for help, and plants illegally competed with one another in recruiting additional labor. The newspapers often denounced managers who "violated civic discipline . . . by paying wages 'under the counter' or by supplementing the regular wage with pay for fictitious overtime."

"Migration" had become a workers' weapon against the state employer. From 1951 on, the directors of the economy complained more and more often about the instability of manpower, about "the incapacity of the enterprises to keep new workers." Knowing that they were indispensable, the workers grew increasingly demanding. In 1951, the female workers of a spinning mill in Budapest gave the following reasons for their departure for another plant: "We know very well that our new plant does not pay higher wages. But the rooms are cleaner, the ventilation is superior, and the working conditions are more sanitary." Managers, who were often inexperienced, thus learned that it was not enough to take care of production and to punish indiscipline, but that it was also necessary to pay attention to the conditions under which their employees were living and working. "A manager who wants to keep his workers must see to it that the rules of hygiene and the measures provided for the prevention of accidents are conscientiously carried out," said an article in *Szabad Nep*. "He must keep his factory clean, secure flawless food for his workers, as well as clean and pleasant quarters for newcomers." But there was more: "It is incumbent on the managers, the foremen, and the workshop superintendents to create for the workers technical conditions enabling them to earn their living honorably." The newspaper named several plants in which work was organized so poorly that the new workers could achieve only a very low output, and, hence, very low wages. "Is it surprising, then, that many of them deserted the plants?"

Other newspapers accounted for "the permanent displacement of workers who look for opportunities elsewhere" by "the bad distribution of wages." The capitalist pattern, as discovered by Marx, can thus be said to apply to the people's state: in developing the productive forces, in increasing the workers' army, it develops its own contradictions, it strengthens the elements which tend naturally to burst the too narrow framework of the social organization and to force the leadership to acknowledge the legitimacy of their demands.

The high labor turnover, the migration of workers, and absenteeism, by which the young proletariat of the Eastern countries manifested, in an unorganized fashion, its will to defend its interests against the state employer, seriously hindered the Communist efforts to increase productivity. Worst of all, they made it impossible for workers to acquire superior training and to become familiar with the specific features of a given plant.

Soviet industry faced similar problems as early as 1931, and never succeeded in completely solving them. What was called in Hungary and other satellites the struggle against "indiscipline," against "the Social Democratic influence in the plants," and against "fraudulent" or "dishonest" workers was but an aspect of the smoldering conflict within the plants between the government authorities and the mass of the workers striving for better conditions. It is this chronic conflict that partly accounts for the events of East Berlin in June, 1954, of Poznan in June, 1956, and of Hungary in October, 1956.

The inadequacies of the leadership at higher levels resulted in the multiplication of supervisory bodies and continual reorganizations. In 1951, the government structure of Hungary was reshaped and brought closer to the Soviet structure. Several new ministries of industry were created by splitting up those already in existence. But the continual changes in the administration of the various branches of industry led to disorder and confusion. The managers of enterprises and the party militants in the plants (often incompetent men who owed their positions to their proletarian origin and to services rendered to the police or the party, rather than to their skill) were bewildered by the large number of instructions, often contradictory, with which they were showered.

All this is well illustrated by the events that took place at the great plant Telephone in Budapest. Early in 1951, the management and the party committee of this plant were the object of a severe purge, on the ground that they had been "infiltrated by the class enemy." The engineer in chief and several of his assistants were arrested and charged with sabotage committed in the service of the Americans. The plant was given a new management and a new party committee, which were told to concentrate all their efforts on the increase of production. Judging by the newspapers, they set about their task with zeal and with some initial success. But early in 1952, *Szabad Nep* attacked the new committee, castigating it for neglecting "political work proper," i.e., organization and propaganda, and for devoting itself exclusively to "production work." It appears that the new committee, misinterpreting its instructions, had concerned itself with technical questions of management which were not within its province, while neglecting the work of recruiting new members for the party, organizing political lectures, etc. According to *Szabad Nep*, this neglect had adversely affected production and discipline: absenteeism, which had been decreasing, became rampant. Once again the entire management and the party committee were replaced.

There was a steady stream of complaints about the lack of co-ordination between the various branches of industry. There were delays in the supply of raw materials, which could not be accounted for merely by shortages, but by bureaucratic red tape. Factories had to wait a long time for needed spare parts; this caused partial stoppages of production and further delays. Newspapers often reported that a given mine which had received imported machinery did not know how, or did not want, to use it. Attempts to electrify the mines ran into all sorts of difficulties. As a rule, the plants were not given sufficient time to digest the new methods, and this resulted in at least temporary drops in output. On the other hand, the workers could not afford to lose wages—especially since those wages were low. Their natural conservatism did the rest.

The system of compensation on the basis of output, and the pressure under which the managers were to increase output, gave rise to a general tendency to sacrifice quality to quantity. Foreign trade was the first to suffer from this state of affairs. Deficient goods were often returned. As early as the spring of 1951, the minister of foreign trade sounded the alarm: "The honor of the Hungarian workers is at stake," he declared. For among Hungary's customers—as was the case with all the satellite countries—the Soviet Union held first place; and the Russians, always suspicious, reacted violently each time they received a shipment of deficient goods. They interpreted the shoddy quality of the cotton thread or the electrical appliances sent them as evidence of hostility or sabotage, and demanded that those responsible be punished. The poor quality of Hungarian products also created obstacles to the economic expansion of the Eastern bloc on the markets of underdeveloped countries.

Then the authorities opened a drive for the qualitative improvement of production. But if they were to be taken literally, this would have involved a new reorganization of the methods of work and control, which would have resulted in a lowering of output—a particularly reprehensible crime. To make things even more complicated, any action, for whatever motives, that harmed the smooth operation of the industries was regarded as sabotage. In the last analysis, it was fear of reprisals that accounted for "the irregular pace of production," about which the economic leadership so often complained.

In most factories production started off slowly at the beginning of each month. Then it increased gradually. Toward the end of each month, management, realizing that it was dangerously behind schedule, gave the signal for the great final sprint. This would start stampedes similar to those which had been eliminated only with the greatest difficulties from Soviet industries—where they had been provoked by the same causes. This stampede occurred at the end of every month, and sometimes at the end of every week. At the beginning of these periods, a considerable part of the machinery lay idle, and many workers "hung about" doing nothing. But at the moment of the stampede everybody worked overtime. The nefarious consequences of such practices were denounced with particular violence by Erno Gero on January 12, 1952, as leading to increases in industrial accidents, abusive use of machinery, exhaustion of men ("this most valuable capital," in the words of Stalin), shoddy quality of the goods produced, greater amount of waste products, and, what seemed even worse, increased production costs, which played havoc with financial planning. These were but parts of the frustrating, vicious circle of difficulties that resulted from the irregular pace of production.

Plant managers and chief engineers—the latter were upgraded to become first assistants of the managers—were under constant pressure from the authorities, who added to their responsibilities without providing them with the means of exercising them. This brings us to the subject of industrial organization proper.

Between 1945 and 1949, most of the nationalized enterprises were managed by a triumvirate—the notorious "triangle" —consisting of the plant manager, the party representative, and the secretary of the workers' committee. The triangle usually drew up the collective contract and had it ratified by the workers; it also set the work quotas. The trade-union and Communist members of the triangle tended, for reasons of popularity, to side with the workers' point of view. The managers, fearing to be denounced by the workers' representatives as saboteurs or bourgeois agents, in most cases complied with the wishes of the two other members of the triangle. This practice resulted in the weakening of the manager's authority: he was now merely an executive agent, not of the government (as would have been preferred in high places), but of the plant committee. The managers acquired the habit of passing their responsibilities on to the two other members of the triangle. Such behavior, while compatible with the principle of industrial democracy, was less compatible with the imperative need to increase productivity, which is the supreme law of all people's democracies.

Around 1949, there arose a tendency to abolish the principle of tripartite management and to return to "individual" management. The party organizations in the plants were summoned "to place themselves at the vanguard of the struggle for the realization of one-man responsibility." "It is of capital importance that the managers be obeyed unconditionally, failing which we shall have only disorganization and incoherence," said the official organ of the Hungarian Communist party in October, 1951. But since party representatives were asked at the same time to control the work of the plant managers and the execution of the plans, the respective responsibilities were not clearly demarcated, and the Communist militants continued to encroach upon the authority of the managers.

The government's principal weapon in the plants was the party organization. But the Communist militants were too few to be successful in their double task of indoctrinating and policing the workers. They were often looked upon as an alien body within the factory, government deputies rather than bona fide workers. Only a short time before, the interests of these workers had been more directly represented by their trade-unions, which almost all Hungarian wage earners had joined after the Liberation. It is natural that the people's state should have displayed particularly great vigor in endeavoring to use

the popular and experienced unions for its own political purposes, and to transform them into auxiliaries of the party and
the government in the task of re-educating the working class.
Indeed, only with the help of the unions could the government
acquire popularity and influence; only their co-operation could
secure collective sanction of the doctrine according to which
the working class, through the party, is in effective control of
the government. For according to this doctrine, all measures
decided upon by the government, including measures that
seem to injure momentary interests of given groups of workers,
are ultimately beneficial to the working class as a whole.

The problem of re-educating the trade-unions, and, through
them, the working class identified with the state, was more
easily solved in theory than in practice. Between 1946 and
1951, the Labor government and the leadership of the trade-
unions in England ran into difficulties similar to those beset-
ting the satellite governments. The main difficulty was that the
immediate advantages the governments could offer to the
working class were insignificant, deceptive, or of interest to
only a small minority: for they aimed at industrialization and
called for a policy of austerity and freely accepted sacrifices
on the basis of a very low standard of living. It was very difficult to persuade the majority of the workers that the government had the right to use the national income as it pleased.
The trade-unions and party militants knew that if they adopted
the government point of view regarding wages, output quotas,
and work discipline they would run the risk of losing all influence in the factories. Occasionally, the government itself
seemed to realize the dangers inherent in the failure to dis-
criminate between government and trade-union functions. But
it was in a hurry, the tasks were urgent, the workers were discontented; therefore the state authorities and the party did
everything to suppress every stirring of independence in the
trade-unions. The struggle for their control is one of the most

striking features of the life of the Hungarian people's democracy.

The trade-union statutes of 1950, which followed the Stalinist model, clearly reflected the government's aims with regard to the trade-unions. Under these statutes, the primary duty of the trade-unions was:

"(a) to organize and extend Socialist emulation among workers, to struggle for a better organization of work, for the strengthening of discipline, for the improvement of the quality of goods produced, for the decrease of production costs and wastage, and for the increase of productivity;

"(b) to see to it that workers acquire greater technical knowledge. . . ."

The Labor Code, a copy of the Soviet Union's, also entrusted the trade-unions with the task of concluding collective contracts and agreements on work quotas. In actual fact, the central administration and the plant management alone drew up the contracts and set the quotas, which the trade-union delegates accepted after a discussion that was most often purely theoretical. The administration sometimes had a local trade-union organization propose new quotas, only to declare later that some of these proposals were "exaggerated." The trade-union leaders were not pleased with such procedures that made them lose face before the workers. In some cases, the party, feeling that it was losing influence in the factories, attacked the "bureaucratic methods" of the trade-union leadership, charging it, for instance, with "displaying a criminal indifference, unworthy of Socialist industry, toward the issue of protecting workers against accidents." [2]

By voicing the workers' grievances the trade-unionists ran

[2] Cf. *Szabad Nep,* January 27, 1952. Early that year there was "an alarming increase of industrial accidents in Hungary," particularly among young workers recruited in the villages, "whom no one bothers to enlighten on the necessary precautions to be taken."

the risk of arousing the anger of the party, which kept them under strict supervision. On the other hand, by complying with the wishes of the management, the state employer, and the party, the trade-unionists lost the confidence of their comrades, who no longer regarded them as their representatives, but as mere tools of the management. According to the official party view, the trade-unions were supposed to discuss each contract or change in a contract with the workers before signing it in their name. "Only in this way can the collective contract become a true constitution, a fundamental law for the factory, which everyone is bound to respect," said *Szabad Nep*. But the carrying out of such instructions proved difficult, if not impossible. For instance, most metal workers and miners had no idea of the contents of the collective contracts that their trade-union delegates had signed for them.

The trade-union delegates encountered similar difficulties in getting the workers to carry out the pledges they had to make to increase production or improve its quality as a means of demonstrating their love of peace or their indignation at a given act of the "imperialists," or just in commemoration of a given event. It often seemed difficult to ask the workers, already exhausted, to make an additional effort in order to mine more coal or produce another carload of goods. And so it happened sometimes that workers on arriving in the factory had the surprise of reading in the trade-union paper that their plant committee had sent, in their name, a letter with such a pledge to the party secretary. That is why, despite the continual increase of trade-union membership, the real influence of the trade-unions on the workers was steadily declining. Incidentally, the same was true of other mass organizations, particularly youth groups. The workers deserted trade-union meetings that duplicated party meetings; and the Communist cells, which theoretically were supposed to represent only the "vanguard" of the workers, had more members than the union committees. The ever-growing difficulties experienced by the state-controlled unions to gain the adherence of the masses to the government policies, to induce the workers, old and new, to wage an effective struggle against absenteeism and "migrations," confronted the Hungarian rulers with one of their most serious problems. Whatever benefit the new regime gained by subordinating the trade-unions to the state and the party was offset by the fact that it could no longer count on the spontaneous support of the working class. By refusing to accept the risks implied in industrial democracy, with its division of powers and functions, communism gave up important trump cards, without which it is difficult to imagine the survival of Socialist society in the Marxian sense of the term. As Imre Nagy was to acknowledge publicly in July, 1953, the Communist party had become divorced from the workers. These came to regard the party leaders as class enemies, as a new privileged group of oppressors and exploiters who did not even secure for them the low living standards that the majority of the workers had enjoyed under the old regime.

Not until the eve of the 1956 uprising did the intellectuals, speaking for the proletariat, have the opportunity of voicing the indignation aroused among Hungarian workers by the existence of "large and small shops, *salons de couture,* etc., reserved for the high civil and military bureaucracy, and enabling its members to obtain rare or superior articles."

Judith Mariassy, a contributor to the Budapest *Literary Gazette,* drew up an indictment against special privileges. She also brought out some other interesting facts. Thus, "certain highly placed comrades" displayed an "excessive" concern for their security by having their villas and gardens fenced off with barbed wire and guarded by militiamen night and day. The same article disclosed that the barbed wire was extended "as far as the water's edge" to protect certain "bigwigs" lolling about in their residences on the shore of Lake Balaton—an obvious allusion to Matyas Rakosi. Then there was the scandalous behavior of many dignitaries who sent their children to school in official cars or threatened to dismiss teachers who displayed "too much severity" toward their offspring. Similar cases had been denounced in *Partelet,* the internal party organ. "This is very unlike our dream of the Socialist order!" wrote Judith Mariassy.

The official Communist organ, *Szabad Nep,* though it did not undertake the defense of the privileged classes, thought it advisable to level against the writer the ritual accusation of supplying arguments to the correspondents of the London *Times* and *Star,* and thus "playing into the hands of the enemy."

The firmness, the boldness and rudeness, even, of Judith Mariassy's reply to this charge strikingly illustrates the change that had meanwhile taken place in the atmosphere of the people's democracies. In 1956, a comment in *Szabad Nep* was no longer inevitably regarded as a summons to a *mea culpa.* Judith Mariassy retorted that "the scandal does not lie in the fact of *speaking* about special shops and villas surrounded by barbed wire, but in the very existence of these shops and villas. . . . Abolish the privileges and there will be no talk about them." She had received, she added, "countless letters and telephone calls" commending her for her stand and denouncing *Szabad Nep* for its attempt "to discredit" and "silence" her.

This incident showed that de-Stalinization, which its initiators had conceived as a purely theoretical affair, was now a weapon of social critique. The new intelligentsia was supporting the people against the new ruling class, which had acquired excessive powers and privileges as a result of a process of social differentiation that had been inevitable in itself, but insufficiently controlled. On the other hand, it will be clear from the foregoing analysis why the workers' councils created by

the insurrection demanded first of all the restoration of independent trade-unions and the right to strike.

The Peasants

Even before World War II it had become obvious that Eastern Europe was in the throes of an agricultural crisis that
could not be surmounted without a complete transformation
of the economic life of the countries involved. Only large-scale
industrialization could enable the nascent industries to absorb
the rapidly growing population surplus, then estimated at about
fourteen million, and to supply agriculture, at reasonable prices
and under easy conditions of payment, with the needed machines, fertilizers, and other industrial products, and at the
same time to extend its markets.

It must also be noted that beginning with this century Hungary, like the other East European countries, had been going
through the first stages of the so-called biological revolution,
caused by lower death rates, which were not balanced, as in
more advanced countries, by correspondingly lower birth
rates. As a result, agricultural and industrial manpower reserves increased from year to year, causing further economic
and social strains.

In the light of these anguishing problems, the postwar agrarian reform could be regarded only as the starting point of a
development determined by projects affecting the entire economic structure of the region. The majority of the agrarian
economists, liberals and Social Democrats, eager to preserve
the system of small holdings, emphasized the need for intensive
production of pigs, vegetables, milk, and fruits. By means of
a judicious distribution of credits and the fostering of co-
operatives of the Danish type, they aimed at transforming the
former "granary of Europe" into a large vegetable garden dot-
ted with dairies and orchards. Others, more realistic, pointed
to the fact that the East European climate was harsher than

that of Denmark, Holland, and England, countries of intensive culture, and envisaged an intermediary system combining the mechanized large-scale production of grains with the intensive production of vegetables, pigs, dairy products, fruits, tobacco, and industrial crops. These ideas were seductive; but they implied that Hungary would remain part of the European system, and that the Western capitalist countries would, in their own interest, support a planned development of this region. Following the nationalization of industry—completed in 1948—the Communists, after eliminating their political competitors, occupied all the economic key posts. They intended to bring the development of agriculture, of the entire economy, into line with the interests they defended and with their doctrine.

What were these interests and this doctrine that inspired the postwar Communist agricultural policies?

Agrarian reforms had been demanded long before the war by the radical peasant parties and the Social Democrats; by initiating them in 1945, the Hungarian Communists faithfully followed the Leninist-Stalinist program. As is well known, Lenin, for strictly political reasons inherent in the specific conditions of pre-revolutionary Russia, had considerably modified the orthodox Marxist doctrine on agriculture. When Marx discussed agriculture, he referred primarily to its development in advanced Western countries, which had convinced him of the absolute superiority of large-scale exploitation. Small peasant holdings, he thought, would not in the long run stand up against the competition of large estates, for only the latter could afford the investments required for the modernization of production methods. The Marxian doctrine, questionable because it was too exclusive, also had the great disadvantage of making it impossible for the workers' parties inspired by it to exploit the discontent of the small landholders, who were threatened by the development of capitalism, and to whom Marxian theory offered no future. For this reason E. Bernstein and J. David, the German "revisionists," early in this century had criticized the Marxian view, and defended against Kautsky, then the spokesman for orthodox Marxism, the thesis that small exploitations were "viable."

Lenin followed these debates with passionate interest. While approving the orthodox thesis with regard to the development of agriculture in the West, he realized that Russia and other underdeveloped countries faced agrarian problems different from those of Western Europe or the United States. The large holdings predominant in the east, he declared, were not capitalist but feudal in character. In struggling against the latifundia, the peasantry was opposing not capitalism with its technological progress, but backward feudalism which kept it in a condition of semi-serfdom. The peasant struggle, he concluded, had a progressive significance, and this justified an alliance between the revolutionary workers' party and the peasants. The revolution of 1905 confirmed Lenin in this view, which could be criticized on economic grounds—for at that time capitalism had begun to penetrate the great feudal domains of the Eastern countries—but which proved extremely fruitful from the revolutionary standpoint. And it was primarily the latter that Lenin was interested in. He knew that his party could not hope to defeat the bourgeois and reformist parties unless it allied itself with or at least neutralized the peasant masses starved for land. On the basis of these considerations, Lenin devised the revolutionary strategy to which communism is indebted for its greatest triumphs in Russia, and later in China and in all other underdeveloped countries where capitalist penetration had begun to modify the traditional way of life without destroying the material foundations of feudalism or relieving the demographic pressure of the villages. The alliance between the revolutionary proletarian party and the disinherited and oppressed peasants is Lenin's great discovery, and one of the most dynamic ideas of the twentieth century. In summoning the peasants of Eastern Europe to break up the large estates, the Communists of that region were merely applying a strategy the effectiveness of which had been proven by history.

Lenin's decision to support the economic demands of the peasants in the hope of securing their political support did not imply that he had become converted to the revisionist thesis of the viability of small holdings. A partisan of political and economic centralization, and of large-scale mechanized production, Lenin rejected as illusory the view according to which a system of small holdings could be established on the ruins of feudalism. His answer to Kautsky, who in 1918 charged him with deviating from Marxism, was: "The proletarians say to the peasants: We shall help you realize your aspirations oriented toward an ideal 'capitalism,' for the redistribution of land on an equalitarian basis is merely the smallholder's idealization of capitalism. At the same time, we shall prove to you the impossibility of such a system and the need to pass on to a collective cultivation of land" (Lenin, *The Proletarian Revolution and the Renegade Kautsky*).

In other words, Lenin wanted first of all to win the peasants as allies. Then, he thought, once his party was in power, it would be easy to steer the peasantry toward collectivization by means of the co-operative movement (Lenin, *Thesis on the Agrarian Question*, 1920). Moreover, Lenin thought that the destruction of feudalism, by paving the way for a "capitalist" evolution of agriculture, would rapidly create a class antagonism between the poor peasants and the kulaks, or rich, capitalist-minded peasants. By organizing the poor peasants and reducing the influence of the kulaks through coercive measures, the Communists would penetrate the villages and pave the way for collectivization.

Trotsky did not share Lenin's optimism on this point. He did not believe that the antagonism between the various strata of peasantry would grow more acute; on the contrary, he foresaw—and subsequent events proved him right—that the rich and the poor peasants, though hostile to each other, would make common cause against the Communist party and the state the moment they felt their property was threatened. The Communists in their attempts to reconstruct agricultural economy on a sounder basis would find themselves in conflict, Trotsky said, "not only with all the bourgeois groups that might have supported them at the opening stage of the revolutionary struggle, but also with the peasant masses which had helped them to seize power" (Trotsky, Preface to *1905*, published in 1922).

It was no doubt to avoid or at least to postpone that conflict —the crisis of 1921 had given a foretaste of its severity—that Lenin embarked on the New Economic Policy, which involved large concessions to the well-to-do peasants. After his death, the Bolshevik party wavered for a long time between the continuation of the N.E.P. advocated by Bukharin (for whom Imre Nagy has always had great admiration) and Trotsky's extremist emphasis on the role of the workers. Trotsky thought that the conflict between the party and the peasants was inevitable; hence he proposed to concentrate all efforts on fostering the world revolution of the proletariat, on the ground that the Russian party could not defeat the peasants without material and moral assistance from the workers of advanced countries. Stalin's solution of the problem was, to say the least, surprising: while actually unleashing a war of the party and the state against the peasantry—the very war Trotsky had foreseen —he claimed that it was waged by the poor peasants (whom Lenin had wished to have as allies) against the kulaks. Stalin began this war of collectivization without waiting for the world revolution, and conducted it with unprecedented brutality, overriding the almost unanimous protests of the Soviet peasantry.

The foregoing historical survey will shed some light on the

Hungarian Communist party's attitude toward the peasants. Their position in Hungary at the moment of Liberation was in some ways analogous to that of the peasants in pre-revolutionary Russia: great feudal domains were still in existence, thus making it possible to apply the Leninist policy of dividing the land. But there were important differences. For in 1945, even though the objective conditions favored a revolutionary mass movement, the peasants had just emerged from a twenty-five-year period of police and ideological pressure, which had left them mentally crippled, disoriented, and without hope. The poor peasants and the farm hands were entirely under the influence of the rural "bourgeoisie," the kulaks, and the police, whose nationalism and virulent anti-communism they shared. Most important of all, the peasants were informed about Russian developments. They did not believe that the Communists were sincere champions of the division of land into small holdings. The presence of non-Communists in the government only half-reassured the peasants. This accounts for the morose atmosphere, characterized by distrust, hesitations, and doubts, in which the Communists, urged by the Red army, carried out the agrarian reform in 1945.

Nevertheless, the Communists did divide the land: this enabled them to gain a foothold in the countryside, and to neutralize the peasant masses which for several years were busy consolidating their acquisitions. Between 1945 and 1948, the Communist leaders rejected as "base reactionary slander" the rumors that they were planning to begin the second stage of the revolution, i.e., to set up collective farms on the Russian model. For instance, at an electoral meeting held in Pecs on May 11, 1947, Matyas Rakosi promised that "as long as the Communists are in power, no force in the world will take back the land that was given to the 700,000 beneficiaries of the agrarian reform." On the same occasion, he said that it was imperative to secure once and for all the right of small and medium landholders to the continual and hereditary enjoyment of their properties.

Then came the Cominform resolution condemning the Yugoslavs, among other things, for their failure to nationalize agriculture. This resolution caused as much consternation in Hungary as in Yugoslavia itself. "The nationalization of agriculture would be a catastrophe," declared Boris Kidrich, economic dictator of Yugoslavia at the Fifth Congress of his party. "Our accusers are trying to push us into disaster." Rakosi might have said the same thing. In condemning Tito, the Hungarian leaders condemned their own policy of 1945–1948 and put themselves in an embarrassing position. By carrying out the measures advocated by the Russians, the Hungarian Communists ran the risk of destroying the very foundations of their influence, and causing very serious disturbances in the villages, which would adversely affect deliveries of foodstuffs. They had had trouble enough trying to consolidate their power against a hostile majority of the population, and now they saw themselves compelled to wage a struggle on a new front, with the result that they would become more than ever dependent on Soviet Russia. But that is perhaps the very reason why the Soviet delegates at the Cominform meeting in Bucharest showed themselves intransigent on the question of collectivization and imposed their views on the others. No doubt the Soviet decision to compel the "fraternal parties" to collectivize agriculture reflected a general plan for speeding up the assimilation of the satellites to the Soviet Union. The Kremlin could not permit Communist-governed countries to pursue a path considered impracticable by the Stalinist doctrine, namely, that of coexistence of a nationalized industry and a private agriculture.

Some Hungarian leaders tried to limit the damage caused by the Cominform resolution by solemnly proclaiming the necessity of collectivization, but adding that it would of course be a long-term process. But the masters of the Cominform

brooked no delays and refused to content themselves with
academic proclamations. What they required was acts—if not
collectivization, at least the persecution of the kulaks, which
was to be the prelude to collectivization.

That was a seemingly simple way out. Still, it was necessary
first to find the kulaks. It proved difficult to establish a distinction between two categories of peasants—"the fairly well-to-
do" and "the well-to-do." Finally, it was left to the discretion
of local officials to determine who was and who was not a
kulak. This brings to mind a cynical statement made by
Lueger, onetime mayor of Vienna and notorious anti-Semite
whom Hitler regarded as his master. Once when he was criticized for having Jewish friends, he declared haughtily: *"Wer
Jude ist bestimme Ich"* [It is I who decide who is a Jew].

Where kulaks did not exist they were invented. In line with
Russian teachings, an attempt was made to set the poor peasants upon them. But the poor peasants of Hungary showed
themselves just as unwilling as those of Russia had been before
them. True enough, they disliked and envied the well-to-do,
but they also respected and feared them, and were ready to
take their side against the "city gentlemen."

In the end, the task of hounding the kulaks fell upon the
government and the party. They were subjected to crushing
taxation, and then to all sorts of harassment. With the formation of the first co-operative the persecution of the kulaks was
intensified everywhere, and ever greater numbers of them were
thrown into prison under various pretexts. In some cases they
were driven from their land with their families and forbidden
to join the co-operatives even if they had applied for membership. In this way immense damage was done not only to many
peasant families, but also to the co-operative movement and
the provisioning of cities. For even though the ensuing unrest
among the peasants remained unorganized, and did not mani-

fest itself by spectacular protests, it resulted in a decline of agricultural production.

Joys and Sorrows of Collective Farming

The anti-kulak drive was but an expedient. Following the anti-Yugoslav resolution of the Cominform, the Hungarian Communist party was thoroughly reorganized. The adversaries of the new agrarian policy (Rajk and the Debrecen group, and the national Communists Kadar, Kallai, and Losonczy, who were imprisoned between 1949 and 1951) were "liquidated," and by 1949 the party had become an effective instrument for the application of the new line. From then on, collectivization made considerable advances. But even though nationalization of agriculture had been considered in 1948, the project had created such unrest among the peasants that the Cominform partisans beat a retreat. While continuing to denounce Tito, they were forced to recognize that his arguments against the principle of nationalization were valid for Hungary as well as Yugoslavia, and that these countries could not follow the Russian example. The Russian peasants of 1918 had welcomed nationalization, because in Russia this measure was anti-feudal rather than anti-bourgeois, and the abolition of the large estates made the peasants *de facto* owners of the lands they had cultivated. But the Hungarian peasants wanted not merely *de facto* but also *de jure* ownership of the lands they had acquired by virtue of the agrarian reform of 1945. They would have opposed this reform if it had been carried out in the guise of nationalization, which they were not sophisticated enough to distinguish from outright confiscation of their lands by the state.

For this reason, the Communists, in urging the peasants to form agricultural co-operatives or collective farms, carefully avoided any mention of nationalization. Under the statute governing these co-operatives, each member had the right to secede, and was entitled to a share of profits proportionate to the area of land he contributed to the community. Four different types of co-operative were provided for. In the first type, each member retained ownership of his land and livestock, and contributed only his farm machinery for which the co-operative paid him a rent calculated on the basis of its income. In the second type, the amount of rent was established on the basis of the value of the land. In the third type, each member received his share of the total income, but retained title to his land. Finally, in the fourth or "highest" type, the members had no right to withdraw, and their land and livestock were the property of the co-operative.

The "inferior" types were intended as transitional stages, enabling the peasants to realize the advantages of collective farming. For similar reasons, the government encouraged the formation of groups which cultivated in common only certain special crops, such as tobacco, rice, or industrial crops; members of such groups continued to cultivate other crops on an individual basis.

On paper, most Hungarian co-operatives were of the first or second type, i.e., they paid rent to their members. But in very many cases the rent was not actually paid, for the landless peasants and agricultural workers who could contribute only their labor power to the co-operative were opposed to such a system, which perpetuated their inferior status. On the other hand, those members of the co-operatives who owned land fiercely opposed the removal of the boundary stones that marked out their properties. The peasants' attachment to their individual plots made it extremely difficult to reorganize agriculture on a rational basis, and without such a reorganization the advantages of collective exploitation remained insignificant. The peasants also refused to send their livestock to the collective stables, preferring to slaughter their animals.

Under the statute governing the co-operatives, each member

was authorized to retain a plot of ½ to 1½ acres adjoining his house, and to raise, for his own consumption, one cow, one calf, one sow with its litter, one pig for fattening, five sheep or goats, poultry, rabbits, and bees. This provision turned out to be another stumbling block. It aroused the resentment of the landless members; as for the others, particularly in the wine-growing regions where the plots retained for individual exploitation were often larger than provided for in the statute, they devoted all their energies to cultivating their own properties, thus robbing the co-operatives of badly needed labor power. Moreover, in most cases only the head of a peasant household joined the co-operative, while his family remained outside, and took no part in the collective work. In 1952, 260,000 households supplied the co-operatives with a total membership of only 400,000. The failure of peasant wives and children to join the co-operatives, in conjunction with the mass exodus of the rural population to the cities, caused a labor shortage that was felt most acutely at harvest time. The authorities tried to remedy the shortage by reducing the areas of individual land allotments. At the same time, local party officials and chairmen of co-operatives were instructed to bring the peasant families into the co-operatives. Where promises of substantial increases in the benefits failed to sway the peasants, various forms of pressure were applied to persuade the wives and older children of members to do their share of at least the most pressing seasonal tasks.

The internal organization of the co-operatives (which corresponded to the Russian kolkhozes) differed from that of the state farms (the Russian sovkhozes). According to Stalin, "the sovkhoz is a state enterprise, whereas the kolkhoz is a voluntary co-operative association of peasants, managed by the peasants." In Hungary, the state farms were run jointly by the manager and chief agronomist responsible for the technical details. The co-operatives, on the other hand, were run by a board of directors, which was elected by a general assembly of the members; the directors appointed a chairman, whose functions were executive. Such at least were the provisions of the statute. In actual fact, the management of the co-operatives had from the outset shifted from a democratic to an authoritarian basis.

The democratic organization was preferable for propagandistic reasons; but the peasants who had most often joined under compulsion made too frequent use of their statutory rights to evade collective work. The non-Communist chairmen appointed by the peasants were anxious to please them; the Communist chairmen were often incompetent and tried to make themselves popular with the members by favoring their individualistic tendencies. In some cases, local Communist militants or officials imposed chairmen of their own choice; then the organization of the co-operative scarcely differed from that of a state farm, and the management had to face the open hostility of the peasants who protested against the violation of their rights. Time and again the Central Committee had to rebuke local officials for their failure to respect the voluntary and democratic character of the co-operatives. The Communists knew that the peasants' greatest fear was that by joining the co-operatives they would completely lose their independence, and be transformed from landed proprietors into farm hands working for large estates.

It was obvious, however—and the Communist leaders realized this quickly—that the literal application of the statute was incompatible with the principle of rentability, all the more so because zealous officials often recruited adherents by offering them privileges in the form of income tax exemptions, government loans, reduced delivery quotas, etc. In some cases, these privileges had official sanction: for instance, co-operatives were obliged to deliver to the state only 188 kilos of wheat per acre, while individual peasants delivered 224. But local officials went beyond that, privately assuring the peasants that they would not have to effect even those reduced deliveries. Government collectors actually often exempted co-operatives at the expense of individual peasants whose delivery quotas were increased. Members of co-operatives took advantage of such practices: instead of selling a considerable part of their crops to the state at low prices, they divided the produce among themselves and sold it on the black market. As a result, many co-operatives vegetated, while their members were prosperous. In April, 1952, Andras Hegedus declared that "the output of several co-operatives was lower than that of individual peasants in the same region." Instead of "several," he could safely have said "almost all."

To remedy this situation, the co-operatives were completely reorganized during the winter of 1951. The authorities, while paying lip service to "internal democracy," strengthened the powers of the chairmen by instituting so-called Control and Discipline Committees composed of active party militants. Managers were authorized to inflict on undisciplined or "fraudulent" members sanctions ranging from fines to expulsion. Moreover, the co-operatives were subjected to strict control by local party organizations and government offices. Finally, the system of distribution of income was radically revised. Between 1949 and 1951, profits had been divided on the basis of the number of working hours contributed by each member. Late in 1951, the co-operatives adopted "the Socialist principle of distribution," based on the number of working days and the output quotas. Members who exceeded the quotas were rewarded with bonuses. Furthermore, the members of the co-operatives were grouped into permanent work brigades like those of the state farms. Each brigade (fifteen to twenty men in dairies, and fifty to eighty in the fields) was in charge of a given piece of land, and a given quantity of equipment and livestock. The brigade chiefs, directly responsible to the chairmen, were given disciplinary powers, just as was the case in the Soviet Union, which had adopted this system in 1932.

At the beginning of 1950, there were 1,760 agricultural co-operatives in Hungary; at the end of that year, this number rose to 2,229, with a membership of 90,000 former smallholders and a total area of about a million acres. In the winter of 1950, there were 260 "Socialist" towns and villages, among them four large peasant agglomerations, 70 per cent of whose population (from 13,000 to 28,000) belonged to the co-operatives.

In the spring of 1951, collectivization picked up speed. During the weeks preceding the Second Party Congress, local officials, eager to please their superiors, coerced large numbers of peasants to join the collective farms, causing unrest in the villages. To reassure the peasants, a decree issued on March 10, 1951, prohibited the formation of new collective farms, and even the recruitment of new members for old farms. An article by Imre Nagy (he had been ousted from the Politburo, and held the chair of agricultural economy at the University of Budapest), published in the party's theoretical organ, sounded the alarm: "While industry is now sufficiently developed to do its part in the mechanization of agriculture, the state farms and agricultural co-operatives have not yet reached an adequate level of development to serve as an example and to attract the rest of the peasants." But the sole result of such warnings was to induce the party congress to take a cautious position, condemning both the danger of "unwise haste," i.e., of forgetting that "small and medium holdings are playing and will continue, in the immediate future, to play an important part in supplying the industry and nation with foodstuffs," and the danger of "an opportunistic policy of waiting." The party came out for "the liquidation of the backward state of agriculture," but at the same time emphasized the fact that "this process can be accelerated only by means of persuasion and conviction."

To solve this problem, similar to that of squaring the circle (what should have been done was, as Nagy proposed, to stop collectivization), the Hungarian rulers hit on a seemingly ingenious method. They decided to issue an urgent appeal to those peasants who were party members. Early in 1951, these numbered about 100,000. The nearly 100,000 members of the Union of Toiling Youth and the 300,000 members of the Communist-controlled National Union of Toiling Peasants and Agricultural Workers were also mobilized.

Up until then, recruitment for the party had not been associated with recruitment for the collective farms. On the contrary, thousands of small and medium peasants had joined the party or Communist-controlled mass organizations in the hope that this would protect them from possible pressures. But the reprieve that had been granted them was coming to an end. The party congress decreed that "the Communist peasants must give the example to the other peasants."

In December, 1951, the minister of agriculture announced that Hungary had 4,653 collective farms, with 360,000 members and a total area of 1,500,000 acres. But at the same time Rakosi acknowledged that "the majority of the peasants who joined early in the year under threats work little and badly," and that "in many collective farms 30 to 40 per cent of the members were absent at the moment of the most urgent harvest work."

According to an article in *Tarsadalmi Szemle* of April, 1952, the number of collective farms and co-operative groups had by then reached 4,950, of which 1,839 were of the "inferior" (first or second) type. During the winter of 1951–1952, 35,000 households had joined. But whereas the tillable area of the collective farms doubled in 1952, their livestock increased by only 60 per cent. This shows that in Hungary, as in the other people's democracies, it was cattle breeding that suffered most from collectivization. The peasants slaughtered or sold their livestock before joining the collective farms; moreover, the depleted livestock of the collective farms often wasted away as a result of poor care.

Such was the extremely critical state of Hungarian agriculture when Imre Nagy was summoned to succeed Rakosi as premier in the summer of 1953. The great majority of the members of the agricultural co-operatives doggedly resisted collective work, to which they had subscribed only under pressure. This resistance manifested itself not only by the slaughtering of livestock, but also by careless work, absenteeism, refusal to obey the chairmen, etc. It compelled the government to adopt ever more stringent disciplinary measures, and to strengthen the authority of the men in commanding posts. The battle which had at first been fought between the state and the free peasants attached to their plots of ground was now waged within the collective farms themselves.

From then on, the members of the agricultural co-operatives acted as if they were bent on proving the falsity of the Communist thesis that large collective exploitations are economically superior to small family holdings. In the course of the first years of the experiment, the small holdings successfully competed against the "socialized sector" both in output per acre and production costs. Indeed, most of the collectivized farmers helped the free peasants to win that battle; and the peasant family asserted itself as a more effective working unit than the improvised brigade of the collective farm.

The struggle waged by the peasants against the Communist form of co-operation brings to mind their onetime opposition to the half-feudal and half-capitalist large estates. At that time the superiority of the smallholders lay in their greater flexibility and the fact that they could work more intensively. Moreover, the large estates of the Eastern countries most often lacked capital and skilled personnel needed for modernization.

This was to some extent also the case on the Communist state farms and collective farms. Even where machinery was available, the other conditions of rational exploitation were often absent. For all the differences separating the people's state from the previous regimes, it was their true heir in granting priority to industrial development, particularly to heavy industry. The cult of technological progress and the will to develop productive forces, which are inherent in Marxism, thus continued a tendency that had asserted itself under the old "nationalist" regime. Investments appropriated for agriculture were insufficient to take immediate advantage of the possibilities offered by a more rational exploitation of the land and the concentration of labor. Despite undeniable efforts to step up the training of agronomists, there was a shortage of skilled personnel. The output of the chemical and mechanical industries was still inadequate to meet the demands of the collectivized sector. Such deficiencies could of course be corrected as industry continued to grow; but in the meantime agricultural production was decreasing instead of increasing. According to the report of the Geneva Economic Commission of 1951, it was still noticeably below the prewar level, and this at a time when stepped-up industrialization—which had already absorbed almost the entire rural population surplus—had considerably enlarged the domestic market, and when Hungary should have increased her agricultural exports in order to obtain in exchange the needed machinery and raw materials.

To be sure, even without communism, under a purely capitalist development, a large part of the smallholders would have been compelled to give up their unprofitable operations and to seek employment in factories or on large farms. In the United States, the number of farmers exploiting areas under two hundred acres decreased by 15 per cent between 1945 and 1950;

an identical tendency can be observed in other capitalist countries. Even if we do not grant that large-scale exploitation in agriculture and cattle breeding is always more economical, we cannot deny that progress leads toward concentration. On this point, the facts have somewhat corrected, but not refuted, the predictions made by Marx and Engels.

The modernization of agriculture, with crop rotation, rational use of fertilizers, and mechanization, is one of the major effects of capitalist development. The weakness of East European capitalism and the foreign capitalists' lack of interest in East European agriculture largely account for its backwardness. Viewed from this angle, the effects of the Communist agrarian policy in Hungary appear as a specific and particularly unfortunate form of capitalist penetration of agriculture.[3]

In Hungary, where industry, banking, transportation, and wholesale trade were nationalized, agriculture could not be modernized without help from the state. Sooner or later the state would have got the better of the peasants refusing to comply with its demands. But the Communist state was impatient, it was in a hurry to complete the task in hand. That is why it sent to the countryside, along with propaganda brigades, its squadrons of machines and tractors, which seemed like incarnations of the conquering power of state capitalism.

[3] In a letter addressed to Danielson in 1892 Engels wrote: "The fact that Russia is the last country affected by large-scale capitalist industry, and that it is at the same time the country with the largest peasant population, will make the upheaval caused by this transformation more acute there than anywhere else. The replacement of some 500,000 landowners and about 80,000,000 peasants by a new class of bourgeois landholders will necessarily entail terrible suffering and social convulsions. But history is the most terrible of all divinities: she drives her victorious chariot on piles of corpses not only in wars but also in the course of supposedly peaceful developments." If we replace in this passage the term "bourgeois landholders" by "representatives of the Communist state capitalism" (party members, local officials, organizers of state farms and collective farms), we shall have a correct picture of the upheaval which began in Russia in 1929, and has been spreading into countries with a similar social structure.

The boundary stones marking out the minutely divided land were no serious obstacle to the march of these great machines, which showed them off as ridiculous anachronisms. The torpor, the millenary stagnation of the villages slumbering under the protection of castles, churches, and rural police, was gone. Mechanized civilization, in the form of a curious mixture of American technology and Asiatic military mores, set the rural masses of Eastern Europe in motion.

Under "private" capitalism, the violent destruction of small holdings that cannot keep up with technological progress assumes a purely economic form, such as the foreclosure of farm mortgages by banks, so eloquently depicted in Steinbeck's *Grapes of Wrath*. In Hungary, where the capitalist was the state, the same process assumed political, i.e., bureaucratic and police, forms: unbearable taxation, increase of compulsory deliveries, threats of eviction, of deportation, etc. But such acts of violence were incompatible with the humanistic principles of Marxism; hence the Communists did not openly expropriate the peasants, but disguised their true aims as co-operation, even though the principle of co-operation had always been branded as bourgeois by the Bolshevik specialists in conspiracy, terrorism, and civil war (according to Lenin, "co-operation begets the Menshevik and Socialist revolutionary elements"). But the resulting ambiguity did not deceive the Hungarian peasants, who knew what had happened to their brothers in Russia, and who from the outset had looked upon co-operation as the first stage of the seizure of their land by the state. In their eyes, the true master of the collective farms was not the assembly of the former landholders, but the state —the chairman appointed by the state, the party secretary representing the state, the chief of the tractor station sent by the state.

That was the crux of the matter. Under capitalism, the smallholder crushed by debts and driven from his land resigned himself to his fate, because this fate was implemented by the operation of an anonymous force governed by rules he accepted. But in Communist Hungary, the peasant, even if he was treated less harshly than under the capitalist regime, resisted more vigorously because he did not understand or accept the rules of the Communist game, and because he was not convinced of his failure as a smallholder. Moreover, the concessions made by the Communists, as spelled out in the statute of the co-operatives, enabled the peasants to wage an effective struggle against the state. Private enterprise scattered the expropriated peasants, while the state capitalism of the Communist countries concentrated them, and thus organized them against itself.

This was clearly realized as early as July, 1953: the co-operatives created by the new regime were subject to the concentrated hostility of their members, who had no interest in making them a success. As soon as the pressure of the state, for reasons of doctrine or opportunism, began to relax, a very large number of peasants manifested their wish to recover independence. Many co-operatives disbanded without waiting for official authorization. The movement was spreading. Then Rakosi forced Nagy's hand and intervened to stop the dislocation of the collectivized sector and to reorganize the movement on a new basis. While some co-operatives were permitted to dissolve, others were reconstituted and consolidated, *manu militari* if this was necessary. In March, 1955, after Nagy had been ousted from office, Rakosi, Gero, and Hegedus (*quos vult Jupiter perdere* ...) resumed the campaign that they had abandoned in 1953, and decided to collectivize the greater part of Hungarian lands before 1960. It is hardly necessary to stress the fact that this decision helped to prepare the ground (particularly in the army, which was largely composed of sons of peasants) for the uprising of October, 1956.

Religion

According to the Christian scholastics, philosophy is the handmaiden of theology. Communist scholasticism regards all culture as the handmaiden of Communist philosophy and politics. In pursuing their task of indoctrination, the Communists were bound to come into conflict with the Roman Catholic Church, which had considerable influence in Hungary. It is certain, however, that when Rakosi set himself up as a champion of the secular state he was not merely combating certain undeniably anachronistic privileges of the Church. In attacking its secular power, the Communist state sought to undermine its spiritual independence. Totalitarian Stalinism was a mortal threat to the religious spirit.

In 1948, an article in *Szabad Nep* described the decree nationalizing the schools as "a measure of self-defense," and in a sense this statement was sincere. The Communists were waging difficult battles on several other fronts, and wished to reach a *modus vivendi* with the Church, postponing a final settlement of accounts to a more favorable moment. But the Church, feeling itself more seriously threatened than ever before in its two-thousand-year history, not merely by guns but also by a doctrine, did not wait for a deterioration of relations between the West and the East to open hostilities. Its intransigence toward Yugoslavia is known from the Stepinac affair. Its attitude toward the Hungarian government between 1945 and 1947, though this government was far less extremist than that of Yugoslavia, was no more conciliatory.

The Church was represented by Cardinal Mindszenty, a dignitary whose fiery nature and zeal in defending the material and spiritual interests of the clergy recall the great figures of the Counter Reformation. He protested vigorously against the extension of the agrarian reform to Church domains, which before the war had enabled the Hungarian high clergy to

enjoy an aristocratic standard of living and complete independence in relation to the state.[4] Later, Mindszenty also protested against the proclamation of the republic, on the ground,
as he said in a letter addressed to Canon Bela Verga, member
of the National High Council, that it was "incompatible with
the thousand-year-old Hungarian constitution," and publicly
stated his attachment to the monarchy. His relations with the
new government grew progressively more strained. In December, 1947, he returned without opening it a letter from the
President of the Republic, the Smallholder Zoltan Tildy. On
January 1, 1948, he refused to send the Church's customary
congratulations to the head of the government, and later emphatically rejected an official proposal to negotiate a settlement between the state and the Church. The Communists
riposted by launching a campaign for the nationalization of
parochial schools.[5]

The Communist strategy aimed at forcing the Roman Catholic clergy to dissociate themselves from the Vatican and, in
the absence of a concordat, to sign agreements securing their
co-operation with the new regime, actually their submission to
it. After 1948, this task was all the more urgent because all
other non-Communist political, social, and cultural organizations had been liquidated, and the Roman Catholic Church
was the only institution taking its political directives from
abroad and opposing the spiritual hegemony of the Communist party. Moreover, the Church had gained in popularity as

---

[4] Out of the 348,000 acres of tillable land that had belonged to the Roman
Catholic Church, it retained only 80,000 in addition to the 23,000 allotted
to the rural parishes. This provision of the agrarian law was considered very
moderate by the Communists, but the high clergy found it inacceptable. In
August, 1951, all the land that had been retained by the Church under the
reform of 1945 was transferred to the state; parish priests were allowed to
keep for their personal use a plot of ground not exceeding 75 square yards.

[5] The Church controlled 4,332 primary schools (65 per cent of the total
number of primary schools in Hungary), and 427 secondary schools (50 per
cent of the schools for boys, and 78 per cent of those for girls).

a result of its anti-Communist stand. Catholic churches and meetings were more crowded than ever before. It was to the Church that the expropriated landowners, the former official-dom, the frightened petty bourgeoisie, and the peasant fearing the loss of their lands turned with their grievances, and it was on the Church that they pinned their hopes. Others supported the Church out of patriotic resentment. This unexpected popularity encouraged the Vatican and the hierarchy to resist the regime with increasing firmness. In the eyes of the world, the Church fought a just battle, while the Communists charged it with conspiracy and agitation. In actual fact, the Church was more or less compelled to oppose the regime, for the majority of the lower clergy, despite its nearness to the people, or perhaps because of it, was even more uncompromisingly anti-Communist than the hierarchy.

To bring the Church to its knees, or at least to force it to compromise, the Communists had powerful means at their disposal. Following the secularization of the Church's possessions, the clergy materially depended on state subsidies. The state showed itself generous: bishops and priests were offered emoluments even higher than those enjoyed by their colleagues in many capitalist countries. Although the *Osservatore Romano* referred to the Communist proposals as "attempted bribery," they could not be rejected outright.

At the same time, the Communists strove to drive a wedge between the higher and the lower clergy. On the one hand, they demanded that the bishops punish and remove from office priests hostile to the new regime of the party; on the other hand, they encouraged the organization of a union of priests "partisans of peace" and favoring co-operation with communism. The state was thus enabled to exert a growing pressure on both the episcopate and the lower clergy. It was only after all those means had proved ineffective that the Communists resorted to direct, physical pressure—indictments for espionage or illegal financial dealings, and severe sentences. They were reluctant to make martyrs, but since the Church did not seem to shrink before a test of strength, and since the prestige of the party was at stake, they had to surmount their reluctance.

The open hostilities between the Church and the government began late in 1948. Cardinal Mindszenty, the most militant of the Hungarian prelates, riposted to the nationalization of the schools by excommunicating a pro-Communist priest of the Szekesfehervar diocese, and by ordering all priests employed as teachers to leave the secularized schools. More than 2,500 priests and monks complied with this order. The government took up the challenge. On December 26, 1948, Mindszenty was arrested. It seems that, warned of his impending arrest, he handed a note to one of his faithful—who later sent it abroad—which said:

"(1) I have never taken part in any conspiracy. (2) I shall never resign from my office. (3) I shall refuse to answer questions. (4) In the event, however, that anyone should read or hear reports to the effect that I have confessed or resigned, and even if my signature should be made use of to suggest the authenticity of such confessions or of my resignation, these facts must be attributed to my human weakness. I declare them in advance to be null and void."

Whether this statement attributed to Mindszenty is genuine or not, it faithfully reflects the prelate's probable state of mind while he was waiting to be arrested. Later, in January, 1949, the world was surprised to see the primate adopt an attitude before the People's Court in Budapest which was not quite compatible with the impression created by his previous statements and actions—that of a man of unshakable courage and boldness. In the glaring light of the reflectors he appeared as a broken man. He clumsily defended himself against the details of the indictment, and against the interpretation given by the court to some of his actions, but he never tried to raise the fundamental issue at stake—the incompatibility between the Communist state and the Roman Catholic Church, of which the cardinal, as proven by all his behavior, had remained profoundly convinced.

This change of attitude could no doubt be imputed to the use of various pressures to break the cardinal's moral resistance. (In October, 1956, after being released by the insurgents, he said that he had been subjected to humiliations and tortures during his imprisonment.) But on the basis of the record there is reason to believe that the most effective means of pressure used against him was a strictly juridical exploitation of some contradictions in his attitude and his activities. He was, for instance, charged with having speculated on a war between the West and the Soviet Union, in the hope that such a war would liberate Hungary. The cardinal acknowledged that he had envisaged such a possibility, and expected to head the government if a *vacuum juris* were created by the departure of the Soviet troops. To be sure, for the Communists the very fact of envisaging such possibilities was equivalent to desiring and preparing for war. And yet the cardinal declared that he had not wished for war and had done nothing to bring it about. If this is a contradiction, it is inherent in the Hungarian situation during those troubled years, when the majority of the population undeniably hoped for a Western military or diplomatic intervention to rid them of a hated regime. Cardinal Mindszenty had shared in such an anxious, obsessive hope.

But how could this be justified from the point of view of canon law or the Hungarian code? To defend himself with greater vigor and clarity, he would have had to proclaim that the Hungarian government was illegal. He had no right to do so, and the Vatican would probably have disavowed him.

Therefore, all Mindszenty could do was to assert the purity of his intentions and to acknowledge that he had committed certain actions that could be interpreted as violations of the laws of the republic. Staring vacantly, he expressed his regrets in a broken voice, and begged that peace be granted to his Church. He was sentenced to life imprisonment.

After the trial, a meeting took place between representatives of the Church and of the government, but no settlement was reached. A year later, the government seized all monasteries, evicting about 12,000 monks and nuns. The Church authorities were faced with an almost insoluble housing problem. In June, 1950, the episcopate entered into negotiations with the government; and on August 30, a first agreement was signed, under which the Bishops' Council recognized the regime and the constitution of the republic, condemned all subversive activities "of whatever source," summoned the faithful to contribute with all their strength "to the grandiose task in which the Hungarian people, headed by its government, is engaged," and stated its support of the "peace movement." The government for its part undertook to secure for the Church "freedom of activity," promised to restore to it eight Catholic educational establishments, and authorized the male and female members of the teaching orders to teach in those establishments. Finally, in line with agreements concluded with the other denominations, the government declared itself willing to defray the material expenses of the Roman Catholic Church for eighteen years, until it was capable of meeting its needs on the basis of its own resources.

The agreement was signed for the episcopate by Msgr. Groesz, archbishop of Kalocsa, close collaborator of Mindszenty. However, less than a year later, in June, 1951, Groesz suffered the fate of Mindszenty. At that time, the government was no longer satisfied with the Church's neutrality. The arch-

bishop of Kalocsa aroused the ire of the regime by his attempt
to safeguard the hierarchy's authority over the lower clergy,
which the government had been propagandizing. His trial and
the charges against him were a crude version of the Mindszenty original. Mindszenty, even when displaying humility
and great sorrow, had preserved some vestiges of his episcopal
dignity. The old archbishop of Kalocsa was but an automaton
confessing everything he had been asked to confess. "I have
always been against the agrarian reform," he said. "I have
systematically fought against an agreement with the state. . . .
I entered into negotiations without sincerity and with fraudulent intent. . . . My aim was to restore the latifundia, to return
the nationalized establishments to their former owners, to re-
constitute the former rural police, to deprive women, workers,
and peasants of their right to vote, and to achieve all this by
means of foreign arms, particularly American. . . ."

The aged prelate thus condemned himself in terms that
would have done credit to a *Szabad Nep* editorial writer. The
record of the Mindszenty trial is a bewildering document. The
record of the Groesz trial, which the Hungarian government
bureaus diffused abroad, is a repulsive document.

On the day Groesz was sentenced, Msgr. Hamvas, bishop
of Csanad, who was implicated in the trial and was in prison,
sent a letter to the head of the government, in which he expressed regret over his past activities, and pledged himself to
bend all his efforts to establish peace between the Church and
the state. A few days later, the entire Hungarian episcopate
swore allegiance to the People's Republic.

The Communist pressure on the Church was relaxed only
after Imre Nagy's accession to power in 1953. But it was not
until 1956 that Groesz was released, rehabilitated, and restored to his office. That was too late to make the Hungarian
Catholics forget the persecutions and harassments of the preceding years.

The Battle for the Soul of the Youth

The Communists did a great deal for public education, and yet their efforts resulted in failure. Despite the constant pressure exerted on schoolmasters, teachers, and students, despite the compulsory courses in Marxism-Leninism, despite the fact that the study of the Russian language had been made obligatory, the Communists failed to capture the minds of the youth: in 1956, the students formed the vanguard of the uprising. Less than two months before the uprising, Gyorgy Lukacs, who had been in disgrace since 1949, declared on being restored to his post of professor of aesthetics at the University of Budapest that "the positions of Marxism have been considerably weakened." And it is true that Communist control of education has been more harmful than beneficial to the spread of Marxism in Hungary.

This paradoxical result can be attributed, first of all, to the mediocrity of the intellectual, educational, and propaganda leaders. By their servile imitation of Russia they extirpated all living traditions and spontaneous national movements in Hungarian pedagogy. The Communists suppressed both the Eotvos Teachers' College and the people's colleges founded after the Liberation. They suppressed pedagogic science and psychology; dismissed or imprisoned the best teachers, such as Tibor Merey; and reduced to a dangerously low level the once famous national universities. It is not surprising that in 1956 teachers and students were unanimous in their condemnation of Communist educational methods.

The Communist objectives in the field of education were to destroy the privileges of the former ruling classes, and, by filling the schools with children of workers and peasants, to create that new intelligentsia devoted to the regime, which, as Stalin had said, "no ruling class can dispense with." At the same time, the technological level of the population was to be raised, and the schools transformed into vehicles of the Stalinist doctrine. As applied in the people's democracies, this doctrine fostered a so-called patriotism which implied unconditional devotion to the Soviet Union, love for Stalin, and the determination to fight for one's country. Only the last of these objectives was achieved. The Hungarian youth was to fight for its country—against Stalinism, and against communism.

After 1948, the government concentrated its efforts on the democratization of secondary and higher education. Before the war, only 5 per cent of the university students had been of working-class or peasant origin. On the other hand, despite the shortage of physicians, veterinaries, and other professionals, intellectuals suffered from widespread unemployment. One reason for this was that many poor students, whose highest aspiration was to enter government service, studied law. Other professions attracted fewer young people. Business careers were considered undignified, and were despised even by those whose fathers were porters, janitors, or policemen; and industry was not sufficiently developed to arouse any interest in industrial careers. The prewar governments, anxious above all to preserve political and social stability, took various measures (directed in particular against the Jews) to limit to the utmost the number of pupils admitted to secondary schools and establishments of higher learning.

As early as 1945, Communist propaganda emphasized the need to replace the former intelligentsia by a new stratum of intellectuals and technicians coming from the ranks of workers and peasants. By this propaganda the Communists alienated many engineers, physicians, and professors whose political ideas were not too clear, and who, though prejudiced against communism, actually asked only to be left alone and to be allowed to continue their professional work. Frequent dismissals that were justified by no professional misconduct; hostile utterances and threats against bourgeois intellectuals;

criminatory measures against their children (who were refused admittance to colleges and often to secondary schools)
had discouraged the former intelligentsia and induced thousands of cultivated persons and technicians to go abroad.
(After the Twentieth Congress, the national Communist Geza
Losonczy became the most vigorous spokesman for this "bourgeois" intelligentsia at Petofi Society meetings and in *Szabad
Nep*, demanding their rehabilitation as a social class.) To these
dissidents we must add a large number of intellectuals who had
been demoted, purged, imprisoned, or sent to concentration
camps for political reasons. This will explain why as early as
1950 the Communist leadership felt obliged to denounce the
abuses that had been perpetrated, without, however, putting a
stop to them.

Independently of the policies adopted in relation to the
former intelligentsia, the realization of the long-term economic
plans made it imperative to train additional top personnel in
industry, trade, the party, and of course the educational field.
The first Five-Year Plan provided for the accelerated training
of highly skilled technicians. For this purpose, a large number
of new schools and colleges were created in record time. According to a report of the National Statistical Office, dated
May 8, 1955, the educational system had developed considerably in the course of the period covered by the plan, and
at its end the number of students in various establishments
reached over 1,700,000. The number of nurseries and children's homes increased by 1,000 between 1949 and 1954.
Several hundred primary schools and numerous secondary
schools had been founded during those five years. The number
of establishments at the college level had increased at an even
higher ratio. The number of pupils in nurseries had risen by
20 per cent, the number of primary school graduates by 50
per cent, and of secondary school graduates by 73 per cent.
The number of public school teachers had risen from 26,000 in

1937–1938 to 46,000 in 1954–1955. This meant one teacher for every 26 students, as against one for every 42 before the war. At the end of the school year 1937–1938, there were only 52,300 high-school students; in 1954–1955, including the students of evening schools and correspondence courses, there were 162,000. High-school pupils of working-class and peasant extraction represented only 4 per cent of the total in 1937–1938, and 63 per cent in 1954–1955. Quarters in students' homes were provided for 27 per cent of these high-school pupils— those whose families lived in rural areas. Most of these homes lacked all comforts and afforded the students little opportunity for serious work. For this reason they became, as was realized in 1956, true hotbeds of rebellion. As for the universities and other establishments of higher education, they had 47,500 students in 1954–1955, i.e., four times the prewar number. More than half of them were quartered in the same homes, and over 28,000—84.1 per cent of the total registered for the day courses—benefited from scholarships. The scholarships, however, were insufficient to enable the students to live decently, all the more so because many of these students, sons of poor peasants or aged workers, had to contribute to the support of their families.

Between 1947 and 1954, various courses in professional training enabled 1,187,000 workers to acquire new trades or to qualify for better jobs. About 113,000 young workers acquired the status of skilled workers through industrial apprenticeship. Apprentices and workers could prepare themselves, by taking evening courses, for matriculation at a university.

All these developments gave rise to material problems. The Communists had concentrated all their efforts on quantitative increase; this inevitably affected the qualitative level. They took pride in the high ratio of students of proletarian or peasant origin, but such progress, just and necessary in itself, had been achieved too rapidly to produce the expected results. The living conditions of most poor students were unpropitious for study, which requires a minimum of material stability and comfort.

For this reason, despite active government propaganda, and even despite some pressures exercised on parents, the latter displayed a growing resistance to the continued schooling of their children. Many students after one or two years in high school or college abandoned their studies to work in industry, which actively solicited them because of the acute shortage of labor. Moreover, many students of "desirable" origin, poorly prepared for higher studies, found schoolwork too difficult. A large proportion of these failed in examinations. Then the party charged the teachers with bias against poor students. As early as 1948, many teachers were the object of disciplinary measures for having given bad marks to proletarian or peasant students.

Such measures resulted in a prompt deterioration of the schools, for the teachers, anxious to prove their loyalty to the new ruling class, gave good marks to its children. A further cause of deterioration was the invasion of the schools by politics. Members of the Communist "youth section" or of other students' organizations of the party were too busy to study geography or mathematics. Was it not their mission to indoctrinate their comrades and keep an eye on their teachers? This directly affected discipline, particularly with the steadily more crowded classes. On November 6, 1956, I questioned a student of the Budapest School of Architecture on her arrival at Le Bourget with a group of refugees. When I asked her what was the reason for the violent anti-communism of her classmates, who had all taken part in the uprising, she said: "The main reason is that they—that is, the Communists —did not let us work seriously, that they forced us to devote too much time to the study of Russian and of Marxism-Leninism, which we regarded as totally useless."

In short, public education suffered from the same evils, the same crisis of rapid growth, as the economy. The programs were ambitious, the means inadequate. The curricula, the textbooks were repeatedly revised. Propaganda was given too much importance, to the detriment of serious matters. Teachers, just like plant managers, were continually harassed with new demands, often contradictory. Because of the growing needs of the economy, specialization had to be emphasized at the expense of general culture. The time allotted for study was reduced, and so were the programs themselves; special abridged courses were created, diplomas were handed out right and left: and then the economic leaders were dismayed at the ignorance of the newly graduated engineers and technicans. There was talk of sabotage; new purges were carried out in the ministry of education; new instructions, constantly issued, served only to add to the confusion.

Late in 1950, when industry began to insist on better quality, a campaign was launched for raising the level of education—this other industry, devoted to the production of experts on an assembly line! In *Szabad Nep* of August 29, 1951, Minister Jozsef Darvas complained: "Our students are very weak in mathematics, Hungarian language and literature, and physics. Too often, actual schooling is neglected in favor of senseless political indoctrination."

The solution of all these problems would have demanded time, patience, and the support of the teaching profession, which, despite the multiplication of compulsory courses in ideological training, had not been won over by the regime.

The insurrection of 1956 strikingly demonstrated the Hungarian Communists' failure to "communize" the youth, who did not take long to discover that the Stalinist system had nothing in common with socialism or democracy. Socialist ideas, through the works of Marx, Engels, and Lenin, had actually influenced a number of young people—many of them died in 1956 crying, "Long live freedom and socialism"—but the majority soon realized that Stalin's and Rakosi's communism was merely a crude distortion of that great movement for justice, freedom, and brotherhood which socialism had been, and which they thought socialism should always be.

The youth of Hungary who in 1945 and 1948 had so enthusiastically welcomed reconstruction and democratization did not join the Communist party but rather non-Communist or new nonpolitical associations of a democratic character. Thousands of young proletarians or peasants, who sympathized with the new regime—their parents had never had the opportunity of actively participating in a legally authorized democratic organization—flocked to the groups controlled by Social Democrats, Christian Democrats, or Smallholders. But the membership of the Communist party's youth section was insignificant.

To avoid losing the youth, the party had to adopt new tactics. To begin with, it announced the abolition of the youth section. In August, 1945, Rakosi declared that "the youth should not belong to any political party, but first of all it must learn the elementary rules of democracy."

All the youth was gathered in the Union of Democratic Youth (D.I.SZ.). Officially it was nonpolitical, and most of its leaders were non-Communists. But its secretary and chiefs of the propaganda and agitation sections were party members. At first, it succeeded in attracting a considerable number of young people. A number of other youth groups controlled by the Church, the trade-unions, the scouts, etc., continued to coexist with it. But after 1947, in line with the efforts to transform the democratic republic into a satellite, the non-Communist organizations were swiftly liquidated. By the end of 1948, only the D.I.SZ., still called nonpolitical, was authorized by the government.

In 1949, when Hungary became officially a people's democracy, the youth that had scarcely emerged from the oppressive climate of the feudal and reactionary Horthy regime once again found itself in chains. From that time on, the main purpose of the Communist leadership seems to have been to militarize the youth. Long before the events of October, 1956, the new generation of Hungarians became a potential army. Had not Stalin said in his *Questions of Leninism* that "the future belongs to those who control the youth"? The Communists attempted to control the youth first by bribery, and when this proved ineffective, by constraint.

To begin with, the D.I.SZ. (like its counterparts in other satellites) was transformed into a local branch of the Soviet Komsomol. Its organizational structure faithfully copied that of the Soviet model. The young people who joined this organization after 1949, either by conviction (a minority) or by constraint (the majority), were subjected to systematic indoctrination. According to a Central Committee resolution of 1951, "the youth organizations must intensify their activity with regard to the political education of their members, make sure that they acquire complete knowledge of the lives and works of Marx, Lenin, Stalin, and Rakosi, and keep them regularly informed of the political events and the successes achieved by the U.S.S.R. in the building of communism."

Other satellite parties published similar resolutions in the course of 1951. They were obviously taken in accordance with a central plan, drawn up in Moscow, with the collaboration of Soviet experts.

One of the major propaganda themes during those years was the great misery of the youth in the "imperialist-capitalist" countries. A hysterical campaign was launched against "Tito's Fascist gang," and to support this campaign, history textbooks were revised. The Yugoslav regime was described in terms of abuse, and often compared to that of Hitler. Finally, in order to strengthen national defense, the authorities created a para-military organization in which teen-agers practiced target shooting and grenade throwing. In 1956, the youths showed that these lessons had not been lost on them.

The cult of Stalin, supreme incarnation of Russia, was propagated among the youth with an intensity equaled only by the French Communist party. In Hungarian schools, teachers and pupils had to stand up each time Stalin's name was uttered. Choruses sang cantatas to Stalin, set to religious airs. His name was spelled out in rhythmic shouts. All youth meetings were conducted in the manner of a Catholic mass, with versicle intoned by the priest, and responses chanted by the faithful to a musical accompaniment. Hence the frenzy with which the youth in October, 1956, tore down the great Stalin monument in Budapest.

A people's democracy was once defined as a regime in which everything that is not forbidden is compulsory. The Hungarian adolescents could confirm this definition. All their life was "organized," even that outside schools or factories.

They went collectively to shows, which were most often of Russian origin. Between 1951 and 1955, 80 to 90 per cent of the motion pictures and plays came from the U.S.S.R. There were several "Soviet Culture Weeks" each year. Participation in cultural activities was more or less compulsory, and the press often criticized the young who failed to attend. In the end, they detested everything Russian.

Their summer vacations had nothing in common with vacations in a Western country. Students and young workers had to become volunteer laborers. They spent two or three weeks toiling at some "great Socialist project" or were sent to perform some urgent task in an agricultural co-operative. After this free contribution to the building of socialism, they were allowed two weeks of "genuine vacations," but even during this time they were subjected to the interminable chore of attending political courses.

In theory, religious teaching, which was optional in schools, was not only tolerated but unsupervised. Still, in order to worship, one had to have the time necessary to attend Mass, Sunday school, etc. The authorities saw to it that the young had no time for such things, by organizing more or less compulsory Sunday-morning games or cultural activities. Thus the regime's anti-religious campaign continued under a mask of progressive education. Patriotic priests were persecuted. This persecution, which made a martyr of Mindszenty, increased the prestige of the Church among the young more than any propagandistic campaign could have done. Hungary witnessed a true renascence of religion, for spiritualism was a challenge to the stupid materialism which was inculcated into the youth.

However, at the end of 1952, the regimentation of the youth in the D.I.SZ. seemed to have been fully accomplished, and some Communist leaders made statements predicting that in another few years all the young people would be "sincerely convinced of the truth of the doctrine of Marx, Engels, Lenin, and Stalin." These leaders were apparently unaware of the youth's hostility to Stalinism and chose to ignore certain difficulties that had manifested themselves early in 1952, when the economic plans were revised.

These economic difficulties, particularly food shortages, touched off a wave of anger against the regime, even among the rank and file of the party, and more especially among the members of the D.I.SZ. These began to desert and to boycott their organization. In December, 1952, the new "leader" of the D.I.SZ., Istvan Denes, solemnly pledged to make this organization "the vanguard of socialism" in Hungary. On the same occasion, Mihaly Farkas, party secretary and then minister of defense, severely castigated the leaders of the youth movement for their "failure to instill into the young Hungarian proletarians internationalism and love for the party." He also deplored the existence of "a strong pro-Western current among the university youth," and summoned the party militants to display more energy in the struggle against "cosmopolitan and pro-imperialist propaganda."

Then, at a meeting of the D.I.SZ.'s central committee held in June, 1953, one of its secretaries, Istvan Gosztonyi, reported that his organization's work was particularly deficient in rural areas, and that only 9 per cent of the young peasants belonged to it (as against 11 per cent in 1952). To remedy this situation, the populist writer Pal Szabo, a friend of Imre Nagy, proposed in 1954 that the D.I.SZ. be severed from the party and placed under the aegis of the Popular Front. This suggestion angered Rakosi, who declared that the party would never let the control of the youth slip from its hands. The result of Rakosi's policy soon became apparent: the overwhelming majority of the young lost interest in the D.I.SZ.

To escape from the pressures of the regime, many young Hungarians took to alcoholism and crime. In recent years, the number of young workers and peasants found lying in drunken stupors in the streets reached alarming proportions. Criminality was rising, particularly among the sons of party leaders and high officials. But the press kept silent about these symptoms of a crisis among the youth, and before 1953 no journalist dared refer to them any more than to the youth's growing hostility to the regime. On the other hand, the press sometimes printed violent condemnations of bandits who were "in the service of Tito" or of "American imperialists." These young "bandits," however, were neither spies nor saboteurs, but merely rebels. Rebels against what?

First of all, against the lying propaganda. In schools, youth organizations, and elsewhere, the young were constantly told about freedom, democracy, political rights. But they read a great deal, and despite the government's unremitting efforts to Sovietize them, they did not fail to discover that freedom and democracy were not what the Russians pretended them to be. They wanted to learn more about the world, about those young who were "suffering under the capitalist yoke." It is no accident that one of the major reforms demanded by the three thousand Hungarian students of the University of Szeged, who met on October 20, 1956, was freedom to travel abroad, in Western as well as in Eastern countries.

Between 1949 and 1953, the regime hoped that its program of rapid industrialization would sever the youth from its religious and national traditions. For several centuries, since the time of the Turkish invasions, Hungary had not seen so many persons change their places of residence. Young peasants were leaving their villages to enroll in high schools and colleges, in preparation for military or teaching careers. Tens of thousands of young workers after a short period of schooling were given posts in the administration, the army, or the agricultural cooperatives. Their place in the factories was taken by the children of the former bourgeoisie, who had been barred from higher studies as a result of the measures mentioned above.

The exact figures concerning these migrations of the young are unknown; it is a fact, however, that the overwhelming majority of persons holding posts in the administration and the army were between twenty and thirty years of age. But all this pampering of the youth did not result in the dissolution of the family, or in the uprooting of the new generation. On the contrary, the sons of workers and peasants always kept in touch with their families, with their class. Even though they underwent a profound transformation, this was not always to the liking of the Communist leaders. For the young workers, peasants, and intellectuals who were thrown together came to know one another and to understand one another's problems. Before 1945, those social classes had rarely been in contact.

In 1956, after eleven years of social change, they were no longer isolated from one another. In this rapprochement the youth played a predominant part. This accounts for the unanimous stand of the youth against the regime, which was one of the surprises of the national uprising of 1956.

Each regime has its profiteers; the totalitarian Communist regime is no exception. In 1956, when "the hour of truth" struck, even the Communist press confirmed the existence in Hungary of a "new aristocracy" of sons of influential officials. These young aristocrats stayed in the cities after graduation instead of being sent to villages or industrial centers. With the help of their influential parents, they obtained soft jobs or could lead an idle life. For those children of the new ruling class, education had become a prerogative, a matter of prestige rather than a means of earning one's bread.

Needless to say, this gilded youth was favorably disposed toward the regime. It was from its ranks that came the bulk of the security police, the AVO, so heartily detested by the rest of the population. Numerically, this class of young people was only slightly superior to the Communist fanatics, i.e., they were a minority.

Despite the general exodus to the cities, a large number of young peasants stayed at home with their families, and continued to be influenced by the Church. Most of them were politically neutral (only the sons of peasants who had benefited from the agrarian reform sympathized with the regime). But later the forced collectivization transformed this neutrality into hostility. This hostility was political as well as economic: for the peasants' standard of living had remained practically as low as before the war. On the other hand, the process of Russification offended the traditional nationalism of the young and drove them to seek the help of the Church. It is no accident that the failure of Russification was more complete among the young peasants than among the workers and students of proletarian origin.

These young peasants were generally uneducated, and their political and economic ideas were rudimentary. But illiteracy had virtually been eliminated from the villages. And since the young peasants sent to study in the cities maintained contact with their families, they influenced to some extent the state of mind of those who had remained in the villages.

Further, since they comprised the majority of the youth, these young peasants greatly influenced the decisions of the government. They and their parents constituted the so-called basic element, and they were sufficiently strong to display effective resistance to the party's anti-peasant policy. Early in 1956, when the party launched a great campaign for collectivization, the firm attitude of the young peasants compromised the success of the operation.

This is not to say that a majority of the youth was opposed to the social advances made between 1945 and 1948. Only a minority of young people, those belonging for the most part to the former privileged classes, were not only anti-Communist, but also anti-democratic, reactionary, and counter-revolutionary. They regarded themselves as the most reliable adversaries of the Communist regime, and some elements among them attempted to capture the leadership of the revolutionary committees of 1956. Their bitterness is understandable, but their resistance to the regime was negative in character, and in October, 1956, when they emerged from illegality, their influence on the mass of the insurgents was actually insignificant.

A far more important tendency that asserted itself among the Hungarian youth might best be described as "progressive nationalism." Before World War II, the Hungarian nationalists were chauvinistic, anti-Semitic, and pro-Fascist. The Communist regime, in its efforts to promote Russification, practically eliminated chauvinism. But in the course of recent years, a progressive, pro-Socialist form of nationalism was born in Hungary.

The new nationalists did not form a cohesive group. They could be found in all strata of the youth, but the vanguard of this movement was formed by intellectuals of proletarian or peasant origin, who owed everything to the regime, particularly the opportunity to study and to raise their social status. They were often party members, but this did not stop them from protesting against Russification and excessive planning. They drew their inspiration from the Hungarian classics: Petofi, Madach, Vorosmarty, Ady, Attila Jozsef, and from contemporary poets and writers, such as Gyula Illyes, Aron Tamasi, Peter Veres, Laszlo Nemeth, Ferenc Jankovich, Sandor Weoreos. Undeniably, these new nationalists were hostile to any return to prewar conditions. They accepted the agrarian reform, the nationalization of industry, the separation of Church and state, but rejected the Soviet-controlled regime. After 1953, heavily represented at the medium and high levels of the administration and the army, they exerted a steadily growing influence on the party leadership. Imre Nagy sympathized with their movement and had been subject to their influence before trying to channel their enthusiasm. In fact, Imre Nagy, alone among the Communist leaders, realized as early as 1952 that the majority of the young workers supported the national-progressive movement, and that the party, in order to survive and take roots, must above all "nationalize" itself.

The nationalism of the youth came into the open during the discussions following the Russian Communist party's Twentieth Congress, particularly at the meetings of the Petofi Society, a branch of the D.I.SZ. numbering several hundred young Budapest intellectuals. Spokesmen for the Hungarian youth in May, and June, 1956, demanded the abolition of para-military preparation, an end to the recruitment of young people for work brigades, and the elimination of politics from the youth organizations.

Furthermore, even though the overwhelming majority of the youth had accepted the principle of separation of Church and state, they opposed religious persecution and demanded religious freedom. This demand was particularly stressed by a number of young writers of peasant extraction.

As for the teachers and students, they demanded the de-Russification of teaching, a radical revision of textbooks, the opportunity to visit Western countries and to study the life of the young there; the abolition or at least reduction of courses in Marxism-Leninism in the schools; an increase in the importation of Western motion pictures, plays, and books; the free circulation of English, French, and other Western periodicals; and a more objective and less conformist press.

Only one step separated these demands from a cry for free elections and neutrality. In October, 1956, the youth in arms took this step in the midst of the exaltation of the revolutionary battle.

3

LIBERAL INTERLUDE: THE NAGY EXPERIMENT

> All of us are ready to die for freedom and
> socialism.
>
> *From a broadcast by an illegal station
> monitored in Vienna, November 11,
> 1956*

IT was only after Stalin's death, when the Soviet Union revised
her policies, that the leaders of Hungary acknowledged their
errors. Several years of misrule had unbalanced the economic
life of the country, and the resulting social crisis had opened
a gulf between the Communist party machine and the masses.
Repressive measures were of no avail: the Stalinist myth of
the indestructible identity of the party with the working class
did not hold up against the insurrections of Pilsen, Brno, East
Berlin, Halle, Jena, and the violent demonstrations staged by
the workers of the Matyas Rakosi establishments in Budapest.
The Communist leaders were realizing with despair that they
were detested by the workers.

A striking picture of the isolation of the Communist leaders
at that time was given later, in October, 1956, by Jozsef
Darvas, minister of culture, in an article published in *Szabad
Nep,* relating a number of incidents he had witnessed during
an electoral tour in his native region in 1953. On that occasion, he addressed fifteen thousand peasants at a meeting in
Nyiregyhaza. The peasants listened in complete silence, and
after he had finished his speech they dispersed just as silently.
Then the minister canvassed a number of farms in the neigh-

boring villages. The peasants ignored him, did not even answer his greetings. In one house, he found only an old woman who was doing her laundry. She, too, ignored his presence. Darvas asked her, "But what have you got against me? What have I done?" The woman walked up to the cupboard, took a piece of black bread, threw it on the table, and snapped: "They've taken all our flour, everything we had, and now it's this they've given me in the store to feed my family with!"

On his return to Budapest, Darvas published an article in which he denounced the writers who, he said, depicted "the situation in the country in too black colors, forgetting the social achievements of the regime." But the situation in the country was becoming unbearable. It was urgent to replace the myth of the party's infallibility by a new myth. The panic-stricken party machine sought refuge in the bosom of Imre Nagy, whom up until that moment it had despised.

The appointment of Imre Nagy as premier on July 4, 1953 —a few days after the Berlin riots and the fall of Beria— marks an important date in the history of Hungary. This appointment, which implemented the decisions taken by the Central Committee on June 28, initiated an experiment the main purpose of which was "to restore contact between the ruling party and the masses, particularly the peasant masses." To supply raw materials and equipment to the heavy industry which had been expanded beyond all reasonable limits, the government had increased agricultural exports. The peasants had been subjected to Draconian measures. After the harvest of 1951, their granaries—collective and individual—had been emptied. As a result, the villages suffered an unprecedented shortage of bread and potatoes.

The anger of the peasants, the despair of the famished workers were reaching the point at which an explosion seemed unavoidable. The relatively abundant harvest of 1952 had postponed the crisis, but an increasing number of Communist leaders realized the necessity of revising not only the plan for industrialization, but the party line as a whole. In 1950 and again in 1951, Matyas Rakosi had defeated the opponents of Gero's policy of super-industrialization by handing them over to the security police or having them executed by firing squads. In 1952, the opposition within the Central Committee became too strong to be liquidated by police methods.

This opposition was headed by the party's best agricultural expert, Imre Nagy. A Communist of the Muscovite old guard, Nagy, perhaps because of his rural background and his experience as an industrial worker, was more sensitive to the voice of the people than the ideologist Rakosi. As early as 1948, Nagy had opposed the collectivization drive. After the expulsion of the Yugoslav Communist party from the Cominform, he lost his seat in the Politburo. In 1951, he was rehabilitated and at once resumed his attack on the economic policies of the Rakosi government. He may have been encouraged by Moscow, where some experts had become alarmed by the growing unpopularity of the Hungarian regime. Stalin's last work, *The Economic Problems of Socialism,* which was published in September, 1952, unwittingly supplied the Hungarian "right-wing" Communists with additional arguments. In this book, Stalin discussed the possibility of a conflict between the Communist government and the working classes—such a conflict, he said, could be caused by "erroneous policies."

The period of wavering that set in at the top levels of the Soviet government and party after Stalin's death accelerated the maturing of new projects in Hungary. For several months the rulers of Hungary were left to their own devices. Rakosi, Gero, and their partisans attempted to profit from this interregnum to consolidate their position. In May, 1953, they called general elections, according to the old formula, as though nothing had changed in the Kremlin and the rest of the world. The Rakosi team was even bold enough to draw up, without consulting the rest of the Politburo, a new plan, which reflected the same frenzied ambitions as the preceding one.

Imre Nagy and his friends reacted violently. Rakosi, Gero, Farkas, and Dobi were summoned to Moscow, where Malenkov arbitrated the dispute. Quick action was imperative if Hungary was not to become the scene of events like those of Pilsen or Berlin, and if the unrest was not to spread to the provinces. Rakosi was asked to submit to collective discipline by surrendering his premiership to Imre Nagy; and Imre Nagy was encouraged to put into effect a new line, modeled after the N.E.P., and in conformity with the policy of appeasement that had been inaugurated by the Malenkov team.

Toward Collective Leadership

On the delegation's return to Budapest, the Central Committee meeting on June 28 adopted a number of resolutions calling for a change of leadership and the application of a radically new program. On July 3, 1953, Rakosi resigned; and on July 4, his successor Imre Nagy appeared before Parliament. His inaugural speech caused a sensation. He sharply condemned the policy that had been pursued by his predecessor, and announced that "the forced march toward industrialization" would be replaced by a new program. Its principal objectives were higher standards of living and the return to a rule of law.

Here are the crucial passages of this speech, which Nagy had the merit of delivering almost three years before the famous Krushchev report, and in which we find a number of truths about Stalinism that Bukharin, Imre Nagy's intellectual master, would certainly not have disavowed:

Economic development. "Nothing justifies excessive industrialization. Such an attempt to achieve industrial autarchy, particularly when we do not possess the necessary raw mate-

rials, surrenders the possible advantages resulting from a more
lively exchange of goods on the world market, from trade with
capitalist countries, and above all from economic co-operation
with the Soviet Union, the people's democracies, and China.

"On the other hand, we shall have to put greater emphasis
on light and food industries, while considerably slowing down
the pace of development of heavy industry.

"We shall also have to change our agricultural policies. Excessive industrialization has hindered the normal development
of agriculture; and agricultural production, which has remained stationary, is clearly insufficient to meet the industry's
needs for raw materials and the population's needs for foodstuffs. The government is resolved to increase the amount of
agricultural investments."

Promises to peasants. "One of the causes of the stagnation
of agriculture is the too rapid development of agricultural co-
operatives, which is unjustified economically and politically.
Our agriculture is based on small individual holdings, and we
cannot do without them. Therefore, the government intends
to support those small holdings by giving them fertilizers,
tools, seed, etc.

"To assure the peasants that they will be able to live peacefully and will not be forced to join co-operatives, the government has decided to authorize members of co-operatives to
leave their group at the end of the agricultural year, if they
so desire. Moreover, co-operatives will be allowed to disband
if a majority of their members wishes to do so.

"We shall void the greater part of the sanctions inflicted on
co-operatives and individual peasants for failure to make deliveries. The fines (ca. 600 million florins) were often imposed
without justification.

"The new system of collections will fix delivery quotas for
several years, so that the peasants will know their obligations
in advance."

Higher standards of living. "The problem of raising the standards of living must be the central problem of planning. Consumption of foodstuffs and industrial products must be increased. The government intends firmly to fight against the high cost of living. We have already reduced prices of certain seasonal products below their 1947 levels. We guarantee that before the end of the harvest season, adequate amounts of flour, sugar, meat, and fats will be put on sale. An effective improvement will be felt in the fall. But prices of certain industrial articles have already been reduced by 15 to 30 per cent. The government does not confine itself to promising an improvement; it has begun to carry out its promises."

Concessions to workers. "We shall revise the Labor Code, and abolish fines as means of coercion of workers and office employees. We shall see to it that the prescribed distributions of clothes and foodstuffs are carried out, and we shall punish those who divert the funds destined for the protection of the workers' health to other purposes. We shall do away with unjustified overtime and Sunday work. Forty per cent of rents will be used for maintenance of workers' dwellings."

More freedom for intellectuals. "It is unfortunate that intellectual workers and particularly former intellectuals often fail to be appreciated as they deserve. The government will radically change this situation. Even though there is a shortage of competent men in almost all walks of life, honest intellectuals have been deprived, in an unworthy manner, through unjustified purges, of the opportunity to use their knowledge for the benefit of the country. The government will proceed with vigor to put an end to such inadmissible procedures."

Religious freedom. "We must display greater tolerance in religious matters. The application of administrative measures in this field is inadmissible; yet this was the case. Here the government will adhere to the principle of tolerance, whose instruments are persuasion and enlightenment. The application of administrative or other coercive measures is condemned by the government and will not be tolerated."

Strengthening of legality. "The government in all its activities bases itself on the legal order and the law as set down in the constitution. The government faces important tasks bearing on the correction of errors committed in the past.

"The government organizations have the duty to protect the security and inviolable rights of our laboring people. They must see to it that every citizen enjoys his rights as stipulated by law. But the principle of government by law has not always prevailed in the work of our judicial and police organizations, and of local councils.

"The abuse of judicial prosecutions and administrative methods, the excesses committed in the field of tax collection, the confiscations for nonpayment of taxes, the drawing up of lists of kulaks, and other vexatious measures have offended the people's sense of justice and shaken its confidence in the law, thus causing an estrangement between the laboring people and the government bodies."

Abolition of internment camps. "The institution of internment has undermined the rule of law. This was possible because we have not created a Supreme Court functioning as the constitutional guardian of the law.

"It is in a spirit of pardon, in the interest of conciliation, and in order radically to correct the injustices and illegal acts committed in the past, that the government is introducing a bill providing for the release of all those whose crimes are not too heinous, and whose freedom will not imperil the security of the state. The same bill provides for the abolition of the institution of internment, and the dissolution of all internment camps.

"The government also wishes to normalize the situation of the deportees, and will permit them to choose their places of residence."

Reduction of the powers of the police. "It is urgent that Parliament set up a Supreme Court. Police jurisdiction is incompatible with the principles of a people's democracy, which cannot permit that the investigating body should also be the judge. The government will abolish that inheritance of the old regime by means of legislation."

Was Rakosi ordered to withdraw for tactical reasons, or did his resignation and the adoption of the Nagy program imply a radical change of objectives? There have been endless discussions on this subject among both partisans and opponents of the regime. In fact, the question is misleading. For since the advent of the Soviets, communism has always had two faces according to whether it attempted to impose its domination by terrorist means or tended to take roots by a policy grafted onto the genuine aspirations of the working class. Even though both Imre Nagy and Matyas Rakosi aimed at keeping the party in power, they often had opposing ideas as to the means to be used in order to achieve that end. Rakosi could not conceive of a dictatorship without terrorism. Nagy dreamed of a regime enjoying the wholehearted support of the people.

In July, 1953, Imre Nagy emerged victorious from the contest. But his victory was far from complete. Taking the U.S.S.R. as their model, the Hungarians replaced personal by collective leadership, i.e., by a policy of balance and compromise. While some overzealous partisans of the old policy were ousted from the Politburo and the government, its chief protagonists, Rakosi and Gero, were not. Rakosi was appointed secretary, then (in August) first secretary of the party; Gero retained his post of first vice-premier and was entrusted with the ministry of the interior, the importance of which need not be stressed.[1]

The Rakosi faction was forced to retreat, but it was not

[1] In July, 1954, Gero resigned from his ministerial post, but retained his vice-premiership.

routed. It was not slow in exploiting the effervescence aroused in the country by the sudden change of course. On July 11, 1953, Rakosi, addressing a meeting of party militants, declared that the leadership was by no means ready to surrender the controls. He acknowledged that errors had been committed in the past; he asserted the need for a new policy and gave his blessing to the Nagy government; but he pointed out that the new policy would have to be compatible with the party's authority and prestige. The most important passage in his speech was addressed to the Communist officials in the rural districts. He made it clear that even though the collectivization drive had to be suspended for a time, collectivization remained the supreme goal. The Communist party, he said, would firmly oppose the disruption of the entire collectivized sector; only a few co-operatives formed under compulsion and utterly unviable would be authorized to disband. In fact, the government had to take measures against the desertions from the co-operatives which in many regions had assumed the proportions of a mass movement at the height of the harvest season.

The New Popular Front

From the summer of 1953 on, Hungary's entire political and economic life was marked by the ambiguity inherent in a government in which two conflicting tendencies—the reformist and the Stalinist—were represented. In this struggle, Imre Nagy was supported by several Politburo members, particularly Antal Apro, former chief of the trade-unions, and Mihaly Farkas, who joined him for opportunistic motives; by the majority of the intellectuals, whether Communists or fellow travelers; and finally by the unorganized public, which after some wavering recognized in him a champion of its aspirations, and hoped for a kind of Hungarian Titoism. But Nagy was opposed by most high party officials, who thought that the liberalization started by the new government might quickly spill over beyond its proper limits. The party leaders had become accustomed to ruling a terrorized population, and feared that it might interpret concessions as a sign of weakness, and sweep them out of office.

The founding of the Patriotic Popular Front, which Imre Nagy announced to the party congress held in May, 1954, was the result of a compromise between the two rival camps within the Communist leadership. Imre Nagy and his friends, among them Pal Szabo and Peter Veres, writers of peasant origin, had originally conceived the Popular Front as a mass organization; while wishing to retain control of it they seemed inclined to grant a large share in its leadership to nationalist-progressive intellectuals. In this way the new organization might have served to bridge the gap existing between the government and the country, and make up, to some extent, for the absence of a peasant party. The revival of such a party entailed risks that Imre Nagy himself did not wish to take.

However, even this timid conception of the Front could not win the support of the Rakosi faction, which feared that control of the organization would slip into non-Communist hands, that the Front would develop into a second party, and that such a party would become the instrument of genuine democratization. After long discussions, it was decided that the Front would not be a mass organization, but merely a group including Communists, fellow travelers, and some carefully selected independents who would be admitted on an individual basis. Moreover, the Front was not to have local branches, but only committees which would be made "representative" by taking the preferences of the local population into account.

This plan was actually carried out, and except for a few isolated cases the Communists managed to control the local committees by comfortable majorities. Nevertheless, the Front's purpose, which was to induce passive and indifferent elements of the population to engage in politics, was partially achieved, for the Front committees included a number of non-Communists, members of the old and new intelligentsia, and even some former notabilities who had been deprived of their positions after 1947. The kind of committee the Communist leadership wished to form is well illustrated by the composition of the Budapest Front committee. Its chairman was a former mayor of the capital (a non-Communist); its vice-chairmen were the secretary of the Budapest party committee and the vice-president of the municipal council; its secretary was the secretary of the Budapest Peace Committee; its other members included two plant managers, a university professor, a Catholic canon, a Protestant bishop, a general, a Stakhanovist worker, a journalist, a sculptor, and the secretaries of the youth organization, of the trade-unions, and of the Women's Union. Other local committees were similarly composed, as were the municipal councils elected on November 28. The elections were held under the auspices of the Popular Front, whose emblem was a tricolor cockade with the inscription, "Independence."

The functions of the Front after the elections remained vague. The Nagy faction hoped to transform the Front into a living organization, which would become firmly rooted in the cities and villages, and which would serve as a counterpoise to the predominance of the party machine. The Front's official organ, *Magyar Nemzet,* was edited by several prominent journalists, among them Geza Losonczy, former state secretary who had been released and rehabilitated; this newspaper proved a formidable competitor to *Szabad Nep,* organ of the party. But the Rakosi-Gero faction strove to transform the Front into an instrument of propaganda, which would serve to supplement the activities of the Peace Movement. The intraparty conflicts on the subject of the Popular Front grew more embittered during the winter of 1954–1955. Pointing to the oppositional tendencies that manifested themselves in several Front committees and Front-sponsored peasant clubs, the Rakosists charged the Nagyists with being "the liquidators" of communism, and asked the Kremlin to arbitrate the dispute. The Russians took their side against Nagy.

Economic Balance Sheet

The two factions clashed during the discussion on the government's economic policies, which began on October 15, 1954. These policies were the subject of a report presented by Bela Szalai, member of the Politburo and head of the planning commission. His report may be summarized as follows: As a result of the measures taken since July, 1953, the government had increased the purchasing power of the population, particularly that of the peasants, but had failed to give a sufficient impulse to light industry and agriculture to meet the increased demand for consumer goods. Now, the growing gap between increased purchasing power and output created a danger of inflation, which made it imperative for the government to revise its entire economic policy.

As regards the standards of living, the results of the Nagy experiment were unquestionably positive. The government had decreed two price cuts, the first covering eight hundred articles of clothing, the second ten thousand other items. Thanks to the resulting general decline in prices, the population had saved a total of 1,500 million florins. The amounts of the quasi-compulsory loans of 1953 and 1954 were considerably reduced. The government had also taken spectacular measures to appease the peasants and carried out its agricultural program. At the same time, the wages of certain categories of workers, particularly miners and metal workers, were raised; this amounted to a total annual increase of 762 million florins. Pensions were revised accordingly. Housing construction was stepped up, the network of retail outlets was extended, and about 100,000 small craftsmen were licensed to reopen shop. As a result of these measures, the income of wage earners rose, during the first six months of 1954, by 15.8 per cent as against the same period in 1953, when it had dropped to its lowest point since 1949. During the same period, prices of consumer goods dropped by 8.3 per cent. Although beef, fats, and canned meats were still in short supply, bread, flour, and sugar were available in considerably greater quantities than before.

Such were the positive results of the experiment. The negative aspect was expounded in a resolution of the Central Committee, published on October 31, 1954. (This was, incidentally, the last Central Committee meeting at which Nagy's partisans won a majority of the votes, despite the vigorous resistance of the Rakosi followers, who were supported by the Gero-led technocrats.) Here are the essential passages of this resolution:

"The policy of out-and-out industrialization has not been completely liquidated . . . and the reconversion of industry with a view to increasing the production of consumer goods and agricultural equipment has proceeded with extreme slowness. . . . Investments in light industry and agriculture still lag behind those in heavy industry. The system of wages and prices, and the distribution of raw-material supplies and credits, set up in the period of super-industrialization, have not yet been readjusted to the new requirements. The total level of industrial production has scarcely been raised, and the quality of the goods produced is often poor. The value of consumer goods produced in enterprises controlled by the ministries of heavy industry and machine-tool construction has been inferior to the provisions of the plan by several hundred million florins; the same is true of the amount of machinery that has been delivered by those enterprises. This situation, as well as the inadequate application of the principle of the material interest of the producers, accounts for the failure of agricultural production to meet requirements; the delays are particularly great in the output of bread crops and the development of cattle breeding. . . . Productivity of labor has declined and production costs have increased in the course of last year."

Some of the data cited by Bela Szalai in his report to the Central Committee illustrate this situation. Production costs in the industries mentioned above were, during the first half of 1954, 2.8 per cent higher than the 1953 averages, while under the plan they were to drop by .2 per cent. The rising production costs were essentially due to lower productivity, which dropped by 3.3 per cent for the first eight months of 1954 in relation to the same period in 1953. The report also mentioned a substantial increase in the number of employees, glaring examples of wasteful use of raw materials, and an increase in appropriations for state expenditures which had risen at a considerably faster pace than the national income. The number of state officials had increased by 16.4 per cent since 1949, and was greater than actually required.

"Because of delays that occurred in reconversion and production," the resolution went on to say, "while we needed a sufficient amount of goods to meet the demands of increased purchasing power, important resources originally intended for investment had to be diverted to consumption. But this has not permanently solved our economic difficulties, which can be brought to an end only by a radical liquidation of all vestiges of super-industrialization, and by a resolute and consistent application of the new policy. Only by eliminating disproportions, by vigorously carrying out reconversion, and by increasing industrial and agricultural production, shall we be able to secure permanent harmony between the available stocks of goods and an appreciable rise in standards of living." Though couched in extremely moderate language, the document constituted an indictment of the Rakosists who had sabotaged the Nagy experiment.

False Conceptions

In conformity with the views of Nagy and his friends, the Central Committee resolution accounted for Hungary's economic troubles by "the hesitation displayed in carrying out the new policy, and the more or less camouflaged resistance it encountered. This resistance fed on erroneous conceptions, without theoretical foundation, which proposed to solve the economic difficulties by a shrinkage of purchasing power, i.e., by a reduction of the standards of living of the working class and the peasantry."

The resolution subjected these erroneous conceptions to a detailed criticism. It pointed to the fundamental law of socialism which demands "the maximum gratification of the continually growing material and cultural needs of society." It stressed the immense importance of the inevitable alliance between the workers and peasants, and the need to extend market exchanges, that is, to increase the ratio of agricultural products sold directly by the peasants on the free market. "The reduction of peasant purchasing power, the restriction of the free market, would not contribute to the prosperity of the working class and strengthen it. On the contrary, our people's democracy would be weakened, the working class would be isolated from the rural population, and cities would be exposed to the threat of famine."

The next paragraph of the resolution condemned a number of other "erroneous conceptions," which "interpreted the new policy as implying the abandonment of industrialization. . . . Behind such conceptions, one discovers the false idea that was at the basis of the mistaken economic policy of before June, 1953, when it was assumed that industrialization could be carried out only by the one-sided development, and the development at all costs, of metallurgy and machine-tool construction." What was in question, the resolution specified, was not industrialization as such, but only industrialization as it had been practiced before June, 1953, when its pace·had been too rapid, when the actual potentialities of the country had not been appreciated, and when the available resources and the existing needs had not been realistically estimated.

According to the Central Committee (i.e., the partisans of Nagy), the false conceptions listed above "not only stood in the way of the solution of our temporary difficulties, but were also their principal source. Our party has the duty to struggle most resolutely against all manifestations of that resistance, which gravely injures the interests of the working class and of the entire population."

All this shows that toward the end of 1954 the Nagy experiment was doubly endangered. On the one hand, there was a real inflationary threat, which could be averted only by an energetic and straightforward policy; on the other hand, Stalinist elements were waiting for the psychological moment to appear as the saviors of the country for whose desperate plight they themselves had been largely responsible.

It was those Stalinists—Rakosi, Gero, and their henchmen —who won the day. With the support of Khrushchev, who regarded Nagy as Malenkov's liegeman and a dangerous Bukharinite, they quickly took advantage of the situation created in Russia by Malenkov's resignation, and in March, 1955, forced Nagy out of office. But that was a Pyrrhic victory. The winning team were so blinded by their doctrine and by their hatred for the "Bukharinist" Nagy, that they hardly noticed the strange, dangerous silence with which the country reacted to their triumph. From one day to the other, the Patriotic Popular Front, which Rakosi was planning to keep under his firm control, was deserted by the intellectuals and the masses; the party militants were appalled, discouraged; the people said to themselves: "We were deceived when we were told that Stalin was dead. He has survived in Hungary." And as though to confirm this opinion, Andor Berei, the Stalinist who had been appointed head of the planning commission to succeed Bela Szalai, a moderate Nagyist, declared in Parliament on November 15, 1955:

"The historic resolutions [of March, 1955, condemning Nagy] have torn the mask from anti-Marxist, rightist, and opportunistic conceptions which advocated the abandonment of the development of heavy industry and collectivization. The party resolutions state clearly that the teachings of Marxism-Leninism are fully valid for our country. For the building of socialism is possible only by means of Socialist industrialization and the Socialist transformation of agriculture.

"During the first year of the Second Five-Year Plan we must above all advance the building of socialism, and we cannot achieve this unless we give a more important place to Socialist industry in our economy, unless we strengthen and extend our state farms and agricultural co-operatives. This is also the most important condition for the development of our agricultural production. In 1956, we must further raise the workers' standards of living, but such a goal can be achieved durably only if the amount of manufactured goods, and the value of production per worker, increase, and the production costs of the various goods decrease.

"The resolutions of the Hungarian Workers' [Communist] party explicitly condemn those who have tolerated or directly encouraged carelessness, indiscipline, wastefulness; and they assert that the work of building socialism can bear fruit only if strict discipline and a spirit of thrift are observed in all fields. Our plan for 1956 meets these requirements."

By applying this program, which was as ambitious as it was stupid, the Rakosists brought to the boiling point the discontent of the three classes on which rested the alleged people's government—the working class, the intelligentsia, and the peasantry. The Hungarians were all the more dismayed by this return to Stalinist methods because it seemed so in flagrant contradiction with the policy of liberalization that the Russians had pursued even after the demotion of Malenkov, and that had been spectacularly asserted in their reconciliation with Tito, the champion of national communism.

The Rehabilitation of Rajk

On March 29, 1956, *Szabad Nep* published the summary of a speech delivered a few days earlier by Matyas Rakosi at one of the many meetings organized all over Hungary to explain the historic decisions of the Russian party's Twentieth Congress to the Communist militants.

To denounce the cult of personality was a ticklish task for the Hungarian leader: both by inclination and by opportunism, Rakosi was one of the most ardent zealots of this cult, and of all the titles he had gladly assumed the one he preferred was that of "Stalin's leading Hungarian disciple." He was indeed a good disciple, of irreproachable loyalty; he mustered all his energy, all his shrewdness to apply his master's methods in Hungary, practicing that art of government which is made up of ruse, malice, and ferocity.

Matyas Rakosi had spent ten years instilling into his party that supreme truth which identifies communism with Stalinism. For him, only the Stalinist way was the correct one. Outside it, everything was heresy, treason, defeat. He regarded Stalinism as a monolith, and everything in it, even its most irrational elements, the most difficult to assimilate for a Western mind, as necessary, inevitable. The madness of Stalinism was for him profound wisdom; its fanaticism, a basis for unanimous action. Inspired by this faith, Rakosi had formed his party machine, composed of young men who swore only by him because they owed him everything. It was thanks to these young party officials—Andras Hegedus, premier; Bela Szalai, minister of light industry; Lajos Acs; and Bela Veg, secretary of the Central

Committee—that Rakosi restored his position that had been
threatened by Nagy after Stalin's death. He had encouraged
Nagy to promote measures that were later held against him,
seized every opportunity to thwart his plans, and sabotaged
his economic policy and attempts to liberalize the regime.
Staking his political career on the rising star of Khrushchev,
Rakosi had waited for the opportune moment. His victory over
Nagy on March 4, 1955, surprised only those who had underestimated his genius for intrigue and utter ruthlessness.

At the same time, Rakosi tried to divert "the struggle against
the cult of personality" from its true purpose. He launched a
crusade against "the little local Stalins and Führers," who
"think they are infallible, do not tolerate any criticism, and sur-
round themselves with flatterers, toadies, and careerists." But
even though Rakosi was bent on proving to his faithful that the
anti-Stalinist decisions of the Twentieth Congress were not in
contradiction with his own policy, he had to destroy his former
idol. After a long, delaying battle, he also had to consent to a
review of the Rajk trial, which in 1949 had enabled him to set
up his personal dictatorship in the shadow of Stalin.

The rehabilitation of Rajk had long been demanded by the
Hungarians and also by Tito, who had not forgotten that he
himself had been the real target of the Rajk trial. Rakosi suggested that the rehabilitation was not a new development, but
merely the result of the Nagy policies—in other words, according to him, these policies had borne fruit "despite the rightist
deviations that the party had condemned in March, 1955,"
i.e., despite Imre Nagy! For Rakosi, the rehabilitation of Rajk
was a natural consequence of the measures taken in 1953 to
strengthen Socialist legality. "After exposing the activities of
the imperialist agent Beria and those of the Gabor Peter gang
in Hungary," he explained, "the party leadership took the initiative of reviewing the Rajk trial. It has been found that the
Rajk trial originated in a provocation. That is why the Supreme

Court, on the basis of a party resolution of June, 1955, pronounced the rehabilitation of Laszlo Rajk and other comrades." In putting all the blame for the Hungarian-Yugoslav conflict on his chief of police who had been imprisoned in 1952, Rakosi was once again aping the Russians.

Without mentioning the other aspects of the trial, particularly the methods by which Rajk was made to confess his guilt, Rakosi passed on to other matters. He emphasized the need to prevent "the enemy" from taking advantage of "the struggle against the remnants of the personality cult," and to concentrate all efforts on economic problems. The purpose of this maneuver was clear: Rakosi wanted at all costs to avoid a thorough investigation of the trial, which would have established his own guilt. But the disproportion between the great publicity given to the Rajk trial in 1949 and Rakosi's laconic references to it now was too obvious to pass unnoticed. Even former diehard Stalinists demanded that full light be shed on this affair, "so that we may learn, for instance, how the Rajk trial was staged so carefully that all those present were convinced of the truth of the charges." (*Humanité*, April 27, 1956.) In Hungary, the consternation was even greater. Rakosi's cynicism touched off an explosion of anger among the old party militants and the intellectuals. The spectacle of Rakosi clinging to power despite the sharp rebuke inflicted on him by the events brought their disgust and hatred to the boiling point. He thus unwittingly encouraged the members of his party to hold him responsible for all the crimes it had perpetrated, for all the blood it had shed.

On June 19, 1956, Rajk's widow, Julia Foldi, speaking at a meeting of the Petofi Society in Budapest, made her first public appearance since her release in July, 1955. Her audience consisted of about a thousand old party militants. Despite the fact that the chairman of the meeting was Karoly Kiss, president of the party Control Commission, many speakers voiced their dissatisfaction with Rakosi. In an overheated atmosphere, Julia Foldi, a tall, robust woman with strong features, who had not been broken by six years of imprisonment, took the floor to demand the complete rehabilitation of her husband, and suggested that Rakosi had handled the matter in a rather cavalier manner. Those present were deeply moved when she recalled the heroic episodes of her husband's career—his underground activities in 1932, his role in the Spanish Civil War, in the Resistance, and as a member of the government, and finally his trial and infamous death. "How was it possible to believe, and to make the country believe, all those terrible slanders?" she exclaimed. She denounced "the incredible atmosphere of suspicion that prevailed in the party," and demanded that Rajk be restored "to the honorable place he deserves in the country's history."

A few days later, the newspapers *Szabad Nep* and *Nepszava* seconded the widow's demands, and proposed that Rajk's biography be published, and that streets and co-operatives in Budapest be named after him.

The solemn interment of Rajk and three of his codefendants took place in the afternoon of October 6. Despite icy wind, three hundred thousand persons filed past the four caskets. Rajk's widow stood impassive in front of the coffin containing her husband's remains; next to her was her eight-year-old son. At some distance stood the members of the government and the party leadership, with the exception of Gero, first party secretary, then in the Soviet Union. High-ranking army officers, replacing the police, directed the crowd which slowly and solemnly paid a delayed tribute to the men whom the Central Committee had recently described as "great martyrs of the working class."

The sumptuous wreaths presented by officialdom were completely submerged in a sea of chrysanthemums, which had been brought by Hungarians from all ranks of life. After the last post, Antal Apro, president of the Popular Front (Rajk had been its first president), delivered the funeral oration. He denounced the Stalinist "massacres and errors," and concluded: "Alas, we cannot resurrect the dead, but we can avoid the repetition of similar crimes."

Other friends of Rajk spoke in the name of the veterans of the Spanish Civil War, in the name of the party, in the name of his former schoolmates. After the speeches were over, a man, alone, emerged from the crowd and embraced the widow, who was sobbing. He was Imre Nagy, former premier, who had been expelled from the party and ousted from all public offices, and who attended the funeral as a private citizen.

This solemn funeral was organized by Mrs. Rajk and the group of Hungarian Titoists around her. The Stalinist party machine had attempted to muffle the solemnities by ordering the workers of the great plants not to interrupt their work. But the workers did interrupt their work, and manifested en masse around the coffin that had become a symbol. The police had feared incidents like those of Poznan. But Mrs. Rajk and her friends maintained that nothing would happen. And the fact is that there were no incidents.

Foreign observers voiced their surprise that the ceremony had taken place with such complete lack of disturbance: according to them, Mrs. Rajk had had to utter only a single word to cause the collapse of the Stalinist party machine. They ascribed her and her friends' silence to a kind of cowardice, or to their political ignorance. In actual fact, the organizers of the funeral wanted above all a display of unity, intended to demonstrate the extent of the people's discontent, and also the ability of the national Communists to control and direct it. The fact that with three hundred thousand persons present (university students, writers, white-collar workers, factory workers, handicraftsmen) there was not a single jarring note in the ceremony proves that on October 6, seventeen days before the outbreak of the insurrection, the appointment of Imre Nagy as premier would have enabled Hungary to solve her crisis as Gomulka solved it in Poland.

Minds were overheated, nerves tense. Then, on October 19, Gomulka acceded to power in Warsaw. The event electrified Hungary. The atmosphere was reminiscent of 1848, when the revolutionary flames spread from country to country, setting all Europe on fire. Overshadowing everything else, one question haunted the Hungarians: "Why can't we do the same?"

4

PRELUDE TO THE INSURRECTION:
THE REVOLT OF THE INTELLECTUALS

THE Hungarian intellectuals have a great revolutionary tradition. It may be apposite to recall here the extraordinary career of the poet Sandor Petofi, since workers and intellectuals named after him the society which drew up the program of the insurrection.

Petofi (1823–1849) was an extraordinary poet: he is a wellspring of lyricism, he embodies the spontaneity of youth for whom everything can become a poetic subject. His revolutionary appeals of 1848 alternate with love verses or a haikai celebrating the flight of a bird. All Hungarian children know his songs by heart.

Petofi is famous for having touched off the 1848 revolution in Budapest, for having roused the people against the Pressburg Diet, by haranguing a group of students in the National Museum park—the same park recently destroyed by Russian tanks. It was a market day, large numbers of peasants were in the capital. A steady rain had kept them away from the stalls, and scattered them in the streets. On hearing that a poet was addressing students in the park, they came in crowds, protected by their large umbrellas. This was the beginning of the revolution: it was nicknamed "the umbrella revolution."

Petofi joined the Hungarian revolutionaries fighting against the Russian invader, and was slain in the Battle of Segesvar in

Transylvania. It is understandable that his life and death should have become the symbol of Hungarian independence and socialism.

Several other poets took part in the revolution of 1848. One of them was Janos Arany (1817–1882), a village schoolmaster who became the greatest Hungarian epic poet. The death of his friend Petofi haunted him to his last day.

It is a historical fact that liberal and revolutionary movements in Hungary have always originated in literary groups. In 1918, the spark was given by the Galileo Society, led by the poet Endre Ady and the sociologist Oscar Jaszi. During the short-lived Bela Kun revolution, the office of minister of education was held by the philosopher Gyorgy Lukacs. As in other countries where democratic institutions have no deep roots, the intellectuals regard themselves as the spokesmen for the real aspirations of the people. Because the governments were unpopular, the intellectuals who opposed them and whose ideas were spread in literary journals have always represented a real, if not direct, threat to the authorities.

We may thus speak of an uninterrupted tradition. That is why it is important to analyze the social and political role of the writers in the preparation of the October uprising of 1956.

However paradoxical this may seem, for a period of several months the Hungarian Writers' Union was a kind of state within a state. Its activities, not only literary but also political and ideological, were not controlled by the party. In fact, the writers whose audience had been continually increasing (the *Literary Gazette* has a circulation of 410,000 copies—an impressive figure for a country of fewer than ten million inhabitants) constituted Hungary's second party—all others being banned by the regime. Even though the leading Communist members of the Union regarded themselves, perhaps in all sincerity, as the progressive, Leninist wing of the group, the Writers' Union itself was a national front in miniature, which faithfully mirrored the country as it really was, that new Hungary of workers, intellectuals, and peasants, which had no capitalists and no landowners, but in which the intelligentsia nevertheless played a leading part. At any event, the Union was far more representative of the country than the various spurious mass organizations founded by the party (Peace Movement, Patriotic Popular Front, etc.).

The truth of the matter is that the collapse of Stalinism had created a political vacuum in Hungary. The Communist bureaucracy had not succeeded in restoring contact with the masses, which ignored it. Therefore the writers became the spokesmen for the people, taking advantage of the freedom of criticism which had been granted them after the Russian party's Twentieth Congress. One might almost say that they did not choose to play such a part, and that the part chose them.

In September, 1956, the Hungarian writers spoke to the government on a footing of equality. If the organ of the Central Committee, *Szabad Nep,* leveled criticisms at them, they rejected the censure with a scorn based on their knowledge that the people were with them. And the party leadership was as though hypnotized by this unexpected opposition, all the more so because the writers had devoted allies among the newspapermen, most of whom, including editors of *Szabad Nep,* shared their views and refused to attack them.

We are confronted here with a new social phenomenon which (however lasting) in itself deserves attention. The emergence of such a state within a state might also be interpreted as a symptom of decay (or of a crisis of growth) of the totalitarian system. Of course, the tendency to artistic or intellectual autonomy has never been absent from the Communist world; but in Hungary this tendency for the first time asserted itself in an organized group which had powerful means at its disposal—the press, the radio, the Petofi Society, etc. To be

sure, the dissolution of the Writers' Union and the arrest of
Gyula Hay on January 18, 1957, put an end to this fascinating
experiment. Nevertheless, the revolt of the Hungarian writers
will retain its historic significance, as the prefiguration of an
inescapable evolution—a stage in the search for forms of social
organization more suitable than the Stalinist strait jacket for
the new Eastern societies, born out of the ruins of feudalism
and capitalism, and now in process of coming of age. The
uprising and the part played by the writers in starting it suggest
that the Communist party itself may someday act as midwife
in the birth of a kind of corporate state, organized on the basis
of essential occupations, which will conclude a new "social
contract," and which will be in the image of Proudhon's Utopia
rather than a realization of the deliberately vague prophecies
of scientific Marxism.

The origin of the Hungarian writers' revolt goes back to
June, 1953, when the Hungarian Communist party had somewhat precipitately struck out on the de-Stalinization path. The
effect of Imre Nagy's speech of July 4, 1953, which revealed
the bankruptcy of the regime, was nowhere so electrifying as
among Communist and fellow-traveling writers. These writers,
among them some of the best in the country (Tibor Dery,
Gyula Hay, Istvan Orkeny), had been subjected during the
years 1949–1952 to rigorous indoctrination by the intellectual
experts of the party in an attempt to mold them to the Zhda-
novian norms of artistic creation. Most of them had been im-
pregnated with Western culture; though their party cards and
convictions were Communist, their artistic temperaments were
somewhat anarchistic, and their minds analytic and critical.
It was almost asking the impossible to expect them to transform themselves into Aragons or Fedines, to embrace, under
coercion, that technique which consists in telling the grossest
lies in accents of the most ingenuous truth, in accusing those

known to be innocent while defending forgers or monsters of criminality.

Their "schooling" had begun with the Rajk affair. The day after the infamous verdict, Tamas Nagy of the Central Committee directed an appeal to the writers, which was printed in *Szabad Nep:* "Fellow Magyar writers, let us denounce Rajk to the people for the adventurer that he is, before the Western writers, with their 'humanist' way of looking at things, make a hero out of him. . . . Let us show up this sinister figure so that even future generations will turn away from him in horror."

For numerous writers who remembered the Moscow trials of 1936–1938, to believe in the accusations hurled at Rajk amounted to committing a kind of moral hara-kiri, akin to offering their brains up for sacrifice. How they envied the non-Communists who were only too willing to believe that Rajk, that Communist Saint-Just, was the most infamous of traitors! The reactionaries were jubilant, the opportunists put on a great show of zeal, while the Communists—I refer to the sincere ones—were required to work a miracle, and did. They believed, because "the party cannot be wrong." [1] They believed in a spirit of self-flagellation. They entered into the cult of Stalin as though into a purification bath, after shedding the soiled garments of bourgeois culpability. The armor of their faith, the *credo quia absurdum,* became the distinctive sign setting them apart from the rabble whose nationalist or cos-

---

[1] These were the last words flung at me, on the subject of Rajk, by a very dear friend, that prince of simpletons, the poet André Havas, former secretary of the Hungarian legation in Paris. Recalled to Hungary after the arrest of Rajk, Havas was arrested and tortured to death. I have learned recently that his teeth were broken off one by one; that the son of General Farkas, Vladimir, the Number One sadist of the police, urinated in his mouth ("the ideological specialty" of this Stalinist, it appears); and when Havas, not understanding exactly what was wanted of him nor able to bring himself to believe that his Communist comrades could be subjecting him to such atrocities, went out of his mind, they continued to beat him until he died.

mopolitan, formalist or naturalist, subjectivist or objectivist
deviations they occasionally joined in denouncing. They submitted with infinite good will to the spiritual direction of Revai,
the supreme custodian of the laws of Marxo-Lenino-Stalinist
art. They no longer wrote for the public; they wrote for the
Akademia Ucca, Revai's headquarters. They wrote to please
the party. They lied. They lied in heroic accents.

Then came the moment when all these sacrifices, all this
heroic effort perversely directed at the destruction of their own
consciences, were revealed as having been not only vain, but
positively mischievous. "You would have done the party a
greater service by refusing to lie, by telling the truth, by not
turning your backs on the people," they were told. One can
imagine the sickness and rage provoked by these words of
common sense.

Those who most quickly recovered their presence of mind
were the small opportunists, alert, cunning, facile of pen—they
shall be nameless. They entered upon a truth-telling race. They
vied with one another in hurling the greatest possible number
of unpleasant truths at the heads of the leaders who appeared
to be on their way out. Other, better-informed opportunists
appealed for moderation, warning against excesses in "the
thaw." They cocked a weather eye in the direction of Russia,
where Ilya Ehrenburg had just received a rap on the knuckles
for doing so much thinking.

Nevertheless, "the thaw" went on apace. Encouraged by
Imre Nagy, the writers went to the country, brought themselves
up to date on the situation, reported on it in verse, in newspaper articles, and in fiction. Others rummaged their desks
for works written during the Terror. Orkeny recovered his
gusty satirical laughter of an earlier day, Konya published
On the Great Road, a poem in which he complained particularly about the Russians' having carried off, without compen-

sation, the aluminum wealth of the country—an unusual subject for poetic treatment!

Factions began to form. The Stalinists, headed by Sandor Gergely and under Rakosi's protection, recovered, after some months of silence, their aplomb. They were opposed by a more powerful group composed of "reformist" Communists, backed by "populists." The party leadership intervened several times in quarrels between these factions, preaching a middle-of-the-road policy for writers, and announcing its readiness to grant them "greater liberty" on condition that they did not impair the prestige of the party, but placed it in a perspective of "having overcome its errors."

But how was this directive to be applied at the level of the particular, to each individual work? How was the invincible march of the party toward glory to be shown, for example, in a love song or a sob? "You can't substitute love for the class struggle," Revai had written in 1952. And if one suddenly felt like shedding a tear, one ran the risk of being called a pessimist and a decadent bourgeois. For the party censors, all personal emotion smacked suspiciously of deviationism. The party leaders might be induced by circumstances to accept freedom of literature in theory, but such freedom on the plane of practice would always appear to them extravagant and dangerous.

They were right, it seemed, for the moment the reins had been loosened the writers and journalists began to denounce certain privileges enjoyed by the high aristocracy of state and party. The anxiety of the bureaucracy before this "spirit of anarchy" fostered by writers was expressed by Jozsef Darvas, onetime novelist of peasant life, who had replaced the sick Jozsef Revai as chief of the propaganda machine. Darvas denounced the writers for "denigrating and vilifying the whole party achievement in the building of socialism, and undermining the authority of the leaders."

This counterattack by the Stalinist bureaucracy developed strength after Matyas Rakosi's position had been consolidated by Khrushchev's direct intervention. When Imre Nagy was ousted from the premiership, the reformist writers lost their main political prop. Orthodoxy appeared to have triumphed up and down the line, and it was in threatening accents that it reasserted "the absolute right of the party to take charge of cultural life."

This time, however, the threats fell on deaf ears. The writers realized that, while the new line formulated by Khrushchev called for struggle against deviationists, it also forbade Rakosi to take administrative and police action against the heretics. It was at this point (May, 1955) that Gyola Hay, Tibor Dery, and the young novelist Tamas Aczel, the only Hungarian Stalin Prize winner, took over the leadership of a struggle against "intellectual bureaucracy," that is, against party control over cultural activities. Their fight took a more desperate turn about October, 1955, when the first findings of the inquiry into the Rajk trial began to be known. For many writers, the discovery of the truth, that is, of the fact that the 1949 trial had been "a lie from beginning to end," came as a terrible shock, leading to despair, self-torture, and even nervous collapse. From that crisis was born, as one of them, Otto Major, wrote, "the moral unity of the writers, based on a solemn commitment never to lie again, never to serve an inhuman purpose . . . to tell the truth."

But what was the truth? The word itself had a doubtful ring in the ears of the bureaucrats, for whom it is so easily confounded with untruth which serves or seems to serve their interests. In their eyes, the moral crisis just undergone by many writers was a symptom of petty-bourgeois hysteria. And when one of the young poets of the *Literary Gazette* circle, the proletarian Laszlo Benjamin, was imprudent enough to attack in an acridly satirical poem the sacrosanct person of Rakosi himself, all hell broke loose. Censorship officials ordered the confiscation of the *Literary Gazette,* and its editor in chief, Gyorgy Hamos, was removed for "displaying weakness in his dealings with writers."

This was only the beginning. The secretary-general of the Writers' Union, Sandor Erdei, guilty of having praised Benjamin, was replaced by the ambitious and detested Aladar Tamas. Moreover, the censors forbade the publication of Konya's *Journal*—a superb piece of reporting on the desolation of the Hungarian countryside—and withdrew from the repertory of the National Theater not only a play by Gyula Hay, but also Imre Madach's *The Tragedy of Man,* a national classic written after the crushing of the 1848 revolution. Finally, they blocked the publication of a series of books by outstanding non-Communist writers, such as Tersanszky, Kassak, and Remenyik.

These highhanded measures, inspired by Rakosi, were the last straw. Six members of the Writers' Union executive committee and three of the secretariat, all of them party members, refused to work with the Stalinist Tamas and resigned. At the same time, one of them, Tibor Dery, drew up a memorandum, which was signed by an overwhelming majority of his colleagues, protesting "violation of the Union's autonomy," and calling for "a complete break with prevailing undemocratic methods of control which paralyze the cultural life of the country and are destroying the authority and influence of the party."

This document—the first real evidence of opposition in Hungary—was transmitted to the Central Committee in the fall of 1955. Rakosi, determined to put down this "lackeys' rebellion," pushed a stern resolution through the Central Committee and had it inserted, on December 10, in the *Literary Gazette*. It pilloried Tibor Dery and four of his friends for their "anti-party and anti-people's views," accusing them of having launched a "frontal attack" against the party. Dery, taxed with having committed the worst of crimes, namely, the organization of a faction within the party, was summoned to reflect and to submit. Several minor writers, called together by the Central Committee and intimidated by Rakosi's wrath, did in fact retract their signatures. But Dery, Hay, and Zoltan Zelk held firm and refused to be browbeaten. Fearful of alienating the so-called liberal wing in Moscow, Rakosi was hesitant.

Then the Twentieth Congress took place, with its partly public, partly secret demolition of the Stalin myth, the cult of Big Brother, terrorist methods, and administrative autocracy. Everybody in Hungary, and above all the writers, interpreted the resolutions of this congress as a condemnation of Rakosi, a justification of Imre Nagy, and an encouragement to clean up and democratize public life.

From that moment on, the writers' struggle against censorship was transformed into a wider struggle against the dictatorship. They demanded that the nation as a whole be given a chance to be heard. Rakosi's effort to take over de-Stalinization was greeted by the Writers' Union with an explosion of anger. And when Rakosi, between two sentences on the economic situation, casually "rehabilitated" Rajk, the writer Sandor Lukacsy rose at a stormy meeting of the Union and shouted: "This is an explanation worthy of a Judas."

Three days later, when the writers met again, a representative of the Central Committee, Marton Horvath, announced that Lukacsy had been expelled from the party because of the insulting remarks he had made against Rakosi. A number of writers, including Peter Veres, the president of the Union, protested violently. Horvath proposed on behalf of the party leadership the election of a new secretary, one Csabai, whose name many of the writers had never heard before. The proposal was rejected by one hundred votes to three. Then Tamas Aczel took the floor, expressing "the utter lack of confidence of the Hungarian intelligentsia in Rakosi" and called for his resignation.

Some days later, the Petofi Society invited several of the insurgent writers to give a public exposition of their point of view. This proved a sure way of making their meetings a success: they began to attract increasingly large audiences. During the same period, the tone of the *Literary Gazette* was becoming bolder every week. On May 5, 1956, this journal printed a fiery article denouncing the cult of personality, which had "poisoned our entire body of literature." "It is high time for us," Gyula Hay wrote, "to become converts to truth, to universal, unconditional, profound truth, which alone serves people and party." And a little later, Gyorgy Lukacs delivered a passionate speech in which he denounced the dogmatism of the party's cultural bureaucrats. This dogmatism, he said, originated in "revolutionary defeatism," in a "deep sense of inferiority" with which such bureaucrats approached non-Marxian thought, betraying their "fear of life."

What assured the writers and their *Gazette* of a sympathetic audience was not so much their theoretical affirmation of the utility of "truth," but their courageous stand against the authorities. Dery and his friends were in fact the first Hungarians for many years to conduct themselves as though utterly unafraid, to talk like free men. Yet Rakosi was still very much there, his police force was intact and under the direction of the torturer Vladimir Farkas. The objective conditions of fear were all still present. Dery and his colleagues pretended to be unaware of their existence. Each new issue of the *Literary Gazette* was in the nature of an event. Issue after issue destroyed a taboo, demolished a prohibition. To be sure, in speaking of the great misery of the peasants, of the apathy or even hostility of the workers, of the arrogance of the new ruling class, and "the death of all spontaneity" in the Communist-controlled trade-unions (issues of June 23 and 30), the writers were merely saying what everyone knew, namely, that the Communist party had failed to win over the masses of the people and to take root in the country. But they were saying it aloud: reality had suddenly ceased to be mute. The message of the writers: Speak! Do as we do, out with it! Air your grievances! reached ever wider areas among the intelligentsia. Toward the end of June, after the Poznan riots, the party completely lost control over the Petofi Society, whose regular debates were becoming increasingly more agitated. One meeting of the Society, on June 27, drew more than six thousand people who booed and threatened the representatives of the party secretariat.

Matyas Rakosi then staged one last attempt to save his position and to re-establish party unity under his rule. He called a meeting of the Central Committee and on June 30 had it adopt a motion of censure against the agitators. Two Union leaders, Dery and Tardos, were expelled from the party; action against the others was confined to severe disciplinary measures. Next, Rakosi's emissaries descended on the Budapest factories and those of other industrial centers to explain the June 30 resolution to the workers. These emissaries represented the rebellious writers and intellectuals as "agents of the bourgeoisie" who were attempting to restore capitalism. It was not the first time Rakosi had set about exploiting the traditional anti-intellectualism of the proletariat while posing as the defender of the working class. But this time the maneuver miscarried. Some echoes of the social and political demands made by the writers had somehow already reached the workers. Harangued by the Central Committee emissaries, the workers insisted that they wanted "to look into the matter a bit," and they demanded that texts of the speeches by the incriminated Dery and Tardos be communicated to them. Rakosi, unable to mobilize the faithful, failed to create a climate favorable to the police measures he thought he could still take against the authors of the disturbance.[2]

The Soviets, it appears, advised him in the meantime to stay in the background. On July 17, Rakosi fell from power, as the result of a compromise worked out between Stalinists who deserted his cause (Gero) and the more moderate wing of "rehabilitated Titoists," such as Kadar. Immediately, the reshuffled party leadership published a resolution announcing its desire to speed up liberalization. The new chief of the cultural department of the Central Committee, Gyula Kallai, politely invited the writers—"now that the main thing has been accomplished"—to return to their own field, creation, and to leave politics to the professionals.

The writers responded to this appeal with a certain reserve. Believing rightly that the fall of the idol was their handiwork, and knowing that their audience in the country was growing, and that in any case they were more popular if not more competent than the party leaders, they began to prepare for a national congress by way of emphasizing their independence. They went to the unprecedented length of affirming that they stood ready to take over "cultural affairs in this period of hiatus" while dealing with the party on a footing of equality. "They tell us: Bring your debates to an end, just write some good books," declared the poet Geza Kepes, the secretary *pro tem* of the Writers' Union. "Our answer is: Even while we were debating violently, we wrote some pretty good things and we shall continue to do so. But debate, participation in public affairs, is not only the right but the duty of all citizens, writers included, in a Socialist democracy."

The writers' congress held in September was not merely a professional convention but a kind of revolutionary assembly

[2] It was only on September 30, 1956, that the Hungarian public learned from an article by Sandor Nagy in *Muvelt Nep* that Rakosi had drawn up a plan for restoring his rule by destroying his opponents.

of the Estates-General. Kallai there took it upon himself to
expound the "revised" point of view of the party leadership in
cultural matters. The struggle of the writers against dogmatism, and against administrative direction of intellectual life,
he said, was basically justified. Consequently, most of the
measures taken against "rebellious" writers had been revoked.
Still others would be similarly revoked, he promised, provided
that the real culprits, like Dery or Tardos, acknowledged that
they sinned against party discipline. Other concessions were
dangled before the Union's eyes—authorization to publish
three new reviews, increased emoluments, and grants for study
abroad. On the other hand, Kallai called their attention to that
"error" which consisted in going beyond the party to appeal
to a kind of national consensus. "National union, as well as
unification of literature, can be based only on the strength and
indestructible unity of the party." Which meant: discipline
first, democracy later.

The spokesmen for the writers, while paying homage to "the
good intentions of the new Communist leadership," upheld
uncompromisingly the writers' demand for absolute freedom
of intellectual life, and for autonomy for their Union.

The old Hungarian Communist Gyula Hay, in an article
published on the eve of the September congress which I would
gladly cite in its entirety, it is so beautifully written and courageous, said:

"Yes, we call for complete freedom for literature. The most
complete, the most unlimited freedom conceivable among men
living in civilized society. That is, we want nothing to be forbidden the writer that the laws do not uniformly forbid all
citizens. Naturally, the writer is no more authorized than anyone else to incite to murder, arson, theft, brigandage, overthrow of the republic, racial discrimination, etc. . . . But he
must be free, like any other citizen for that matter, to tell the
truth without restriction; to criticize anybody and anything

whatsoever; to be melancholy; to be in love; to meditate on death; to believe in the omnipotence of God; to deny His existence; to express doubts as to the accuracy of certain statistics relative to the plan; to think along non-Marxist lines; to think like a Marxist even when his ideas developed in that way do not happen to correspond to officially established truths; not to love certain rulers; to realize that the city is tumbling down for want of repairs; to love Stalinville or not to love it; to defend humanity even in situations about which less sensitive minds have been unable to see that there is anything inhuman; to have an original style; and so on, and so on. . . ."

Worthy of note is the fact that the Communist Hay, and with him, save for very rare exceptions, all the Communist writers of Hungary, defended freedom not only for themselves but for non-Marxists as well, for everybody—spiritualists, Catholics, idealists, anarchists, individualists, formalists, pessimists, decadents, nationalists. And if they were asked the reason for this surprising show of liberalism, they called on their own past experience. "In helping the bureaucracy to muzzle non-Communist writers, we prepared our own servitude," they said. "The best among us," said Hay in a speech to the congress, "suffered in this climate of mendacity," in this climate of empty, ostentatious optimism where the supreme duty of writers consisted in spreading the myth of the regime's popularity and the party's phantom successes. "We have paid dearly for our lives; we saw our productivity falter, the level of our work sink, while drifting farther and farther away from the philosophic foundations of our literary existence: Marxism-Leninism. . . .

"I have been a Marxist for nearly forty years," Hay cried out to the congress. "Marxist philosophy has been the basis of my thought, the guiding force of my life. But in these years, the psychic tortures of the recent past have taught me that no philosophy, however just, can be relied on as an automatic safeguard against errors, aberrations, and even against crime and dishonor. Like everyone else, the Marxist, too, must carry on, day after day, his struggle for the truth."

In this stirring confession, the word "truth" appeared as the great rallying cry of insurgent Hungarian writers, taking on an exalted, almost mystical tone. But let there be no mistake. It signified for the best of them a real effort at demystification, at emancipation from propaganda. It marked a point of junction with popular sentiment.

Part Two

THE POPULAR UPRISING OF OCTOBER 1956

1

MEN AND CIRCUMSTANCES

The Uranium Revolution

THE Hungarian insurrection of 1848 was nicknamed "the umbrella revolution"; that of 1918, "the dahlia revolution," because the partisans of the republic then sported dahlias in their buttonholes. The uprising of October, 1956, could properly be called "the uranium revolution."

In the great race for industrialization, which started among the underdeveloped countries of Eastern Europe in 1945, Hungary, as we have seen, had certain considerable initial advantages—a heavy industry that had enjoyed a good reputation even before the war, skilled workers, and capable technicians. But Hungary's low resources in coal and hydraulic energy presented a severe handicap. As a result, the realization of the plans for industrial development, particularly as regards the rational exploitation of the country's rich bauxite deposits, was greatly hindered.

In the summer of 1956, rumors spread in Budapest that important uranium deposits had been discovered at Pecs in the Mecsek mountains near the Yugoslav border. The news aroused a great deal of excitement not only among economists but also among the public at large: it seemed that Hungary would now benefit from a rich source of cheap power. The people thought of Belgium, whose prosperity owes so much to the uranium deposits of the Congo, and dreamed of a better future. Then it was learned that Rakosi had concluded a secret agreement with the Russians, granting them the exclusive right to exploit the new deposits in return for a ridiculously small compensation. The high hopes aroused by the discovery gave way to indignation.

The scandal came into the open in June, 1956, when Professor Janossy, famous physicist, speaking at a meeting of the Petofi Society, violently attacked Rakosi for causing "a major injury to the national interests of Hungary." This friend of Imre Nagy who was vice-chairman of the Atomic Energy Commission revealed that even he had learned of the existence of the uranium fields only from foreign newspapers and some indiscretions of Soviet politicians and experts. A few months later, on November 1, after the ephemeral victory of the insurrection, Janossy confirmed these statements in a broadcast from Radio Kossuth in Budapest. "I know nothing of the contents of the agreements concluded with the Soviet Union," he said on that occasion. But he added that as far as he knew the exploitation of the deposits was only beginning. While it was true, he said, that sixteen tons of ore had been exported to Russia, this represented only an insignificant amount of uranium, although he believed that the ore was of high quality.

More detailed information about the deposits trickled through gradually thanks to disclosures made by engineers and workers in the mines. It was learned among other things that the deposits had actually been discovered in the fall of 1954. Imre Nagy, who was premier at that time, resisted the Soviet demand for exclusive rights to exploit the deposits, all the more so because the Soviet government had then decided to reorganize its economic relations with the satellites on a basis of greater equality. It would seem that Nagy's resistance to the Soviet demands had been one of the main reasons for his fall from power in March, 1955. While it is possible that this version of the events was invented for the sole purpose of raising Nagy's prestige as a patriot, it is certain that an agreement on uranium was concluded only after the ousting of Nagy. The agreement was signed by Rakosi without the knowledge of most of the members of the government that had been formed in March, 1955, under Andras Hegedus, a young careerist devoted body and soul to the party's first secretary.

Under this agreement, the Soviet Union was granted a long-term concession of the Mecsek deposits. The exploitation was entrusted to a mixed Russo-Hungarian company. Seventy per cent of the initial investments was supplied by the Russians, the rest by the Hungarians. Hungary undertook to amortize half the Soviet investments (in the form of mine equipment) by deliveries of uranium; Russia undertook to send back to Hungary 10 per cent of the ore processed in Soviet plants. As usual, Russia reserved the right to set the prices of the equipment delivered to Hungary as well as those of the ore delivered by Hungary. Moreover, the agreement secured Russia's exclusive rights to exploit not only the Mecsek deposits, but also the Polisberosjeno and Balatonfured uranium fields which had been discovered in the interval.

In the fall of 1956, a large number of Soviet technicians arrived in Pecs. The project was shrouded in the strictest secrecy: the Hungarian workers were virtually sequestrated and prohibited from divulging anything whatever about the mines. The very word "uranium" was never uttered; the miners were told to pretend that they were working a bauxite deposit. (Incidentally, the Csepel munitions factory had been similarly camouflaged as a "toy factory"; in both cases the toys were of a rather dangerous kind!)

The Hungarian uranium deposits, added to those of Czechoslovakia, East Germany (which alone supplies one third of Russia's uranium requirements), Romania, and Bulgaria, were a boon for the growing Soviet atomic industry. Unfortunately

for Hungary, this gave Russia an additional motive for not
relaxing her grip on her satellite. In the summer of 1956, however, the Hungarians scarcely noticed this particular aspect of
the problem: by then they had risen in protest against Soviet
colonialism as a whole. But there is good reason to believe
that uranium was one of the main causes of Rakosi's downfall, the straw that broke the camel's back. Hungarian collective consciousness crystallized around that treasure which
could provide a material basis for the country's independence.
This radioactive mineral was a kind of Rhinegold rising from
the depths. It was invisibly present in the insurrection, investing Magyar nationalism with the virtues of the medieval
alchemists who strove to transform mud into gold. At the same
time the presence of uranium gave the movement an ultra-
modern flavor worthy of our atomic age.

The sense of power inherent in uranium was clearly reflected in the demands of the insurgents. On October 26, the
workers' council of the Borsod district, in its very first proclamation, demanded the publication and revision of all foreign
trade agreements, and insisted that "uranium, this national
treasure," should be exploited "in conformity with national interests." Three days later, on October 29, the revolutionary
committee of the intellectuals, whose president was Gyorgy
Markos, one of Hungary's most brilliant economists, similarly
demanded the abrogation of all economic agreements disad-
vantageous to Hungary, particularly those covering bauxite
and uranium deposits. But on October 29 the uranium deposits, like the coal field of Pecs, were already in the hands of
the insurgents, and the Soviet engineers and workers had fled.
As late as November 20, long after the second Russian intervention, Hungarian refugees arriving in Yugoslavia reported
that the Mecsek deposits were held by six thousand young
men, most of them students, and more than two hundred
miners. Surrounded by the Russians, they resisted doggedly,

then retreated to the mountains, and kept on fighting for a long time. It was in vain that the Pecs radio, recaptured by the Russians, repeatedly appealed to the miners to resume work. In December, a delegation of these miners got in touch with the Soviet army commandant in Budapest. The delegates said that they were ready to resume work, but only after the Soviet troops occupying the mines had returned to their bases.

As for Janos Kadar, he tried to minimize the importance of the uranium issue. On November 15, he declared to a delegation of Budapest workers that the extraction of uranium had only begun in Hungary. He promised that the trade agreements with Russia would be made public, and that Hungary would sell uranium at world prices. Moreover, he said, Hungary had not the equipment indispensable for processing the ore. But the worker delegates were not reassured by these statements: they had often been deceived before.

Whether it was a myth or a reality, uranium, even before supplying energy to the Hungarian plants, supplied national energy to the students, workers, and intellectuals who fought under the national flag from which they had removed the hammer-and-sickle emblem and the Soviet star, in order to put an end to the spoliation of their country. For this spoliation was not a myth. It was a reality that can be expressed in figures. For instance, in 1949, real wages in Hungary were three times the Soviet wages; in 1953, they dropped to only three fifths of the Soviet level. This drop in the standard of living, which coincided with a steadily accelerated pace of work, was bitterly resented by the people. It was ascribed to the fact that the Soviets controlled the national economy, manipulating prices, operating mixed companies, exacting war reparations, imposing heavy military expenditures, and keeping the trade balance unfavorable to Hungary.

Public opinion also held the Soviets responsible for fuel

shortages, particularly coal shortage, which became increasingly acute in the course of 1956. Several hundred passenger trains had to be withdrawn from circulation, and many factories closed. At the end of the summer of 1956, Hungary was threatened by unemployment and inflation. The fuel shortage became critical after the flooding of the Nagylengyel oil fields, causing a loss that Jozsef Mekis, member of the Politburo, estimated at equal to the price of one million tons of coal. Now, it was an open secret that the flood had been a consequence of Soviet mismanagement—a consequence that had actually been foreseen. This writer, native of the oil-producing region, which had been opened for exploitation by Standard Oil, in 1947 met one of the Hungarian administrators of the oil field, chief engineer Bittner, who complained about the irresponsible Soviet management and foretold that it would lead to disaster. He reported on the situation to the Hungarian government, with the sole result that he was imprisoned and sentenced to death. A year later, a commission of Soviet experts was forced to recognize that Bittner's warnings had been justified, and production was somewhat slowed down, pending improvements. In 1956, when the floods took place, everyone associated the disaster with the hasty and imprudent exploitation of the uranium deposits, which are situated near Negylengyel.

The Hungarian uranium revolution was an armed uprising —the first—against Soviet colonialism, which had been draining the people's democracies of their national resources under the pretense of emancipating them from the capitalist yoke.

Reform or Revolution?

Was the insurrection inevitable? This is a theoretical question that will be discussed for a long time. Historians still ask whether the Bourbon monarchy could have prevented the outbreak of the French Revolution. In fact, a revolution is merely the penalty a government must pay for its failure to carry out indispensable reforms. The wise legislator, instead of postponing reforms, anticipates the people's demands; the stupid legislator who resists them is surprised and overwhelmed by the events. This maxim is confirmed by all the revolutions of the past, and the recent Hungarian uprising is no exception.

One thing is certain: The men who started the Hungarian freedom movement were not revolutionaries, no more so than the eighteenth-century philosophers who are regarded as the spiritual authors of the French Revolution. Let us take a closer look at some of them.

Gyula Hay, the fifty-two-year-old writer who has been called "the Hungarian Bert Brecht," and who in September, 1956, launched the slogan of "absolute freedom of mind," is anything but a revolutionary. As we know him from his writings and his actions, he is a typical reformist, an aesthete akin to Ruskin, and an anarchist who toyed with Marxism. After a period of wavering between cynicism and despair, he sacrificed his mind on the altar of the party, and then became infected with the spirit of the Budapest youth—those Hungarian young people whose existence he had not noticed until 1956, and in whom he discovered unexpected qualities, treasures of generosity and heroism. Speaking of them to one of my friends, François Bondy, who came to see him during the insurrection, he said: "I felt attracted to these young people by an irresistible surge of sympathy. . . . Our youth thirsts for freedom, and we writers have understood this. Their spirit has perhaps best been expressed by our poet Zelk who said: 'I was too cowardly to remain dishonest.' "

Gyula Hay was one of the leaders of the Writers' Union and the Petofi Society, and a favorite of the regime. Like other Communist intellectuals, he joined the opposition by taste, or, more accurately, by distaste. He became a reformist because he had suffered too much from Stalinist bad taste in art and literature. The same is true of the other leaders of the intellectual opposition, particularly of Gyorgy Lukacs, who joined

the fray with youthful ardor, freely displaying before his students all the brilliance of his long-suppressed mind.

For these refined men of letters, the criticism of the political,
economic, social, and moral aspects of the regime began with
the criticism of its impossible ideological and aesthetic dogmas. But all of them remained emotionally attached to communism with which they had identified themselves for many
years. They were moralists rather than politicians. Their purpose was to improve communism, and to transform Marxism-
Leninism into an instrument of culture and prosperity, to
adjust the official doctrine to the needs of the turbulent youth
who surrounded them, and who clamored for a breath of freedom, for efficiency, and for truth.

It is very likely that these reformists harbored Utopian
ideas. That absolute freedom, that total democracy, which
Lukacs thought he could reconcile with the dictatorship of the
proletariat, was a contradiction in terms; and by coming out,
in the course of a discussion with his students on the eve of
the insurrection, for the monopoly of Marxism in the teaching
of philosophy, Lukacs implicitly disavowed his own theories.
His students, for their part, demanded a regime of free competition between historical materialism and the other modern
philosophical schools. In the field of politics, the Communist
instigators of the reform movement were guilty of even more
flagrant contradictions. After all, they could have foreseen
that it would be impossible to contain liberalization within the
narrow limits imposed by the party. Nor could Lukacs, Hay,
and their friends fail to know that the Communists, without
the support of the political police and left to themselves, would
command the loyalty of at most 8 or 10 per cent of the population. In the course of the above-mentioned discussion, Lukacs
admitted that as a result of the regime's mistakes Marxism had
lost considerable ground in Hungary. Nevertheless, he and his
friends, the national Communists or the patriotic Marxists,

were full of hope, all the more so because the young people listened to them as to oracles. The impressive manifestation of unity in sorrow and hope which marked the funeral of Rajk, the encouragements of Tito, and the success of the Gomulka group in Poland confirmed them in their convictions. Moreover, the non-Communist and anti-Communist forces were numerically insignificant and unorganized. Only the old men, remnants of the former ruling classes, and the most backward peasants longed for the good old times of the Horthy regime or the Hapsburg monarchy; the overwhelming majority of the population, and particularly of the youth, looked forward not backward. A reformed communism seemed possible.

A reformed communism also seemed possible, indeed, indispensable, to some professional politicians closely associated with the intellectuals, above all to Imre Nagy, who had come to be regarded as the symbol of national communism in Hungary. His debonair appearance, his broad face and heavy stance, his open, straightforward eyes are not deceptive: this Communist whom I met in prison in 1932 is not a revolutionist either, at least not by temperament. I have always regarded him—and I was not alone in this—as a reformist, a typical Social Democrat who became a Communist by mistake, as it were, a Communist despite himself. He is one of those Hungarians, particularly frequent in the provinces, who embrace extremist ideas on the basis of theoretical considerations, and remain loyal to them later out of stubbornness as much as out of honesty.

Imre Nagy was twenty-three at the time of the Bela Kun revolution. For this native of the Somogy district, situated in a region where the influence of the Church and the big landowners was particularly strong, communism meant above all the agrarian revolution. Unlike the other leaders of the underground Communist movement between 1919 and 1945, unlike Rakosi, Gero, Farkas, Revai, Zoltan Vas, Zoltan Szanto,

all of them intellectuals of Jewish middle class (or upper
middle class, in the case of Lukacs), Imre Nagy was a peasant, familiar with the life of the peasants, with their poverty,
their needs and aspirations. All his life he has been primarily
interested in the agrarian problem. This accounts both for the
fact that he survived successive party purges (since his supreme ambition was to become an agrarian specialist rather
than a political leader), and for his relatively inconspicuous
position. Around 1934, he was released from prison and went
to Moscow, where he studied at the university and later became a member of the Soviet Academy of Agriculture. In
1935, he was one of the Hungarian delegates to the Seventh
Comintern Congress, but he kept prudently aloof from the
dissensions among his fellow exiles. Two years later he was
manager of a kolkhoz in Siberia. He may have been sent there
because he had fallen into disgrace; but he seemed to have
been interested in his job. In 1940, he was recalled to Moscow.
Rakosi had just arrived there after fourteen years of imprisonment, and set about the task of reorganizing the Hungarian
party in exile, which had been decimated and scattered after
the "liquidation" of Bela Kun. Close co-operation between the
two men was precluded in advance by the difference of their
temperaments: Nagy, the slow, ponderous, Calvinist peasant,
could not become a close friend of Rakosi, who modeled himself on Stalin and dreamed only of power and revenge. In
order not to become adversaries they avoided each other.
What Rakosi found and was always to find irritating in Nagy
was the latter's habit of giving ground without bending, of
submitting without surrendering. No wonder Nagy had to content himself with a subordinate post (but he did not seem to
resent this): he was an editor at Radio Kossuth (a branch of
the Soviet radio broadcast in the Hungarian language; on
October 30, 1956, the Budapest radio station adopted this
name, which is that of the leader of the anti-Hapsburg insur-

rection of 1848). Nagy also published several articles on the agrarian problem in *Uj Hang* (The New Voice), organ of the Hungarian exiles.

Late in 1944, Nagy returned to Hungary in the wake of the Red army, and was appointed minister of agriculture in the Debrecen government, formed on December 23, 1944. In this capacity he prepared the great agrarian reform that put an end to the latifundia. The reform, which was carried out in great haste, is open to criticism in some details; but there can be no doubt that it represents a great step forward. Nagy owes to it his fame and popularity, as well as the friendship of several non-Communist reformists, among them writers of peasant extraction, such as the novelist Gyula Illyes and Peter Veres, president of the Writers' Union, who proclaimed the demands of the nation at the foot of the monument to Jozef Bem, that hero of the 1848 revolution, on the first day of the insurrection.

For some time Imre Nagy—or Uncle Imre, as he was referred to in literary circles, no doubt because of the patriarchal radiance emanating from him—served as minister of the interior. He was entrusted primarily with administrative work, and had nothing to do with the organization of the police. Then he yielded his post to Laszlo Rajk, and was elected chairman of the Assembly. In 1948, he fought against the program of collectivization of agriculture. Like Rajk, but more cautiously, less passionately, Nagy advocated a "Hungarian path" toward socialism. He had firsthand knowledge of the disastrous effects of collectivization in Russia, and wished to spare Hungary this experiment. The peasants could be won over to communism only gradually, he argued, and he called for moderation.

But in 1948 the party policies were no longer determined by free debate. Tito's defection had reawakened Stalin's persecution mania; the Russian dictator, encouraged by Zhdanov, suspected treachery everywhere. In his eyes, the relative independence of the satellite parties constituted a threat to the integrity of his empire. National communism was the enemy: the international Communist movement was reorganized on the basis of extreme centralization, and while the national sovereignty of the satellites was respected on paper, their party machines were completely regimented. Henceforth the people's democracies were to toe the Russian line; since collectivization of agriculture was good enough for Russia, it had to be good for the satellites. Faced with this situation, the Hungarian leaders vied with one another to prove their loyalty to Moscow; and the best method of proving it was to track down and denounce real or imaginary opponents of the new policy. In this race for the Kremlin's favor, Imre Nagy was badly handicapped. Just like Rajk, Nagy found himself deserted by his friends. For some time Rakosi and his policemen hesitated between the two men: they had determined to stage a great show trial, but had not yet decided who would be assigned to play the part of the arch-traitor. In the end their choice fell upon Rajk, who was more prominent, more naïve, and more dangerous to Rakosi as a potential rival, because of his popularity among the party rank and file. Rajk was arrested. Nagy got away with a severe censure, and was dismissed from the Politburo. But his disgrace was only temporary. Some Kremlin leaders, among them Malenkov, who regarded him as a competent and harmless man, protected him, hoping no doubt to use him in the event of the failure of the Rakosi-Gero experiment. Late in 1950, Nagy was readmitted to the Politburo. In 1952, he was appointed deputy premier, and in this capacity, even before the death of Stalin, he came out in favor of a new economic policy.

The subsequent vicissitudes of his career—his attempt to restore the prestige of the party by liberalizing its policies in relation to the peasants, the intellectuals, and the Church; his

condemnation as a deviationist; his stubborn refusal t
nize his alleged errors, which earned him additional po
—have been dealt with in previous chapters. In Octobe
even non-Communists and anti-Communists looked upon Nagy
as a lesser evil. They appreciated his patriotism, and his associates were seduced by his personality, his cheerful temperament, his sound judgment, and his sense of humor.

As a politician, however, Nagy has one great defect: he is
passive, he lacks ambition and initiative, and, above all, he
blindly respects the decisions of the party. Even though he was
firmly convinced of the correctness of his policies, Nagy, after
his expulsion from the party in November, 1955, had done
nothing or almost nothing to communicate his conviction to
the people at large. To be sure, writers and journalists from
among his friends, students, economists, and experts who
shared his views, contributed a great deal to publicizing them,
and thanks to their efforts a Nagy legend was created in Hungary—just as a Gomulka legend was born in Poland in the
course of recent years. But behind the Gomulka legend there
is a vigorous and determined man, who skillfully exploits his
political trump cards in behalf of his own career as well as of
his country's interests. Moreover, the Polish liberal Communists ignored the official ban on intra-party factions; whereas
Imre Nagy's followers submitted to the ban, and remained
prisoners of the party discipline. This is, incidentally, the principal criticism leveled against Nagy and his friends by the
anonymous authors (formerly members of Nagy's brain trust)
of a confidential document which was circulated among Hungarian intellectuals after the crushing of the insurrection, and
of which I received a copy in January, 1957. One passage of
this document says:

"In 1956, the internal opposition against the party leadership was stronger in Hungary than in any other country,
including Poland, even though in Poland the opposition com-

prised numerous partisans within the Central Committee. It is to the credit of the Hungarian oppositionists that they subjected the Rakosi regime to a detailed criticism, thus paving the way for the democratic October revolution during which the people in arms expressed their agreement with the opposition. . . . Thus history sided with the opposition. But at the same time history severely condemned the opposition for failing to organize itself as an independent force. While the party continually stigmatized alleged anti-party factions, the opposition confined itself to debates. It debated the question whether or not it should form an independent group. It did nothing to establish contact with the people, nothing to gain a foothold among the workers. . . ."

It is the last-mentioned point that seems crucial. No doubt the workers did not believe or no longer believed the slanders spread about Nagy by Rakosi's agents, who represented him as a friend of the peasants and an enemy of large-scale industry, and hence of the proletariat. Nevertheless, Nagy and his followers remained isolated from the proletariat, and enjoyed organized support only in the Writers' Union, the Journalists' Union, and among the student members of the Petofi Society. The party cells and the factory organizations were in the hands of the Rakosists, who systematically prevented the Nagy partisans from expressing their views. Neither Nagy nor his friends did anything to remedy this state of affairs. Convinced that he was right, conscious of his popularity (perhaps even fearing it), Nagy patiently awaited his readmission to the party, his appointment to the premiership. In the interval, he had given much thought to the policies he would follow as head of the government; at the same time he had demonstrated an amazing lack of realism. Unlike Gomulka, who knew that he would be helpless unless he controlled a powerful party machine, Nagy behaved like a functionary waiting for his appointment to be entitled to start a revolution. To be sure, on October 23, 1956, when the immense crowd assembled in front of the Parliament building clamored for him, he appeared and addressed it—but instead of being equal to the occasion, instead of clearly formulating the obscure aspirations of this enormous, rumbling mass of people so as to be able to channelize and guide them, Imre Nagy, profoundly disturbed by the riot, thought only of appeasing his audience: "My friends, keep calm, the Central Committee will take steps, leave everything to us. . . ."

Later that evening when, following Gero's speech, threatening crowds surrounded the Budapest radio station, Nagy displayed a similar lack of initiative. His friend Geza Losonczy telephoned to him asking him to address the people. Nagy declined. "What could I say?" he asked. "At best I could speak only in my own name. The Politburo has entrusted me with no mission. Let us wait till it makes up its mind."

"I can see your point, Uncle Imre," said Losonczy, who was only half convinced by Nagy's argument.

There can be no doubt about this—Nagy is anything but a revolutionist, a leader of men, a tribune of the people. His background, his temperament, his erudition fit him for the role of a servant of the state, not a wrecker or a founder. He would be perfect as an enlightened despot. But he was totally unprepared to lead an insurrection. Much the same can be said of the men who surrounded him at the crucial moment. Among these, Zoltan Szanto seems to have been the most capable. This tired, disillusioned Communist, cultivated and sensitive, had always been opposed to Rakosi; in 1954, Nagy appointed him head of the propaganda department. Previously, he had served as Hungarian ambassador in Belgrade and in Paris. Rakosi, who regarded him as a dangerous rival, had sidetracked him soon after the Liberation, and he had no influence whatever on the party machine.

The most dynamic of Nagy's associates—most of them were

journalists, such as Miklos Vasarhelyi and Miklos Gimes, former editors of *Szabad Nep,* or writers such as Gyula Hay—was Geza Losonczy. A man of fiery temperament, steeled by his work in the anti-Nazi underground, he served as state secretary of information; after 1951, he was imprisoned by order of Rakosi. He was released in 1954, and spent more than a year in a nursing home recovering from a nervous breakdown and the tortures to which he had been subjected. An excellent speaker and journalist, he wrote for *Magyar Nemzet,* organ of the Popular Front, and won great popularity among the intellectuals whose cause he championed. In September, 1956, he distinguished himself by polemizing against Istvan Friss, one of the most ferocious Rakosists. He perhaps possessed the qualities of a political leader. But he was isolated; his attempts to create an organization were frustrated by his timorous friends.

The national Communists were all the weaker because after Rakosi's resignation they split up. In July, 1956, a number of them, including Janos Kadar and Gyula Kallai, joined Erno Gero. And yet Kadar after 1954 had played an important part in the struggle against Rakosi, and it was largely thanks to him that Rakosi's plan for exploiting the Poznan riots of 1956 to restore the party authority was frustrated. At the Central Committee meetings held between July 18 and 21 of that year, Kadar led the moderates who demanded a policy reflecting the views of Khrushchev and Mikoyan and compatible with a Yugoslav-Hungarian rapprochement. But Kadar did not aim at doing away with the dictatorship of the party machine; the enemy for him was Rakosi and his policemen, whom he hated personally. Even though he had disapproved the expulsion of Nagy in 1955 and occasionally voted with the latter's partisans, he never regarded himself as a Nagyist. It is necessary to keep this fact in mind in order to understand the subsequent events.

Kadar, like some other Hungarian Communists, is a child of the anti-German underground, of which Laszlo Rajk was the most brilliant representative. Unlike his friends, who are of middle-class origin, he was born into a proletarian family. He joined the party in 1929, as a twelve-year-old boy. For some time he worked as a carpenter. Honest but narrow-minded, tormented by an inferiority complex, he became a professional revolutionary under the German occupation. His character seems to have predestined him for dangerous missions. In 1944, the party charged him with establishing contact with Tito's guerrillas, but he was arrested at the border and imprisoned. After the Liberation Rakosi, who wanted to exploit his envy of Rajk, appointed him member of the party secretariat. In 1947, Kadar distinguished himself by courageously affronting a crowd of angry strikers at Miskolc and restoring order.

In 1948, on the eve of the purges, Rajk was appointed minister of foreign affairs, and Kadar succeeded him as minister of the interior, despite the fact that Kadar was regarded as a close friend of Rajk. In keeping with the classical Stalinist procedure, the most Titoist of the Hungarian Communist leaders was chosen to preside over the witch hunt organized against the Titoists.

To be sure, Kadar, in his capacity as minister of the interior, was only the nominal head of the police. The real chiefs of the AVO were Gabor Peter, a former tailor intoxicated with his new power, and the torturer Vladimir Farkas. Both were under the direct orders of General Byelkin of the Russian service. But Kadar had to lend his name to their sordid activities.

In order to compromise him, the party made him sign warrants of arrest against his best friends. The diabolical Rakosi, abusing Kadar's credulity and his naïve faith in Stalin and the party, charged him with the most hair-raising tasks. In the

summer of 1949 he was sent to Rajk, who still stubbornly resisted his torturers bent on wresting from him false confessions
incriminating Tito. Kadar told him: "We shall never succeed
in making the people accept the new line unless we simplify
things. The people must not doubt, must not discuss. We shall
tell the people that there was treason; this will appeal to the
imagination. The party has chosen you for the role of traitor,
you must sacrifice yourself to the party. This is terrible, but
after all you are an old militant, and you cannot refuse to help
the party." [1]

The episode is worthy of the pen of Koestler. It confirms
the revelations made as early as 1939 by V. Krivitsky, former
chief of the Soviet counter-espionage, in a book published at
that time. But apparently this did not prevent the Soviet inquisitors from using the same methods several years later. It is
probable that Kadar believed every word he said to Rajk.
He was convinced that Rajk had committed mistakes, and
that he had been wrong in opposing Rakosi who was supported by the majority of the Central Committee. Kadar was
also capable of thinking that if he had been in Rajk's place he
would have done what the party asked of him, all the more
so because Rakosi had assured him that Rajk would not actually be executed. "You will confess everything and we shall
sentence you to death. But the sentence will not be carried out.
You will emigrate to a friendly country under an assumed
name, where you will be able to work in peace." That is what
Kadar was asked to tell Rajk.

Later, when Rajk was hanged, Kadar complained indig-
nantly to Rakosi, who merely shrugged his shoulders with contempt. He had no use for sentimental Communists. A few days
later the minister of the interior was in turn imprisoned and

---

[1] This incident was reported by close friends of Kadar to the Polish journalist, Wiktor Woroszylski. (Cf. *Nowa Kultura,* November, 1956.)

charged with complicity with Rajk, Tito, Churchill, and Allan Dulles's Central Intelligence Agency. Several of his fellow prisoners told me that Kadar was more cruelly tortured than any other victim of Rakosi's police. His nails were torn off his fingers one by one. No doubt only his ferocious hatred of Rakosi saved him from a nervous breakdown—he was more resistant than Geza Losonczy. On his readmission to the party in 1954, Kadar at once began to demand that the so-called Titoists be rehabilitated and the torturers punished. Tito encouraged him: from 1955 onward, the Yugoslavs pinned their hopes on Kadar rather than Nagy, who seemed to them "too soft." During a meeting of the Central Committee, when Kadar renewed his demand, Rakosi sent for the tape recording of Kadar's conversation with Rajk in prison. "I am taking the liberty of treating you to this bit of entertainment," he said, "which proves that Comrade Kadar, then minister of the interior, has his share of responsibility in the Rajk affair."

Kadar defended himself, declaring that he had been carrying out orders, and that he would not have tried to convince Rajk if he had known that he would be executed. He continued his fight against Rakosi until July, 1956, when he succeeded in overthrowing him with the help of Gero. There can be little doubt that he allied himself with Gero at that time only for the purpose of overthrowing Rakosi. Kadar could not have much sympathy for Gero, the most inhuman of all Stalin's henchmen, who felt only contempt for the Hungarian people, for all peoples. Kadar had a strain of humanity and patriotism in him; for Gero, people were merely the raw material for his mad technocratic dreams.

In 1956, however, Kadar wanted to act realistically. He knew that the Soviets distrusted Nagy, that Gero had strong supporters in the Kremlin, and that Kaganovich never failed to ask his Hungarian visitors how his dear friend Gero was doing. Now, after Poznan, the positions of Kaganovich, Molotov, and the other diehards were strengthened. Gero took advantage of this, and Kadar thought it inopportune to demand a radical purge of the Stalinist elements. He hoped that by means of his alliance with Gero and other moderate Rakosists, such as Karoly Kiss and Antal Apro, he would gain a foothold in the party machine, and gradually eliminate the Stalinists. He also intended to place so-called Titoists or rehabilitated Rajkists in key posts in the party secretariat and the police. Then he planned to play the part of arbiter between the Gero clique and the Nagy followers. As for Nagy himself, Kadar favored his rehabilitation on the same conditions Ochab had laid down for the rehabilitation of Gomulka: he was to be absolved of all personal guilt, but his ideas were to be condemned. Kadar thought that the party would recover some of its prestige by exploiting Nagy's popularity, provided, however, that the former premier broke with the confused and dangerous intellectuals surrounding him. For this reason Kadar opened negotiations with Nagy, and asked him to recognize his errors that had been condemned in 1955. This, too, was a ticklish and painful task: for Nagy was just as obstinate as Kadar, "stubborn as a Calvinist," as the saying goes in Hungary. "Why should I recognize my errors," Nagy argued, "when I was right all along?" And he refused to discuss the matter before being reinstated in the posts from which he had been dismissed after his expulsion from the party, namely, his post of professor of agronomy at the University of Budapest and his seat in the Academy. The negotiations dragged on, until Gero and Kadar were compelled to yield under pressure of the party, the intellectuals, and the public at large. Nagy was readmitted without conditions. But much valuable time had been lost. . . .

Between July and October, Kadar, if he had taken the place of Gero, might have played the role of a Hungarian Ochab. But actually he was manipulated by Gero just as he had been manipulated by Rakosi. What was worse, Kadar retained the support of some of his old comrades who might have considerably strengthened Nagy if they had joined him. For instance, Gyula Kallai did everything he could to persuade the rebel writers and newspapermen to submit to party directives.

Another close friend of Kadar was François Munnich, the Fouqué of de-Stalinization. A former provincial notable, picturesque, elegant, amateur of women, good food, and vintage wines, he became a Communist out of a taste for adventure and conspiracy. In 1956, Munnich became the head of the veterans of the Spanish Civil War, that is, those who had survived the purge that had decimated their ranks after the Rajk trial. The part Munnich played in the Rajk affair is far from clear: it has been reported that he had helped the policemen who investigated his former companion in arms, and that he was rewarded for this help by being appointed ambassador to Moscow in 1949, though others looked upon that appointment as a sign of his disgrace. However that may be, Munnich was prominent in the agitation that followed the Twentieth Party Congress in the Soviet Union. He was one of the speakers at the Rajk funeral, and on the eve of the insurrection he was regarded, despite his seventy years, as a man of the future.

The Party Machine in Panic

The national Communists were unorganized; with no clearly formulated program of action, they were unprepared to take over the government. The agitation they carried on, particularly among the intellectuals and students, was not directed against the regime as such, but only against the Stalinists, against the party bureaucrats, and against the Red aristocracy, the so-called *kucsera*, whom Gyula Hay denounced in the September issue of the *Literary Gazette*. But the bureaucracy was an integral part of the regime; indeed, the regime was founded on the privileges of high and low functionaries. To be sure,

Hay and other critics distinguished between the *kucsera* who traveled in luxurious cars, lived in modern apartments, and benefited from all kinds of special favors, and the lower functionaries whose living conditions were modest enough. Nevertheless, the overwhelming majority of government and party officials felt themselves threatened by the opposition, all the more so because the latter demanded the dismissal of all Rakosists and Stalinists, and raised the question of their responsibility for the crimes of the regime. Many functionaries, including party secretaries of factory committees, administrative departments, and collective farms, chairmen of people's councils in the provinces, and, above all, former workers who held key posts in the army, in the police, and in the diplomatic service, were anxiously wondering whether the anti-Stalinist purge, though seemingly directed only against the bigwigs, would not soon be extended to themselves.

This anxiety, this great fear of the bureaucracy, was one of the most characteristic features of Hungarian public life in the fall of 1956. It affected tens, perhaps hundreds, of thousands of men more or less compromised by the Rakosi regime. On October 7, 1956, Jozsef Darvas, minister of culture, published an article in *Szabad Nep* in which he dealt with this situation. This son of poor peasants and author of proletarian novels, who had become chief censor and intellectual inquisitor and had been ousted from the executive committee of the Writers' Union, pointed out that it was necessary to reassure the civil servants, who were ready to join the opposition provided that the latter received them. But even before this article was published, Istvan Friss, a Rakosist who had joined Gero and was moving closer to Kadar, had violently protested against the Nagyists' attack on the party machine. Friss was particularly angered by an article Losonczy had published in *Muvelt Nep,* demanding the dismissal of all functionaries guilty of the errors that had been condemned by the party resolution of July.

"Losonczy, to be sure, demands the dismissal of only those functionaries who displayed excessive zeal in carrying out inhuman policies," Friss wrote. "But how will it be possible to establish clear distinctions between those functionaries who merely carried out a bad policy in good faith and those who exaggerated and distorted this policy? . . . And if we call the sectarians to account, will it be possible not to call to account the opportunists, too? No, this is not the way to defend and consolidate the unity of the party. Whatever Losonczy's intentions may be, this would lead to a general persecution of the party and government functionaries, to a new witch hunt. . . ."

Losonczy hastened to declare that his attacks were not aimed at the bureaucracy as a whole, but only at the chief culprits. And Gabor Tanczos, secretary general of the Petofi Society, writing in the October 14 issue of *Muvelt Nep,* rejected the charge that the anti-Stalinist intellectuals were hostile to the functionaries. "The opposite is true," he said. "The best among the young intellectuals have the greatest respect for the public duties that the functionaries perform in a spirit of self-sacrifice. . . . It is precisely because we feel friendly toward the functionaries that we ask them to join us in our struggle, to fight with us against all those who will not or cannot serve the people."

Such statements, however, were too vague to reassure the bureaucracy. What was needed was a frank exchange of views between responsible leaders of the opposition and representatives of the civil service. Such a confrontation had taken place in Poland between the partisans of Gomulka and the members of the various administrative departments, including the officers' corps and the political police, but nothing of the kind was done in Hungary. On the eve of the insurrection, the functionaries, particularly those at medium levels, felt more and more isolated, and more and more threatened by an anti-bureaucratic St. Bartholomew's night. Under these circumstances, most high-ranking officials had no choice but to run away from their responsibilities: they either fought desperately against the people, or hid in cellars. Whereas in Poland a peaceful transformation of the regime was secured thanks to the fruitful contacts that had taken place between the opposition and the old bureaucracy, in Hungary, tens of thousands of functionaries thought that such a solution was out of the question. The Rakosists exploited the blunders of the opposition by representing themselves as the only true defenders of order, of party unity, of continuous progress, thus rewelding the bonds of solidarity between the Stalinists at the top and the bottom. Their appeal to solidarity in the face of danger influenced even some centrists, such as Karoly Kiss, who had good reasons to fear that the popular movement after eliminating the Stalinists would cause their downfall, too. In October, the national Communists were faced with the task of controlling the agitation. Unable to master this task, they hesitated until the last moment between two methods of dealing with the events. The first was to meet the demands of the masses at once; the second, to restore order and unity in the party, and to make concessions later. And since they could not make up their minds in favor of either of these methods, the outbreak of the insurrection threw them into utmost confusion. In the light of the foregoing considerations, Gero's and Hegedus's request for Soviet intervention does not appear as an accident or even as a crude provocation (although, as we shall see, provocation played a part in the events), but as the fatal consequence of the isolation and despair of the entire bureaucratic machine, its cry of mortal anguish.

The Hesitations of the Kremlin

We still have to analyze briefly the state of mind that prevailed in the Kremlin on the eve of the insurrection. To do this it will be necessary to go back somewhat, even beyond

the Twentieth Congress of the Russian party, whose decisions
largely determined the course taken by the events in 1956.

Actually, the new Soviet line with regard to the satellites, including Hungary—we might call this line "the Khrushchev-
Mikoyan experiment"—went into effect as early as the fall of
1954, to be exact, soon after Khrushchev's and Mikoyan's
visit to Peiping. According to reliable reports, it was Mao
Tse-tung who devised this new policy which aimed primarily
at the gradual decolonization of the satellites. At the first
meeting of the Komekon, or Council of Mutual Economic
Assistance, held in Budapest, Mikoyan disclosed that Mao
Tse-tung had sharply criticized the Soviet Union for her exploitation of the European people's democracies by means of
the so-called mixed companies established after the war. Mao
Tse-tung described this exploitation as a vestige of "great-
power chauvinism," which, he thought, should be eliminated
from the relations among Socialist countries, thus taking up
one of Tito's favorite ideas. At the same meeting, Mikoyan
announced the impending dissolution of the mixed companies,
which were actually abolished a short time later.

Mao's idea was, roughly speaking, this: One of the major
tasks of the Communist bloc is to strengthen its cohesion and
defensive potential. To achieve this, it is necessary first of all
to help China develop her industry. Therefore the policy of
dropping, even temporarily, the principle of the priority of
heavy industry is erroneous. To adhere to this principle is a
matter of life and death for the Soviet-Chinese bloc. But since
the acceleration of the pace of the development of heavy industry imposes further sacrifices on the populations of the
Eastern countries, which must thus renounce a rapid improvement of standards of living, it is necessary to stimulate them
by appealing to their nationalism. "Restore national pride to
the people, give them the illusion that they are independent,
and they will work more efficiently." At the same time the

Communist intellectuals must be given greater freedom and be permitted to express themselves in their own language, and in accordance with each country's traditions. The Chinese thought that many taboos set up by Stalin were harmful and unnecessary.

It may be said that the Sino-Soviet plan put into effect at that time provided for a progressive transformation of the Soviet empire into a kind of Communist commonwealth. The countries composing it were to regain their sovereignty and national independence within the limits compatible with the one-party system.

Needless to say, this transformation was to be carefully supervised, in order to avoid convulsions such as the Czechoslovak and East Berlin riots of June, 1953. It was only under this reservation that the Soviet strategists gave their blessing to the desatellization suggested by Mao. The importance attached by the Kremlin to strategic considerations is best illustrated by the military and diplomatic negotiations that were conducted between the Soviets and the satellites from 1954 onward, and that ended with the conclusion of the Warsaw Pact in May, 1955. While the text of this pact underlined the independence and equality of the signatories, it included a secret clause, which in advance limited this independence, and which was not disclosed until October, 1956, when the Soviet army intervened in Hungary. Under this clause, the unified Soviet forces commanded by Marshal Konev, i.e., the Soviet army, had the right to come to the "assistance" of any Communist government threatened by a popular movement capable of imperiling its existence and the military security of the Soviet Union. In other words, for the architects of desatellization the future independence of the Eastern countries was consistent with the maintenance of Soviet bases in their territories. The subsequent developments in Hungary and Poland showed that such a conception of independence was not easily accepted by the public opinion of the countries concerned.

However that may be, it was only after taking all those precautions that Khrushchev, Bulganin, and Mikoyan went to Belgrade to effect a reconciliation with Tito, now rehabilitated as the first apostle of "relations on a footing of equality among Socialist countries." The Soviet rulers at that time were sincerely convinced (no doubt under Mao's influence) that they would be able to obtain Tito's support in the task of desatellization, which was in line with the official Yugoslav doctrine, and which offered Tito's diplomacy an unexpected field of action.

The policy of reconciliation with national communism met with strong opposition. A number of Soviet leaders, particularly Molotov, saw no objection to restoring diplomatic and economic relations with Yugoslavia; such a restoration was compatible with the general policy of "coexistence" which applied to all countries, Communist or non-Communist. But to Molotov, the cosignatory with Stalin of the famous letters of 1948 charging Tito with heresy, Tito remained a cause of dissension, and national communism was the most dangerous of all deviations. Molotov had said so before Khrushchev's departure for Belgrade, and repeated it later at a meeting of the Russian party's Central Committee, held in July, 1955, which was of capital importance for the subsequent fate of the satellites, and which foreshadowed the Twentieth Congress.

A former Polish high official, Seweryn Bialer, who went over to the West in January, 1956, has seen the minutes of that meeting; and his account of it was later confirmed by other satellite officials. One of the principal items on the agenda was the revision of the relations between the Soviets and the people's democracies. Once again Mikoyan acted as the chief advocate of such a revision. He criticized the institution of the mixed companies, the "tactless" behavior of

Soviet experts sent to satellite countries, and the discrimina-
tory clauses in the Russian trade agreements with those countries. Seconded by Khrushchev, Mikoyan launched a sharp
attack on Molotov, charging him with responsibility "for inadmissible Stalinist practices." Molotov, supported by only a
minority of the Presidium, was on the defensive, but made it
clear that he did not share the optimism of Khrushchev and
Mikoyan, who, for their part, were firmly convinced that de-
Stalinization would result, after some inevitable upsets, in an
increase of Soviet prestige.

The lifting of a number of Stalinist restrictions in Russia
had not touched off a violent reaction against the Communist
system, as the Stalinists had feared; on the contrary, in the
course of discussions preceding the Twentieth Congress, the
Soviet intellectuals had displayed a great deal of restraint,
suggesting that for them the possibility of improving the Stalinist regime was beyond dispute. Khrushchev and his partisans
were convinced that they could channelize and exploit the
growing liberal movement, which was primarily directed
against the sectarian features of Stalinism—the rigid control of
science and art, and the countless falsifications of history. They
had come to believe that such practices, which paralyzed intellectual production, were actually harmful.

This view proved correct as regards the Soviet Union. But
in the people's democracies, particularly in Poland and Hungary, where standards of living had dropped in the course of
recent years, the policy of de-Stalinization touched off a wave
of unrest which threatened to upset the regime. For instance,
how could Rakosi make Stalin the scapegoat for all the crimes
and disasters of the recent years without implicating himself,
and the party as a whole? To be sure, Rakosi did everything
conceivable not to be dragged down by the fall of his former
idol. Like his Soviet and Czechoslovak counterparts, he tried
to take refuge behind the wall of the party leadership's col-

lective responsibility. But after all, this so-called collective responsibility was a fiction: Stalinism consisted precisely in the usurpation of power at the expense of the collective leadership, not to mention the fact that the crimes in question were too monstrous to be described as errors or blunders, and any reference to them implicitly condemned the party as a whole.

De-Stalinization might have run a smoother course both in Hungary and in Poland if it had coincided with important changes in the leadership personnel and a substantial rise of standards of living. As regards the latter, neither Rakosi nor Ochab could make concessions, for Malenkovism had been condemned, and the priority of heavy industry had been established as an inviolable dogma. As regards the former point, the influence of the Kremlin diehards was still strong enough to prevent the return of Nagy and Gomulka, and to secure the positions of the Natolin group in Poland, and of the Rakosi clique in Hungary. As a result, the Communists were deprived of all the benefits they might have drawn from the ideas launched by the Twentieth Congress. Instead of serving as new cement to unify the party, and a basis for a new social contract between the government and the people, these ideas had become a source of dissension and weakness. As early as June, 1956, the Hungarian Communist party, just like the Polish, was hopelessly divided. This was pointed out by one of the leading spirits of the Petofi Society, Tibor Tardos, in a speech delivered on June 27.[2] "For some time there has been no unity in the party," Tibor Tardos said. "We can observe two distinct currents. The first is represented by the comrades who have reflected on the situation following the death of Stalin, and greeted with enthusiasm the program of June, 1953 [i.e., the program of the first Nagy government]. . . . These comrades,

[2] The speech was not printed in Hungary; the text quoted here was given to me by a person who had attended the meeting and taken shorthand notes. Tibor Tardos was arrested in January, 1957, by order of Kadar.

as early as the fall of 1954, became convinced that Rakosi, Farkas, and others must be replaced, and by their theoretical and practical work they have created the conditions that make it possible for us to draw the necessary conclusions from the Twentieth Congress, and to apply its teachings. Needless to say, this camp, particularly since the Twentieth Congress, has increased in numbers. . . .

"The second current is represented by the comrades of the old school," Tardos went on to say, "the dogmatists who have assimilated the Stalinist doctrine and believe that it is essentially a good doctrine. They have not yet disavowed the principles of Stalinist policy, they have not analyzed it critically, and they continue it, tempering it by a greater or smaller dose of compromise. The party moves ahead amidst inner dissensions . . . but its advance is painful, very slow, and is like a battle of attrition. The spectacle thus offered to the people causes immense moral damage. And the material damage is even greater."

Rakosi and his faithful had complained that Tardos "had been criticizing the party from the outside." Tardos replied that the complaint was not entirely unjustified, "since we are actually outside the restricted circle which continues to pursue the dogmatic Stalinist policy, which at a pinch makes concessions, but which shows itself unable to renounce its former ideas. But this circle is not the party. The party is ourselves, those who belong to the other current, who fight for the ideas and principles of humanism, and whose aims reflect in ever-increasing measure those of the people and of the country."

And with an eloquence which expressed the enthusiasm, the hopes, but also the illusions of the Hungarian national Communists during that summer of 1956, Tardos exclaimed: "Our allies are innumerable. The people's spreading knowledge, their growing need for more air, are on our side. So are the ancient cultures and modern research, and Lenin, too, who inscribed into history the date of a revolution made to liberate men. And so is Petofi, who, in a house in Lajos Kossuth Street, gave this people freedom of the press: 'Let it be yours, Hungarians,' he said. This freedom is therefore inalienable."

Tardos spoke in the name of Marxism-Leninism, and of the Russian party's Twentieth Congress. But did his lofty invocation of the freedom of mankind, of the freedom of Hungary, actually reflect the views of the Twentieth Congress? The Rakosi camp did not think so. Those slogans of freedom, justice, truth, democracy, patriotism seemed highly suspicious to Rakosi; and they sounded heretical also to Communists such as Kadar. They detected bourgeois influences in them. Freedom for whom? Truth in the service of what? they asked. Although these party bureaucrats were not profound students of Marxism, they knew one thing: the party is at the center of the world, the dictatorship of the party is the ultimate criterion. In their eyes, the interests of the party and those of the proletariat were absolutely identical. They distrusted the intellectuals who despite their protestations put truth above the party.

The Poznan riots of June, 1956, had a sobering effect on the Kremlin: these riots, to which the Polish party had reacted weakly, seemed to justify Molotov and the other Stalinists in their opposition to the policy of liberalization, and to show once again that there is only one step from criticism of institutions in words to criticism of institutions by force of arms. But Khrushchev and Mikoyan blamed the imperialists who, they said, hoping to take advantage of the discussions being carried on in the Socialist countries, "attempted to arouse chauvinistic passions, loosen the bonds uniting the Socialist states, and sow discord among them." (*Pravda* editorial of July 16.) As a result of Poznan, the balance of forces within the Soviet party leadership was altered. The army leaders, worried by the prospect of a dislocation of the Stalinist empire, joined hands with the Orthodox group and launched the slogans of vigilance and unity. But unity was difficult to achieve: for the liberals could plausibly enough blame the popular agitation in Poland and Hungary on the stubbornness of the Orthodox leaders who had resisted the necessary reforms. Significantly, the above-mentioned *Pravda* editorial attacked the Petofi Society, thus condoning the measures Rakosi had taken against the rebel writers: "Some elements hostile to the policy of the Hungarian Workers' party, yielding to the influence of imperialist circles, tried to spread views contrary to those of the party, thus playing into the hands of the enemies of the People's Hungary." However, the editorial went on to say: "We must not close our eyes to the fact that wherever the task of the political education of the masses is neglected, the enemy agents take advantage of this."

This hesitation in fixing responsibility shows that the Russians could not make up their minds about the course to follow. Mikoyan and Suslov were sent to Budapest to investigate the situation, and early in July they proposed a compromise: Rakosi was to resign in favor of Gero, and the unity of the party was to be restored by admitting Kadar and some other victims of Rakosi to the leadership. But, as we have said, these concessions were no longer sufficient to satisfy the Hungarians. They demanded the return of Nagy and a more radical change in the party policies. The agitation that had begun in the intellectual milieus threatened to extend to the rest of society, and it was growing more and more anti-Soviet and anti-Russian. Some Communist leaders ascribed this to the undermining influence of the Yugoslavs. And it is a fact that national communism in Poland and Hungary was considerably strengthened through political and cultural contacts with Yugoslavia. The Yugoslav emissaries made no secret of their sympathies for Gomulka and Nagy, and the Budapest correspondents of *Borba* and *Politika* reported certain turbulent meetings of the Petofi Society in glowing terms.

Early in September the relations between the U.S.S.R. and Yugoslavia grew cooler. On September 3, the Russian party's Central Committee addressed a confidential letter to the satellite parties, warning them against the dangers of certain Yugoslav ideas. The Yugoslavs, after being informed of the contents of this letter (no doubt by their Polish comrades), declared that it violated the spirit of the Soviet-Yugoslav agreement of June, 1955, which had been confirmed a year later during Tito's trip to Russia. On September 17, Khrushchev went to Belgrade to appease Tito and no doubt to explain to him the reasons for the stiffening of the Russian policy. A week later, Tito, accompanied by some of his closest associates, went to Yalta where the talks were continued. Nothing or almost nothing was disclosed about these talks at the time. But it was clear (and later, on November 12, Tito's speech at Pula confirmed this impression) that the situation in the people's democracies was the most important item on the agenda. Khrushchev asked Tito to help him appease the Poles and the Hungarians, and to induce them to adopt a less intransigent attitude toward the pro-Soviet elements which the Yugoslav propaganda described as Stalinists. Otherwise, Khrushchev explained, he and the other partisans of democratization and of a rapprochement with Yugoslavia would lose their majority in the Presidium.

It seems that Khrushchev was willing to pledge himself that the policy of democratization and desatellization would continue; only the pace and the range of this policy were in question. The Soviet Union, he argued, could not afford to weaken the Warsaw Pact as long as NATO was in existence and West Germany was being remilitarized. The Soviet leaders feared that nationalistic elements in Poland and Hungary might win the upper hand over Gomulka and Nagy, and that the Western powers might be tempted to exploit the ensuing unrest to oust Russia from Eastern Europe. Such a development, Khrushchev pointed out, would not be in the interest of the

Yugoslav Communists, for the restoration of bourgeois democracy in Poland and in Hungary would weaken the authority and stability of the Yugoslav regime.

The Yugoslavs were not convinced by these arguments, as is proven by the very length of the talks. While Tito was willing to support Khrushchev against the pro-Stalinists, his view of the developments in Poland and Hungary was more optimistic than Khrushchev's. He believed that a liberalized communism had good prospects in those countries, and that it would not necessarily lead to the abrogation of the Warsaw Pact. He may also have thought that a loosening of ties between those countries and Russia was not entirely undesirable, and that Yugoslav influence would replace the weakened Russian influence. But there are reasons to believe that Tito was less outspoken as regards Hungary than Poland. It seems that he came out emphatically in favor of Gomulka, while for Hungary he was inclined to accept the Gero-Kadar regime of July, 1956. Tito gave proof of his good intentions by agreeing to meet Gero (who "happened" to be in Yalta), by reconciling himself with this former adversary, and by inviting him to Belgrade. While maintaining his reservations, he gave his blessings less to Gero himself than to his team and the Titoists represented in it. Moreover, Zoltan Szanto, a member of Nagy's brain trust, was among the Hungarian delegates who visited Belgrade in mid-October. Thus a bridge was created between Tito and Imre Nagy, whose popularity in Hungary had been demonstrated during the Rajk funeral.

However, within a few days, the mounting popular unrest in Poland and Hungary shattered the precarious understanding that had been reached between Tito and Khrushchev. National communism had become a force that Belgrade could not control any more than could Moscow. The threat of an explosion was becoming ever more real, dispelling Mao's and Khrushchev's dream of transforming the Soviet empire into a Socialist

commonwealth. In the rush of the events, Khrushchev, Mikoyan, and the other champions of de-Stalinization were assum-
ing the status of apprentice sorcerers. It is noteworthy that of
all the Russian leaders who landed in Warsaw on October 18
to appease Gomulka and save Rokossovsky, Khrushchev and
Mikoyan were the most vociferous and intransigent, as though
trying to save their own skins by outdoing the others in patriotic fervor.

Around October 18, Poland avoided Soviet intervention
only by a hair's breadth. Movements of troops took place all
over the country. (A few days later, similar movements were
observed in Hungary, even before the manifestations had taken
a threatening turn.) These movements could of course be interpreted as a means of intimidating the populace, as a warning. But it seems certain that at least some of the Soviet army
leaders were not unsympathetic to the plan advanced by some
Stalinists for a putsch against the national Communists. Agents
provocateurs were at work. The police were striking out right
and left, at random, without co-ordination.

Poland averted disaster thanks to the firmness, coolheaded-
ness, and astuteness of Gomulka and Cyrankiewicz, who were
equal to the situation, and thanks above all to the patriotism
of Ochab, who by lending his support to Gomulka decided the
outcome of the political battle. The role of the Polish working
class, mobilized by the national Communists, was just as
crucial. The Soviet leaders realized that a military Soviet intervention in Poland would at once assume the appearance
of a war of aggression against a united nation which possessed
a strong and well-equipped army. They did not—as yet—run
the same risk in Hungary, where the high-ranking officers were
far more Stalinized, where the political police was still under
complete Soviet control, and where the working class seemed
neutral and indifferent to the agitation carried on by the intellectuals. It is understandable that some Soviet experts on

whom Hungary's fate depended should have been tempted by
such a situation. They were obsessed by the idea of setting an
example in order to restore Russian prestige, which had been
severely shaken by the Khrushchev report and the discussions
that followed. To be sure, the Polish intellectuals irritated them
no less than did the Petofi Society "brawlers"; but the Poles
had got away this time and were safe behind Gomulka's authority. The Hungarian students, writers, and journalists
seemed a far easier prey.

This is not to say that there was a deliberate provocation
for the purpose of restoring the Rakosi system in Hungary. It
is probable that even the most Stalinist among the political
and military leaders of Soviet Russia had resigned themselves
to the abolition of Stalinist colonialism in favor of a kind of
reformist neo-colonialism. But their main objective was to
safeguard the strategic predominance of Russia and the political hegemony of the Communist party. The Hungarian tragedy
must be understood against the background of this Soviet neo-
colonialism. Unfortunately for Hungary, the Russians, no
doubt ill informed about the state of mind of the people, and
advised by Gero, who despised the people and the intellectuals,
found no Hungarian Gomulka capable of persuading his countrymen of the necessity to move more slowly toward independence, to stay within the Soviet bloc, and to refrain from doing
anything that might strengthen the chauvinistic and imperial-
istic tendencies of the Soviet policy makers. The Hungarians
have been criticized for their imprudence. After the Polish
elections of January, 1957, Khrushchev himself contrasted
their recklessness with the "political maturity of the Polish
people." But the recklessness of the Hungarians, the explosion
of their anger, as we shall now see, was the inevitable consequence of the patience and passivity they had displayed over
a long period.

2

REVOLUTION VICTORIOUS

From Effervescence to Explosion

IN the days following the Rajk funeral, fever mounted rapidly in Budapest. Yielding to popular demands, the Communist party lifted its ban on criticisms of Matyas Rakosi, who up until then had enjoyed a kind of personal immunity even though his policies were attacked. On October 13, *Magyar Nemzet,* organ of the Popular Front, printed an article charging the former first party secretary with "having delayed for more than a year the reconciliation between Yugoslavia and Hungary." On the same day, the Hungarian Telegraphic Agency published a statement by Colonel Karoly Rath, veteran of the Spanish International Brigade, charging Rakosi with responsibility "for the death and sufferings of the best party militants." It seemed that Gero was no longer defending either Rakosi or Mihaly Farkas, whose arrest had just been announced. There were reports that Farkas had said to the police agents who had come to arrest him: "You will see that there is no Farkas affair, that there is only a Rakosi-Gero-Farkas affair. Woe to those who have loosened the avalanche."

On October 14, *Szabad Nep* announced that Imre Nagy had been reinstated in the party. "The Politburo took the decision to void the resolution of November, 1955, expelling Nagy from the party," the newspaper said. "Even though Comrade Nagy had committed political mistakes, these did not justify his

171

expulsion. Comrade Matyas Rakosi's personal prejudices played an important part in this expulsion. . . . Taking all this into account, the Politburo readmits Imre Nagy to the party and proposes to the Central Committee that the questions still pending be discussed soon in order to determine to what extent the previous party discussions contained exaggerations and inaccurate statements. . . ."

The same issue of *Szabad Nep* contained a letter addressed by Nagy to the Central Committee on October 4, which said: "I think it absolutely indispensable that the charges made concerning my political and ideological activities be discussed. . . . I am ready to recognize the errors I have actually committed, but the unfounded charges against me must be dropped. . . ."

The opposition was jubilant: it regarded this reinstatement, which was announced a few hours before Gero's departure for Belgrade, as a stage on the road that would lead the former premier to power.

On October 19, it seemed that Hungary was holding her breath. Everyone had his eyes fixed on Warsaw. Newspapers were sold out the moment they appeared on the stands, people waited impatiently for newscasts. The general opinion was that the fate of Hungary depended on the outcome of the battle being waged between Gomulka and his opponents. The report that Rokossovsky had not been re-elected to the Central Committee was greeted with cries of joy. The Workers' Union, the Journalists' Union, and the Petofi Society were in continual session. The *Literary Gazette* of October 20 demanded the immediate convocation of a special party congress, and a complete change in the party's leadership.

The agitation was no longer confined to Budapest—it had spread to the provinces. At a public meeting held in the Jokai Theater at Gyor, an industrial center in western Hungary, Gyula Hay and Lajos Simon demanded that Hungary follow the examples of Yugoslavia, Poland, and China, and adopt a method of building socialism in conformity with her own traditions. "Are you for or against the departure of the Soviet troops?" one of the audience asked Hay. "I am for it," Hay answered. "The abolition of Soviet bases in Hungary is part of an independent domestic and foreign policy, the adoption of which, I hope, will be speeded up by the present negotiations between Hungary and Yugoslavia."

"And what about releasing Cardinal Mindszenty?" asked another member of the audience. Hay replied without hesitation: "I am not a believer, but I am against the settlement of the religious question by administrative methods."

These questions are significant: they prove that the provincial intelligentsia, slower to awaken than that of the capital, is more radical once aroused.

On October 20, three thousand students meeting at Szeged, Hungary's second largest city, decided after a long debate to resign from the Union of the Youth and to form a new "free and independent" student organization. Even though they declared that they accepted the guidance of "the Marxist-Leninist party, in the spirit of the Twentieth Congress," their decision was an act of defiance, and was so interpreted by the party, one of whose leaders, Karoly Kiss, had warned the rank and file against "excessive democratization." "There are still elements in Hungary which aim at restoring capitalism," he said. "These elements have recently been reinforced. Unless the Communists and defenders of the working class realize this fact, it might cause irreparable damage."

Kiss and his friends, who represented the middle-of-the-road tendency in the party leadership and had joined Kadar, hurriedly organized meetings in factories to mobilize the workers against the danger of a counter-revolution which they saw lurking everywhere behind the activities of the opposition. But these meetings turned against the men who had called them. The workers who had been gagged for years now suddenly gave vent to their feelings. They complained about their low wages, and attacked the party bureaucrats and high officials who drew big salaries, rode in cars, and wallowed in luxury. They did not even spare the Soviet Union. When the official speakers mentioned the assistance given by the Soviet Union to Hungary, the Csepel workers merely jeered in reply. "But has not the Soviet Union just granted us a new loan of one hundred million rubles to help us in our difficult situation?" "We need no help from the Soviet Union," one of the workers cried, "we want assistance from the West. With dollars we can buy what we need, while Russia sends us only marmalade." Thus the party leaders realized that the only social class on which, they had thought, they could rely was turning against them.

It was, however, among the Budapest students that the spirit of revolt manifested itself most strongly. "We are engaged in a struggle for independence exactly like the one our forebears waged in 1848," said the newspaper *Szabad Ifjusag*, organ of the youth, on October 19. Control of this newspaper had already slipped from the hands of the party censors. The reference to 1848 was not a mere literary cliché: Petofi was a living example to those students, a contemporary, whose presence was more vivid to them than that of Imre Nagy or Geza Losonczy. For several days now work had been stopped at the university. The classrooms had been transformed into meeting halls. The speakers were intoxicated by their own speeches, which voiced the long-suppressed aspirations of the students. They formulated demands such as the abolition of compulsory courses in Marxism-Leninism, the reorganization of military training, and complete academic freedom.

On October 22, the students of the various establishments of higher learning in Budapest held a meeting at the Polytech-

nic School to discuss a proposal to hold a great demonstration
of sympathy for Poland on the occasion of the accession of
Gomulka. A few speakers opposed the planned demonstration,
fearing that it might degenerate into a riot: too much agitation,
they said, would play into the hands of the Stalinists. But the
moderates were booed off the stage. "If Petofi had been so
timorous on March 14, 1848, Hungary would never have been
independent," one of the speakers cried. On the eve of the
1848 revolution Petofi and his friends had drawn up a twelve-
point program. On October 22, 1956, the Budapest students
drew up a program of fifteen points. The most important of
these were: the convocation of a party congress to elect a new
leadership; the appointment of Imre Nagy as premier; the
maintenance of friendly relations with the Soviets but on a new
basis; the withdrawal of the Soviet troops; the holding of free
elections. This last demand, which goes beyond national communism, was here formulated openly for the first time. It was
a concession wrested from the Nagyists by the students, who
looked upon national communism as only a temporary solution.

The Petofi Society, which held a meeting on the same day,
was more moderate: its ten-point program stayed within the
boundaries of Nagyism. It called for an immediate meeting of
the Central Committee with the participation of Imre Nagy to
determine the new party line; a revision of the Five-Year Plan;
a Popular Front independent of the party; the appointment of
Nagy as premier; the expulsion of Rakosi from the party; the
public trial of Farkas; the revision of erroneous party resolutions; the use of uranium for national needs; the revision of
the alliance with the Soviet Union on a basis of equality; the
democratization of the youth movement. As for the demonstration planned by the students for the next day, the Petofi Society
leaders displayed some hesitation. They hoped to convince the

government to authorize it and thus to avoid a clash between the demonstrators and the police.

On the morning of October 23, all Budapest awoke in an atmosphere of euphoria which was reflected in the newspapers. *Szabad Nep,* the official party organ, approved the resolution taken the night before at the meetings of the youth. "These meetings of the youth," it said, "resemble a rampaging river overflowing its banks, rather than an artificially channelled stream. . . . Our party and *Szabad Nep* wish much luck to the young." It seemed that the denouement of the de-Stalinization drama was near at hand. The script for the last act was ready: Gero, who had just returned from Belgrade bringing excellent advice from Tito, was to convoke an urgent meeting of the Central Committee, just as the Petofi Society had demanded. It was expected that the Central Committee would rid itself of the Hungarian Rokossovskys, including Gero, this former associate of Rakosi. Then the Hungarian Gomulka, Imre Nagy, whose return to office was clamored for by all classes of the population, Communists and non-Communists, would seize control. He would proclaim Hungary's right to choose her own path toward socialism, submit a program of economic reconstruction, and announce his decision to call to account the dethroned tyrant Matyas Rakosi, the chief organizer of the Terror of 1949–1952. Then order would be restored, and the new Nagy experiment would begin in a climate of national unanimity. As for the Russians—well, they had yielded in Poland, why should they not make concessions to Hungary?

Poland and Hungary: never before had these two nations felt more keenly the brotherhood that fate had bestowed on them. Hungary vibrated in unison with Poland as she had under Bathory; as later during the common struggle against the Turks; as in 1848, when the most brilliant general of the Hungarian revolution was a Pole, Jozef Bem; as in 1863, when the Hungarian troops stationed in Poland fraternized with the insurgent population and gave them their arms; or as in 1939, when Hungary welcomed tens of thousands of Polish refugees fleeing from Hitler's armies.

So far the picture was radiant. It looked as though Hungary would conquer her right to independence in a sensible way, in conformity with the nation's proverbial patience and prudence. Then, during the night of October 23, there was a radical change. The exhilarating hope for a peaceful transformation of the regime, for a new era of democratic socialism, was drowned in the rattle of Soviet machine guns. In the early hours of the morning of October 24, the Hungarian radio announced that Imre Nagy and several of his political friends had entered the Central Committee and the government, but Nagy's triumph coincided with a brutal, unexpected, unaccountable intervention of the Red army.

What, then, had taken place on October 23? Early in the morning, lively groups began to form in the neighborhood of the university. It was learned that the Petofi Society had finally agreed to sponsor the great demonstration before the Petofi monument scheduled for 1 P.M. From there the students were to march to Jozef Bem Square to place a wreath at the foot of the statue of the Polish general. In the principal thoroughfares boys were distributing a mimeographed sheet containing the students' demands and inviting the populace to join the demonstrators. The government was hesitating. At first it had decided to forbid the demonstration; then, yielding to the pressure of the Petofi Society and the Writers' Union, it lifted the ban. Gero assured the writers who had come to see him that he would order the police to refrain from anything that might resemble a provocation. At about one o'clock a human tide began to surge at the approaches to the Petofi monument. The crowd intoned the Hungarian national anthem, "God Bless the Hungarians." Imre Simkovics, actor of the National

Theater, climbed on the pedestal of the statue and recited
Petofi's famous poem, "Up on Your Feet, Hungarians." The
crowd repeated the refrain:

> By the Hungarians' God
> We swear
> That we shall no longer be slaves!
> Never! We swear! Never!

Then a girl waved a tricolor flag from which she had cut out
the center bearing the Soviet emblem. Later, innumerable flags,
similarly cut, symbols of the de-Sovietization of Hungary, were
seen. Many young people had tears in their eyes. A worker
hoisted himself on the pedestal and cried in a stentorian voice:
"Comrades, students, writers, we want you to know that the
workers are with you!"

Simkovics read aloud the program drawn up by the students,
and then the demonstrators formed ranks to march to Buda.
For a stretch of about two miles the crowd roared incessantly:
"Nagy for premier! Long live freedom! Long live Poland!"
The young people marched in perfect order, singing old revo-
lutionary songs at the top of their lungs.

After crossing the Danube, the procession joined a group of
students of the Polytechnic School and cadets from the Military Academy. Several thousand people were waiting for them
near Jozef Bem Square. At the foot of the statue young men
were waving Hungarian and Polish flags. The crowd sang the
national anthem and the "Marseillaise," which had served in
Hungary as the workers' anthem and a patriotic song, and had
been forbidden under the Hapsburgs. Then Peter Veres addressed the crowd in the name of the Writers' Union, of which
he was the president. He recited the demands formulated by
the Union. "We have arrived at a turning point of our history,"
he exclaimed. "In this revolutionary situation we won't achieve
results unless the working people of our country observe the

greatest discipline. It is true that the party and government leaders have so far failed to give us an acceptable and efficient program. But the responsibility for this failure falls on those who, instead of creating the conditions required by a Socialist democracy, have stubbornly fought this democracy and are now organizing to restore Stalin's and Rakosi's terrorist regime. . . .

"Therefore, we, Hungarian writers, have formulated the nation's demands as follows:

"1. We demand an independent national policy inspired by the principles of socialism. Our relations with other countries, including Soviet Russia and the people's democracies, must be based on the principle of equality. We demand the revision of all previously concluded economic agreements, in a spirit of equality of rights of the nations concerned.

"2. We demand the end of the policies now in effect in relation to national minorities. . . .

"3. We demand that the government frankly disclose the economic situation of the country. . . .

"4. The factories must be managed by the workers and specialists. The wage system must be reformed. . . . The trade-unions must above all represent the interests of the working class.

"5. Agricultural policies must be revised, and the peasants must be granted the right to determine their fate.

"6. The Rakosi clique must be eliminated from public life. Imre Nagy, this noble and courageous Communist who enjoys the people's confidence, and who in the course of the last years has consistently fought for Socialist democracy, must be appointed to the high post he deserves. At the same time we must take the necessary measures to frustrate all counter-revolutionary plans.

"7. The situation requires that the Patriotic Popular Front actually represent the laboring classes of Hungary. Our electoral system must be brought into conformity with the requirements of a Socialist democracy. The people's representatives in Parliament and in all autonomous branches of the administration must be elected by secret ballot.

"We think that we have thus expressed the wishes of the entire nation," the writer concluded. The assembled crowd shouted, "Long live Hungary! Long live the workers! Long live the soldiers!"

While Veres spoke, trucks carrying young workers were reaching the square, as well as numerous young soldiers of the *Honved*. The leaders of the Petofi Society then asked the demonstrators to march to the Parliament building. The crowd was so thick that it had to break into two groups, each crossing the river by a different bridge. Eyewitnesses estimate the number of demonstrators at more than one hundred thousand. The two groups met in front of the neo-Gothic Parliament building. Once again Peter Veres addressed the crowd which shouted: "Hoist the national flag on Parliament!" Soon the tricolor flag ripped in the center appeared on top of the building. But other cries, more seditious, were also heard: "Russians, go home! Down with Gero! Rakosi to the gallows! Gero to the gallows!" Then, "We want Imre Nagy!"

Someone announced that a delegation of students and writers had left to get Nagy and bring him. Another delegation, followed by a crowd of several thousands, had gone to the radio station, where Gero was scheduled to broadcast a speech at 8 P.M. The students asked the management of the station for permission to broadcast their demands. A negotiation that was to last several hours began. At the same time several members of the Writers' Union, sensing the mounting excitement of the people, tried to persuade Gero to yield the microphone to Imre Nagy. But Gero was stubborn. It was his duty to speak, he said; his failure to do so would be interpreted as a sign of weakness, as the party's surrender to the mob. He locked himself up in a room at the party office, and worked on his speech.

All this time the crowd in the streets was growing thicker, stormier; there could be no question of controlling or organizing it. Someone shouted: "To the Stalin statue!" The cry was greeted by a tremendous roar. The monumental statue of Stalin at the entrance of the Varosliget (City Woods) was regarded as the symbol of the terrorist regime. The decision to demolish it surged up from the very depths of the collective consciousness. Steel cables were thrown around the statue and lashed to three trucks which began to pull. But Stalin—was this an omen?—resisted stubbornly. The demonstrators had to use an acetylene torch. Finally, after half an hour of strenuous efforts, the bronze colossus came down. There was thunderous applause. Then the immense statue was dragged by ropes in a long ride through the city. "The fall of the tyrant literally intoxicated the crowd," writes Dezso Kozak, a Hungarian journalist who participated in the riots. "Young people got into the Communist bookstores and came out carrying loads of pamphlets and newspapers, which they stuffed into the hollow head of the statue, and made a bonfire. They were happy as children. 'Look at the luminous genius,' they cried when the flames spurted from the bronze head."

Meanwhile, the demonstration in front of the radio station in the Sandor Ucca took a threatening turn. The authorities had refused to broadcast the students' program. But at 8 P.M. Gero's speech was broadcast—and it was this speech that touched off the explosion. How could Gero have failed to foresee the disastrous effects of this speech? Instead of announcing the immediate convocation of the Central Committee, Gero stated that it would meet on October 31, and did not even mention Nagy. Instead of announcing a new economic policy and the revision of Hungary's relations with the Soviet Union, he attacked "the provocateurs who try to disturb our friendship with the Soviet Union and the people's democracies, who spread slanders about the nature of our economic relations with the Soviet Union, and who want to defend our independence at all costs not against the imperialists but against our Soviet friends. . . . We want a Socialist, not a bourgeois, democracy," he said, summoning the workers to exert "the greatest vigilance to prevent our enemies from breaking the unity of the party."

The population of Budapest, the demonstrators, the students, intellectuals, workers, and soldiers who filled the streets surrounding the radio station could interpret Gero's speech only as a brutal rejection of their demands—as a provocation. Later, Kadar's spokesmen, while describing Gero's speech as a serious error, tried to minimize its effect on the crowd. The demonstration against the radio station had begun long before Gero made his speech, they argued. However, all eyewitnesses I have questioned agree that without Gero's speech and without the use of arms by the police against the demonstrators, the demonstration would have ended without bloodshed. This is also the opinion expressed on December 28, 1956, by the secretary-general of the Writers' Union, Sandor Erdei, in a report on the events which was almost unanimously approved by his colleagues: "This provocative speech infuriated the crowd," said Erdei, adding: "The students had asked that their demands be broadcast. . . . But the doors of the radio station opened only to enable the Avos who guarded the entrance to fire at the crowd. The armed uprising was only a riposte to this provocation."

"The demonstrators fired first," say the defenders of the Kadar regime. But all the available evidence gives him the lie. Thus it has been established that in the afternoon of October 23 the political police had transformed the radio building into a fortress. There were nearly five hundred Avos inside, and they had been supplied with truckloads of arms. On the other hand, it is not entirely clear why the Avos opened fire. It has not been established that they were ordered to do so, and it is known that the AVO chiefs hesitated as to the course to follow. Whereas the minister of the interior, Laszlo Piros, was for strong measures, his assistant, Mihaly Fekete, told a student delegation that his organization, that is, the AVO, and the army were on their side. He stuck a ribbon of the Hungarian national colors into his buttonhole. Later, the police first tried to disperse the crowd by drenching it with water. But when the young people cut the hoses and overthrew the firemen's trucks, the Avos began to pelt them with tear gas bombs. At 9 P.M. the crowd pressing before the radio building forced the door. Then the Avos fired, and there were casualties.[1] Among the first victims was a young army colonel, in uniform but bearing no arms.

At first there was a wild stampede. The street was emptied in a few minutes. Ambulances came to pick up the dead and the wounded. But soon the crowd surged back to the building, shouting, "Down with the AVO! Down with the murderers!" Stones smashed the windowpanes. One of the ambulances lagging behind the others was slowly making its way through the milling crowd. "God alone knows how the door of the ambulance came to be opened," an eyewitness reports. "Anyhow, the ambulance proved to be filled with ammunition: the AVO was using that stratagem to get weapons. The car was unloaded at once by the demonstrators, turned over, and burned." Now shots were fired from the crowd, but the police

---

[1] Here is the testimony of a radio editor, published in the weekly *Szabad Magyar Radio* (issue of November 1, 1956): "The demonstrators then tried to penetrate into the building, whereupon the AVO commander gave orders for a bayonet charge. We were on the second floor above the entrance and we heard the heart-rending cry of the first to be wounded, pierced through the body by the murderous weapon. A salvo was fired into the air, then the gun barrels were turned against you [the demonstrators]. And the harvest of death began. We shouted and clung to the arms of the Avos, begging them not to shoot. But the blindness of this caste created by the regime knew no bounds. And then you [the demonstrators], you too found weapons...."

did not return the fire. It seems that after the first salvo, which had perhaps been due to panic, the police were under strict orders to use weapons only in case of extreme urgency. Thus for several hours the Avos inside the radio building remained passive, even though many of them had fallen under the demonstrators' bullets. But this moderation came too late. The crowd interpreted it as a sign of weakness or cowardice. Moreover, soldiers who had witnessed the death of the young colonel had gone to their barracks to alert their comrades and to get weapons. A large group of demonstrators rushed to the Lampada munitions plant. Though usually guarded by the AVO, that night (was it an accident?) the plant was unprotected. It was promptly sacked.

In the meantime, Nagy had finally appeared on a balcony of the Parliament building. He had no loud-speaker and his voice was heard only by the front ranks of the crowd. "Dear comrades . . ." he began.

"We're not comrades! We're fed up with the comrades!" someone roared, and the crowd echoed in one voice: "We're not comrades!"

Nagy drew back, very pale. He muttered a few words to the men surrounding him, then started over: "My fellow countrymen, dear friends. . . ."

This time he was acclaimed. But while he spoke, trying to appease this stormy sea of a hundred thousand people, a truck made its way into the square. It was equipped with a loud-speaker which boomed: "Demonstrators are being murdered at the radio building! Help! Help! The police are shooting students!"

According to some witnesses, this announcement was made at least half an hour before the first shots were fired. This would suggest that it was a provocation staged by the police to justify the Soviet intervention then being prepared—which is not impossible, but not proven either. Moreover, in a state of overexcitement, people often do things that resemble provocations. The true provocation on October 23 was Gero's speech, the insults he hurled against the student demonstrators. The provocation consisted in Gero's failure to understand the situation and to grant the concessions that alone could have prevented the worsening of the crisis. After 9 P.M. it was too late. The monumental bronze Stalin, the idol of Rakosi, had already been pulled down; thousands of people rushed forward to trample it, to spit in its face. The statue was surrounded by a delirious crowd when a tall man of powerful build, wearing a green raincoat, climbed on the pedestal, and cried in a strident voice: "The Avos have murdered seven men at the radio! To the radio station! To the radio station!"

The crowd repeated the cry. There was a rush to the trucks that had been brought from neighboring factories to help demolish the monument. When the overloaded trucks set off, the crowd followed them on foot. It was like the Danube during the spring floods. Tens upon tens of thousands of people—students, workers, children, women, old men—screamed, sang, roared, seized by a strange drunkenness. "Kill the Avos!" was their battle cry—the cry that began the revolution.

For at that moment it had become evident that no peace or reconciliation would be possible between this angry people and the police that was the embodiment of the hated regime. The shots fired by the police had produced an explosion: they exploded the dam of fear that had been built in everyone's soul by seven years of terror. At 9 P.M. on October 23, the people of Budapest suddenly ceased to be afraid. And it is in this feeling of deliverance caused by the disappearance of fear that was born, under the impact of the police bullets, that grandiose popular unanimity, that immense, marvelous, and bloody fraternity that characterized the entire insurrection.

After the crushing of the revolt, the Kadar government published a White Book, translated from Russian into Hungarian.

According to this document, the uprising of October 23 had long been prepared by imperialist agents. This version of the events scarcely deserves a critical examination. Gomulka had refuted it in advance on October 20, when he said, referring to the Poznan riots: "Always and everywhere there can be imperialist agents and provocateurs, but never and nowhere can they determine the attitude of the working class." Even less so, we may add, the attitude of the overwhelming majority of a nation, of an entire nation. Not to mention the fact that the official analyses of the events of October 23 bristle with contradictions. On the one hand, we are asked to believe that the siege of the radio building was the work of gangs specially organized for that purpose; on the other hand, we are told that the siege would not have lasted a quarter of an hour if the assailants had known of the existence of another entrance to the building, which was unprotected.

As early as the night of October 23, it became obvious that the government could not rely on the army. True, the troops sent against the demonstrators in front of the radio building did not at once fraternize with the crowd. They looked embarrassed, worried. They did not understand why they had been sent there. "Don't fire at us," the crowd cried to them. "You are Hungarians like us, aren't you?" "We won't hurt you," the soldiers answered. At the same time, other soldiers mingling with the crowd had begun to fire at the policemen hidden behind the smashed windows. At about 11:30 P.M., an army officer was seen on top of a tank stationed in front of the main entrance to the radio building. He shouted something. Suddenly the Avos opened fire. The officer ducked, the crowd sought cover under porches. It was at that moment that the firing spread. Trucks with large amounts of ammunition, automatic arms, and machine guns were arriving in the neighboring streets. These trucks came from the Lampada plant, whose workers were the first to join the battle. The fighting grew continually more intense. The Avos sent up flares and sprayed the crowd with machine-gun fire. The army tanks fired at the radio station. Close to daybreak, several groups of insurgents broke into the building and the battle continued inside. The Avos used their tommy guns and hurled hand grenades. By 7 A.M., the battle was over; the last AVO man was dead.

The young insurgents did everything they could to preserve the studio equipment intact, for they wanted to use it themselves. This battle for the radio had an emotional significance for the young. The radio was the voice of the nation, but it was an enslaved voice, distorted, void of meaning. It was by means of the Budapest radio that the regime had always flooded the country with lies. The Hungarians rose in arms because they wanted the truth to take over the radio. And yet, despite all the bloodshed, the Budapest station continued, during the battle and even after the capture of the radio building, to broadcast, from a new studio set up in the Parliament building, communiqués and appeals which were insults to the insurgents. At 3:30 P.M., on October 24, it spoke of "the attack launched by Fascist and reactionary elements against the public buildings and the armed forces." The new studio was strongly guarded by the AVO and then by the Russians. It was from here that Radio Budapest continued its broadcasts during the days that followed until the Parliament building was occupied by the insurgents.

Request for Intervention

While angry crowds were besieging the radio station, the Communist leaders found nothing better to do than to debate. Gero called an urgent meeting of the Central Committee in the Parliament building. An account of this historic meeting was later given by Thomas Schreiber, Budapest correspondent of the French newspaper *Le Monde,* who was given his facts by a member of the Central Committee. Two points were on the

agenda—the reshuffling of the party leadership, and a proposal
to appeal to Russian troops to restore order. Gero thought that
such an appeal was absolutely necessary. Faced with a dramatic choice, he did the opposite of what his Polish counterpart, Ochab, had done a few days earlier. Ochab at the crucial
moment acted like a Socialist and a patriot rather than a party
bureaucrat. Gero did everything he could, and this was a great
deal, to compromise Imre Nagy's chances.

According to Schreiber, "Gero tried to convince his colleagues that a Soviet intervention was indispensable, because
the 'popular forces' (as Gero called the AVO) were outnum-
bered, the Hungarian army unprepared for civil war, and the
regime in danger. Janos Kadar and his friend Gyula Kallai—
another Titoist who had been released from prison and admitted to the Central Committee in July, 1956—retorted that the
only way to avert disaster was for Gero to resign at once. But
Premier Andras Hegedus, Deputy Premier Istvan Hidas, and
Minister of the Interior Laszlo Piros were against Gero's resignation. Piros described Imre Nagy and his friends as 'accomplices of the Fascists who are rampant in the capital at this
moment.'

"These words were followed by tumultuous scenes, punctu-
ated by the sound of firing coming from the outside. It was
said that some students had broken into the Parliament building and were trying to battle their way to Gero and Hegedus.
They were killed by the guards.

"Gero and Hegedus, who had abruptly left the room, where
small groups continued to talk, came back at 1 A.M. Amid an
icy silence, the first party secretary announced that he had
asked for and obtained the fraternal assistance of the Soviet
troops. In the same breath he proposed the appointment of
Imre Nagy as premier. Most members of the Central Committee were appalled. Several left the meeting in a hurry."

It was amid this confusion that the Central Committee decided to elect Imre Nagy and several of his friends, such as Geza Losonczy, Ferenc Donath, Gyorgy Lukacs, and Zoltan Szanto, as well as Kadar's friends, among them Ferenc Munnich, as new members. The Politburo was also enlarged by the admission of Imre Nagy and Zoltan Szanto. But Gero's partisans were still in the majority. And, most important, Gero refused to resign from his office of first party secretary. Moreover, Andras Hegedus, his liegeman, was appointed deputy premier: this amounted to reducing Imre Nagy and his friends to the status of helpless hostages.

Why, then, did Nagy accept the premiership under such conditions? It would seem that he had not been consulted. He was summoned to the Central Committee at dawn, and was faced with an accomplished fact. His chief aide, Geza Losonczy, was informed of his election to the Politburo only during the morning of October 24, by a telephone call from a member of the executive board of the Writers' Union. During the chaotic days that followed, Imre Nagy and his friends were virtually prisoners of the AVO and the Russians, completely isolated from their partisans. Without their knowledge, the old team of Andras Hegedus, Laszlo Piros, and Istvan Bata, minister of defense, handled all the government business: that is to say, they wrote communiqués announcing the defeat of the "counter-revolutionary" forces and issued ultimatums—with deadlines that were constantly changed—ordering the insurgents to lay down their arms. Control of the administration had slipped from the hands of the Communist leadership both in Budapest and in the provinces. Protected and imprisoned by Soviet tanks, this leadership presented a lamentable spectacle of confusion and dissension. Nagy, Kadar, and Losonczy played the parts of the accused, and at other times of accusers. The question under debate was whether Gero should or should not retain his post of first party secretary. In the end, the Russians settled the controversy. The two great specialists in

Hungarian affairs, Mikoyan and Suslov, flew to Budapest, where after a brief lull the fighting had resumed in the morning of October 25. At 11:30 A.M. that day, the radio announced that Gero had been replaced by Kadar. A few minutes later Mikoyan and Suslov flew back to Moscow.

This change failed to produce the psychological shock it would have produced if it had been announced on the night of October 23. It was clear that the Communist leadership lagged behind the events. As for Nagy, Gero's hurried flight to Russia in an armored car gave him more elbow room. It would appear that Mikoyan and Suslov promised that the Russian troops would withdraw after order was restored, and that later he would be allowed to carry out his program of reforms. Therefore, Nagy sought first of all to resume contact with his followers; his main concern was to put an end to the bloodshed. But his position was ambiguous, and he was handicapped by the fact that his appointment had coincided with the Russian intervention and the proclamation of martial law. In his radio address of October 25, while recognizing that "the young people, workers, and soldiers" had taken up arms, he spoke of a "counter-revolutionary provocation," and said that "the intervention of the Soviet troops was necessary for the sake of preserving the Socialist order." Later, Nagy was to state that he had made this speech under duress, and that even after Gero's departure he had been the prisoner of the AVO and the Russians. This may be true. Nevertheless, during the first days of the insurrection, even Nagy's most faithful friends were bewildered and wondered whether he had betrayed them. They could not understand why he kept company with Hegedus, Marosan, and the other members of the government who were held responsible for the Soviet intervention. The same confusion prevailed in the provinces. This accounts for the paradoxical fact that most revolutionary committees, while accepting and approving the appointment of Nagy, refused to

obey the orders of his government. The insurrection now followed its own logic, turning against those who stood in its way
—the police, the Russians—and this logic dictated the actions
of most of Nagy's followers. It was proving stronger than the
mental habits that had been acquired under the influence of
Marxism-Leninism.

An important immediate consequence of the explosion was
the total disintegration of the Communist party. This party
split into its components—the bureaucratic machine that had
managed the country for seven years, and the large mass of
followers, opportunists and idealists. The Communists of the
latter kind, the majority, took part in the revolt. "Most Hungarian Communists are enthusiastic about the insurrection,"
the Yugoslav writer Cosic observed on October 26. "And how
about the party? What's happening to it in all this?" he asked
a Communist insurgent. "Since the Rajk funeral there has
been no party," was the reply. "The party, it's the bunch of
Stalinists holding meetings in the cellars of the Parliament
building."

As for the members of the party machine, those among them
who felt that they were definitively compromised and hated
by their fellow countrymen went immediately into hiding. The
others hastened to join the insurgents in order to redeem themselves. The party offices were suddenly empty, deserted by the
functionaries; only the Avos stayed to defend them. That was
the penalty the party paid for the policies of Rakosi and Gero,
who had eliminated the opposition from all key posts. In the
eyes of the people, the party bureaucracy, the party organization, was a tool of Rakosi and Gero, that is, of the Soviets, and
hence an anti-national entity. The Hungarian party machine,
unlike the Polish one, had had no time to dissociate itself from
Stalinism and to give proof of its patriotic sentiments. There
were a few exceptions, for instance, the party organization of

the Gyor department, which operated throughout the insurrection and took active part in the creation and the work of the departmental revolutionary committee.

It is the collapse of the party machine that compelled Nagy to revise his program. The Russians and Kadar later criticized him for having made too many concessions to the right, concessions that were incompatible with his ideology. But actually, in the face of the workers' councils and the revolutionary committees that had emerged from the insurrection, and their far-reaching demands, Nagy could rely only on his shaken prestige and on the necessity (vaguely sensed by the insurgents) to preserve the continuity of the government. The party—this party with more than 800,000 adherents—had evaporated.

Let us return to the morning of October 24. Since daybreak Soviet armor had been in action. Soviet jet planes flew over the capital. Their appearance, instead of intimidating the crowd, aroused its anger. Groups of young workers who had battled all night against the Avos went back to their factories and swayed their comrades. This happened not in a few isolated factories, but in practically all of them. This immediate general adherence of the proletariat to the cause of the insurrection doubtless surprised Gero and the Soviet leaders. It is probable that the latter decided to intervene in the belief that the Russian troops would not be long resisted, for the Russians, like Gero, thought that the uprising was confined to students and intellectuals, and that it had to be crushed quickly. Even if young workers had participated in the demonstrations of October 23, they could be expected to calm down after the forces of order had manifested their firing power. But that expectation proved false. In the morning of October 24, the most violent battle between the Russians and Hungarians was fought in the workers' suburbs of Budapest. One of the most important stakes in this battle was the Red Star tractor plant, in which several hundred armed workers and students had entrenched themselves. Around 10 A.M. the plant was attacked by Russian T-54 tanks. Unable to stop them, the insurgents let the armored columns pass and concentrated on the Russian infantrymen who followed in their wake. "Then the battle continued in the halls and corridors of the plant," an eyewitness reported. "But soon we were attacked from behind by Soviet soldiers who had entered through other doors. Our group had to disperse."

Similar battles took place at numerous points in Budapest, including battles for the possession of the Ujpest electrical-appliance factory and the Ganz railroad-car factory. The insurgents were completely unorganized. They rushed against machine guns with an impetuousness that could not make up for their absolute lack of tactics. This was an 1848 uprising against a 1956 army. The city had an unreal appearance, with fires blazing everywhere. Women hurled from the window everything they could lay hands upon—bottles of gasoline, boiling water, heavy objects. The rumbling of tanks and heavy guns mingled with the roar of jet planes and the rattle of machine guns. The streets were littered with corpses. Groups of insurgents scattered at one place only to re-form at another.

Radio appeals coming allegedly from Nagy or Kadar and summoning the insurgents to capitulate, and communiqués announcing curfew hours, were ignored. In vain did Kadar in his radio address of October 24 call on the Communists "to fight and to crush the enemy so that he never dare attack the working class": for the fighters, the enemy was the AVO and the Russians. The working class had already made its choice. On the very first day of the uprising, workers' councils had formed in a number of factories, and the movement spread during the days that followed. Contemptuously, the proletariat swept aside the Communist-controlled factory committees and trade-union organizations, and elected bodies that were its genuine representatives.

It is noteworthy that the workers' councils had everywhere been created before the revolutionary committees, whose members were chosen on a territorial basis and included delegates of the workers' councils. And, contrary to what might have been expected, the movement for workers' councils spread more rapidly in the provincial industry centers than in the capital itself: for the Budapest proletariat had rushed into battle on the morning of October 24 without having had the time to organize, whereas in the provinces the first days of the insurrection were marked by few armed clashes.

The working class was the first to be aroused. Miskolc, a center of chemical industry with a population of one hundred thousand, offers a typical example. As early as October 24, under the influence of the alarming reports coming in from Budapest, the workers of all the Miskolc factories elected a workers' council representing the entire city. This council at once proclaimed a general strike, from which only the public utilities and the hospitals were excepted. Thereupon, a strikers' council was called into being, and all the workers of the district were summoned to join the movement. Only then did the Miskolc students form a "student parliament" which proclaimed its solidarity with the workers. Worker and student delegates seized the Miskolc radio station and all the administrative offices. On October 25, the two bodies were in full control of the district. They drew up a program which they immediately announced over the radio. This program included twenty-one points among which: it demanded the public trial of Mihaly Farkas and his accomplices; the revision and publication of all foreign trade agreements; a revision of the Five-Year Plan; the utilization of uranium for the needs of Hungary; increased wages for various categories of workers; the lowering of the age limit for retirement; increased pensions and family subsidies. Among the political demands proper were those for the immediate withdrawal of the Soviet troops, the formation of a new government, the recognition of the right to strike, and the granting of a general amnesty to the insurgents.

It is noteworthy that the Miskolc workers' council, and later that of the Borsod department, approved the appointment of Imre Nagy as premier, but made a clear distinction between Nagy and his government, and ignored the government orders calling for resumption of work. A similar attitude was adopted by the workers' councils all over Hungary. It was by going on strike that the Hungarian working class contributed to the fight for national independence. This is one of the basic features of the Hungarian revolution, which relates it to the anti-imperialist movements in underdeveloped countries. The Hungarian proletariat, even though emphasizing its economic demands, shared the major goal of the other classes—that of putting an end to Russian domination.

Within the factories, the first concern of the workers was to rid themselves of the representatives of the totalitarian state employer—the party-controlled factory managers, the factory committees, the Stalinist trade-unionists. At the same time they removed the Red star emblems from the factories. When a Yugoslav journalist in Budapest expressed his surprise at the eagerness with which the workers were smashing these emblems, which he regarded as symbols of proletarian internationalism, the workers said to him: "We do not remove those stars because we are against internationalism and socialism. We are Socialists. But the Red star has become for us the symbol of Stalinism and foreign oppression."

Through the formation of councils, the workers took effective possession of the industries that in theory had long been theirs. At the same time, the network of these councils, spreading rapidly throughout the country, became the basis of a new authority, a new social and economic organization. The workers' militias formed by the councils replaced the regular police which had been disbanded or liquidated, and it was those militias that prevented the spread of disorders and lynchings. For instance, as early as October 26 and 27, the Miskolc militia consisting of adolescents rescued a number of policemen from an angry crowd. Thanks to them, the clash between the police and the demonstrators on October 26, in the course of which twelve of the latter were killed, did not lead to greater bloodshed. In the provinces, where demagogues might easily have stirred up the populace, it was the working class that revealed itself as a force of order and moderation.

In the first days of the insurrection I described it as "a revolution marked by the emergence of anti-Soviet soviets." The reports I have studied since then seem to confirm this paradoxical estimate. Even though the insurrection was touched off by intellectuals and students, and even though it centered on national demands, it had from the outset a proletarian character. This popular and national uprising, with its workers' councils and militias, has features strongly reminiscent of the Russian soviets of 1917. To be sure, the Hungarian workers' councils were not Communist; only a minority of their members belonged to the party. At Miskolc, at Nyiregyhaza, and in the other great provincial centers, as well as in the Csepel plants, which became one of the most important strongholds of the uprising, the majority of the members of the workers' councils were Social Democrats. But the majority of the Russian workers' soviets in 1917 was also under the influence of the Mensheviks. In fact, the Social Democrats, despite or perhaps because of the persecutions to which they had been subjected after 1948, retained strong positions in the Hungarian working class. Since the party delegates in the factories represented the administration rather than their comrades, the workers lost confidence in them, and instead trusted the Socialists who had been removed from office. Even prior to the insurrection, the working masses had become completely divorced from the party which had lost its proletarian character and had become a party of bureaucrats. When the workers' councils closed the party offices in the factories, not a single worker protested. This fact illustrates better than anything else the hostility of the Hungarian proletariat toward the social system instituted in the factories by the Communists. The overwhelming majority of the workers rejected Stalinism, without, however, planning to restore capitalism. They had chosen Socialist democracy.

The Hungarian "soviets," i.e., the revolutionary workers' councils, were passionately anti-Soviet, patriotic, anti-Russian, and national, if not nationalistic. They were also democratic in the sense that they supported the struggle waged by the Hungarians against the Russians and the Hungarian police, considering themselves an integral part of a unanimous national and democratic movement. Thus everywhere they encouraged the formation of revolutionary committees representing the other classes of the population, and co-operated with those committees. For instance, at Gyor, which is the site of Hungary's greatest factory of railroad equipment, revolutionary councils of soldiers, peasants, intellectuals, and the youth were formed, along with the town's workers' council. On October 27, a meeting of those five councils made it possible to constitute a provisional national committee of the Gyor department, which from that moment on assumed government functions, and controlled the militia and the town garrison. It was this national committee that negotiated with the Russian commanders.

Because relative peace prevailed in the smaller cities and because the Russian troops there maintained a passive attitude, the reorganization of the government under the aegis of revolutionary committees was effected in the provinces considerably earlier than in the capital, where the insurgents were harassed by the Russians. While the youth and the proletariat of Budapest fought with epic courage, the provinces held demonstrations, organized, and debated. And while the Budapest radio, still in the hands of the AVO, continued its lying propaganda, the free radios of Miskolc, Gyor, and Nyiregyhaza spoke for the nation. It was the Gyor radio that on October 28 proclaimed the two demands that were subsequently adopted by all workers' councils and revolutionary committees without exception—the demands for the denunciation of the Warsaw Pact and the organization of free elections.

These demands reflected a right-ward shift beyond the program of the national Communists. But this was only the logical consequence of Gero's provocation, of the disintegration of the party, and of the Soviet intervention. For the Soviets justified their intervention by invoking the Warsaw Pact, and the Hungarians could see in it only an instrument of foreign domination. As for the demand for free elections, it was a consequence of the workers' complete disappointment with the proletarian dictatorship. They had experienced it for seven years, and in their eyes it was nothing but the police dictatorship of a tiny minority which was exercised against the proletariat and the nation as a whole. Socialism as practiced by this dictatorship meant misery, exploitation, militarized work discipline, and suppression of all rights to protest and to strike. The workers felt that they would be able to defend their rights more effectively in a democratic system than in a system which gave the Communist party the monopoly of power. The granting of freedom to all involved undeniable dangers for the working class and its organizations, and for socialism. But in the heat of the national struggle against totalitarianism, these dangers did not seem immediate. The workers' councils did not indulge in theories, and their will to establish a Socialist democracy coexisted in their minds with the will to give Hungary a truly democratic constitution. The first days of the insurrection were dominated by the idea of national solidarity. Partisan considerations made their appearance only when the insurgents, believing that they had been victorious, passed on to the stage of organization.

The Army and the Insurrection

At the moment of the explosion the Hungarian army was composed of two motorized divisions, one armored division, and nine infantry divisions grouped into four army corps. By joining the insurrection these forces would have assured its almost immediate success. The Hungarian army was numerically superior to the Soviet troops—three motorized and armored divisions that had been in Hungary for several years, and one armored division that had recently been transferred from Austria to the Borsod industrial region. On October 23, these forces were supplemented by a Soviet armored division that was dispatched from Odessa to Szeged, and by two motorized divisions that crossed Hungary's eastern border in the direction of Nyiregyhaza.

As we have seen, almost all high-ranking officers of the Hungarian army were Stalinists: this fact accounts for the attitude of the army during the insurrection. On October 23, the Hungarian generals realized that their troops would not fight against the people, and in accord with the Soviet high command they concentrated their efforts on neutralizing the army, that is to say, on preventing it from joining the insurgents. As early as October 24, most Hungarian units were disarmed. In many cases, the officers in command ordered their soldiers to return home. The thousands of soldiers who participated in the uprising did so in an individual capacity. Almost all of them, to avoid the charge of desertion, had discarded their uniforms and fought in civilian clothes. Only in the provinces, for instance at Gyor, did a few garrisons go over in their entirety to the insurgent camp. On October 26, a unit of the

Gyor garrison was sent to Masonmagyarovar to help the population of that town rid themselves of a group of policemen who the day before had killed eighty-two demonstrators. But even the units that joined the insurgents refrained from fighting against the Russians.

One of the most paradoxical features of the uprising was the *modus vivendi* that was established in many provincial cities between the revolutionary authorities and the Soviet commanders. The latter were chiefly concerned with avoiding fighting. At Gyor, the Soviet officers told the worker delegates who had come to see them: "Don't hurt us and we won't hurt you." The Russian troops stayed in their barracks; the population provided them with food, and both sides were glad to avoid unnecessary bloodshed. Even in Budapest, where the battle was raging, and where the Soviet military police saw to it that there was no fraternization between the Russian troops and the insurgents, the Soviet soldiers were obviously unhappy. For they discovered that their enemies were not Fascists but young workers. Cosic, the *Borba* correspondent mentioned before, relates that he witnessed the following scene. A group of insurgents asked the crew of a Soviet tank: "Why do you fire at the Hungarian people?" One of the Soviet soldiers answered with tears in his eyes: "We don't want to fire at the Hungarian people."

Where the tanks did their inhuman work, the insurgents attacked them with bottles of gasoline, the famous Molotov cocktails. In some cases, clusters of children would hang on to the tanks, and women would lie on the pavement to stop their advance. Such incidents completely demoralized the Soviet troops.

It was not until October 27 that the insurgents made an attempt to create a centralized military organization. In Budapest itself there were only scattered guerrilla groups led by improvised leaders. Among these, the most famous and doubtless the most gifted was Colonel Pal Maleter, one of the few high-ranking officers of the Hungarian army who wholeheartedly joined the insurrection.

Aged thirty-seven, Maleter, a handsome man with an open face and sparkling eyes, was completely unknown when the uprising began. A few days later, all Budapest celebrated his exploits at the great Kilian Barracks which he had transformed into a formidable stronghold. His words were quoted, he was ascribed the qualities of a statesman, and children playing in the ruins of the capital vied with one another in acting out his part; each of them dreamed of being another Maleter. He had become a legendary figure. It was said that in 1936 he had distinguished himself in the Spanish Civil War. But in 1936 Maleter was only seventeen, and had the rank of cadet. At the outbreak of World War II, he was a lieutenant in Horthy's army. In 1942, he was sent to the Russian front, and was wounded and captured by the Russians. There he became a Communist, probably out of resentment against the Hungarian officers' caste, which had snubbed him because of his humble origins. In 1943, Maleter asked to be dropped by parachute in Hungary, where he joined the anti-German guerrillas. He was awarded a high Soviet distinction and after the Liberation was admitted to the Moscow Military Academy, where he specialized in tank warfare.

If Maleter had been ambitious, his military career might have been more spectacular—and more dangerous. His relatively low rank (he was captain, then colonel) enabled him to survive the successive purges that decimated the Hungarian officers' corps after 1949. At all events, nothing in his conduct foreshadowed the future revolutionary leader. Nor did he seem to have been affected by the movement for democratization and decolonization that preceded the uprising; it was as though he kept aloof from politics, holding himself in reserve for the future.

On October 24, when the fighting was resumed in the heart of Budapest, General Bata, minister of defense, ordered Maleter to take his armored unit to Corvin Square near the Boulevard Jozsef, and to help the "forces of order" dislodge a large group of rebels entrenched there. Maleter at that moment was still loyal to the government; he had been told that the rebels were counter-revolutionary Fascists in the pay of foreign powers.

It was then that the miracle of Maleter's second conversion took place. The insurgents whom he had summoned to capitulate sent him a delegation under a flag of truce. He was impressed by their arguments. "We are not Fascists," they told him. "We are students, workers, and soldiers, and our purpose is solely to oust the Rakosi-Gero clique and to restore our country's independence." The leader of the insurgents defending the square was a national Communist, and he declared he would gladly surrender to a genuine patriot.

Maleter withdrew to the Kilian Barracks to think matters over. Then he made up his mind: by his order, the tricolor flag with its Soviet emblem ripped out was hoisted on the roof of the barracks. The troops applauded. Maleter's tanks opened fire on the Russians, who were taken by surprise.

The four days that followed were for Maleter days of exaltation and fame. The Russians stubbornly attacked his barracks, but Maleter set up batteries on the roof, and their fire swept the neighboring streets. His commandos, electrified by his fighting spirit, continually harassed the Russians. Soon the quarter was liberated, and Maleter's troops passed to the attack and took many prisoners. On the night of October 27, the government summoned Maleter to surrender in return for a promise of amnesty. Maleter rejected the proposal: "Let the Russians go first," he said. On October 28, the resistance of the Russians weakened; and when they ordered their troops to withdraw, the Budapest people acclaimed Maleter as their liberator. His prestige was immense. On the night of October 30, eight hundred delegates of the insurgents gathered in Budapest elected him by 798 to 2 votes president of the revolutionary military committee, even though he had declared that he had been and intended to remain a Communist. Possibly the insurgents hoped to pacify the Russians by electing a patriotic Communist as their leader; possibly they elected him without any ulterior motives, merely because they were seduced by this military tribune who, according to all eyewitnesses, emanated an irresistible radiance. The Polish and Yugoslav journalists who interviewed him on October 31 were struck by his political intelligence, and saw in him the inspirer of a new party of the revolutionary youth, the future leading Hungarian statesman.

On the same day Nagy, whose primary concern was to put an end to the general confusion, summoned Maleter, easily reached an understanding with him, and appointed him deputy minister of defense.

The next day Maleter set about his task. He removed those pro-Russian elements that still lingered in the ministry of defense, and took measures to restore order and to disarm several groups of dubious allegiance (for instance, that of the picturesque Dudas, whom Maleter ordered to be arrested). On November 2, he was appointed minister of defense, and took steps to reorganize the Hungarian army on a national and democratic basis. On November 3, Maleter, accompanied by two generals, went to Soviet headquarters to negotiate, in the name of the Nagy government, the withdrawal of the occupation troops. The negotiations opened in an atmosphere of cordiality; everything seemed to go well; then suddenly the talks were broken off. Maleter was seized, and a few days later the Russians launched an all-out attack on Budapest.

Another important military figure of the insurrection was General Bela Kiraly, right hand or rival of Maleter. In January,

1957, at a meeting of the revolutionary council in exile in Strasbourg, which I attended, the forty-four-year-old general, a slender, clear-eyed man with graying hair, related his eventful career. Kiraly is the son of a civil servant; he studied at the Ludovica Akademia, the Hungarian West Point, and during World War II fought on the Russian front. In addition to a regular army unit, he commanded a so-called compulsory labor battalion composed of Jews, Communists, Socialists, and other elements regarded as undesirable under the Horthy regime. They were usually subjected to unspeakably brutal treatment, but the liberal-minded Kiraly did not share the other officers' contempt for these unfortunates, and the men in his labor unit were no worse off than regular soldiers. After the Liberation, several of these men were appointed to important government posts, and thanks to them Kiraly was retained in the new army. He joined the Communist party and soon achieved the reputation of an excellent technician and teacher. The Soviet experts on one occasion praised him for his skill in organizing flawless military reviews. In 1950, he was appointed commander in chief of the infantry; a short time later General Farkas dismissed him from this post and appointed him director of the Ludovica Akademia, and then, in 1951, had him arrested as a spy. He was tortured and sentenced to death. For a whole year he waited to be taken before a firing squad; then he learned by accident, when his wife sued him for divorce, that his sentence had been commuted to life imprisonment. In September, 1956, thanks to the efforts of his former pupils, members of the Petofi Society, he was released on parole, pending a new trial.

Kiraly left prison in a deplorable physical state, and was taken to a hospital for an operation. At the moment of the insurrection he had not yet recovered. But on October 28, his friends of the Petofi Society came to see him in the hospital and took him with them, asking him to help reorganize the army. Kiraly agreed on condition that he was no longer to be a member of the party. On the night of October 30, he was elected with Maleter co-president of the revolutionary military committee. On October 31, Nagy appointed him commander of the Budapest forces consisting of 30,000 regulars and 26,000 freedom fighters, which he immediately organized into a National Guard. But the Russian intervention on November 4 cut short Kiraly's efforts to restore the Hungarian army. The betrayal of General Istvan Kovacs, chief of staff, who went over to the Russians, did the rest. Kiraly withdrew with a few hundred men to the mountains near Buda, then, after waging a desperate battle against the enemy, made his escape to Austria.

It is clear that the regular Hungarian army took only a minor part in the uprising, contributing to its ephemeral success only by supplying the insurgents with weapons and by refusing to fight against them. The military successes of the insurrection were due almost exclusively to the unprecedented heroism of students and young workers. These successes would doubtless have been even greater if the fighters had not been completely deprived of anti-tank weapons. But the absence of these arms further underlines the importance of the results achieved by the insurgents who, after seventy-two hours of street battles, crippled 320 Soviet tanks in Budapest alone (this is the official estimate). In the country as a whole, the insurgents put out of action two Russian armored divisions. Thus they proved that a determined population inspired by patriotic sentiments constitutes a force that can to some extent make up for lack of preparation and military equipment.

The Youth and the Moral Purity of the Revolution

Even the most impassive and impartial historian will find it difficult not to pay tribute to the indomitable courage, patriotism, and contempt for death of the Hungarian youth of

October, 1956. The Yugoslav journalist Cosic voiced his admiration of this youth in an article printed in the Belgrade *Borba:* "Up until this day I thought that no race in the world was bolder, more militant, and more heroic than ours. Well, my dear fellow countrymen, this Hungarian youth has surpassed us." Cosic spoke as an expert: he is a former Communist guerrilla, a companion of Tito. But the most moving eulogy of the young freedom fighters comes from the skeptical poet Milan Fust: "They set an example to the entire world, by showing how the devoted sons of a small, impoverished country should love freedom and their nation," he said. "They also gave an example of endurance and strength. Their ardor was not a straw fire, they were not deterred by the roar of tanks and cannon, they exposed their young chests to steel, they fought until the last moment; and that is how they died."

All eyewitnesses noted with surprise that in this life-and-death struggle the Hungarian youth displayed a consistent, scrupulous will to preserve the moral purity of the uprising. They saw to it that their movement was not blemished by acts of looting or banditry. The goods exhibited in the smashed showcases of the Budapest shops remained intact. These young men who killed the Avos like rats (incidentally, the Avos were colloquially called "rats") treated their fellow countrymen and foreigners with the utmost consideration. They rose above all partisan considerations, they barred any action that might have disturbed their spirit of patriotic brotherhood. There was something sublimely theatrical in their deliberate will to moral purity and unity. This youth that was inspired by Petofi, Vorosmarthy, and Jokai was as romantic as its models; the words "freedom," "fraternity," "equality," "Europe," "the world" had for them new, living, profoundly real meanings. One felt that they were conscious of acting out a magnificent drama watched by the whole world—a world di-

rectly personified in the two hundred-odd foreign correspondents present in Budapest during the uprising.

It is this will to moral purity that accounts for one of the
miracles of the insurrection—the fact that contrary to what
might have been feared, the explosion of popular anger produced no manifestations of anti-Semitism. And yet anti-Semitism was very much alive, particularly among the anti-Communists of the older generation. For several years reactionary
propagandists have made the most of the fact that Rakosi,
Gero, Revai, Zoltan Vas, Mihaly Farkas, Vladimir Farkas,
Gabor Peter, and most other Hungarian party leaders were of
Jewish extraction. For this reason, many among the 150,000
Hungarian Jews who had survived the Nazi massacres were
apprehensive of the fate lying in store for them in the event of
a popular uprising against the hated regime. And yet the great
majority of the Hungarian Jews was victimized by the same
regime. The nationalization of large-scale industries and wholesale trade in 1945 had ruined the well-to-do Jews. In 1949 and
1950, the Jews suffered heavily from the regime's measures
directed against retailers, handicraftsmen, and liberal professions. They also suffered from the purges: among the victims
of the first show trials there were many Jews, such as Rajk's
codefendants Tibor Szonyi, Andras Szalai, and Pal Justus.
This is easily understandable: for the Stalinists were particularly bent upon destroying the old militants who had adhered
to the party for idealistic, Messianic motives, and who were
disappointed by the reality of Russian communism. In turning
against these disillusioned Jews, Rakosi, Gero, Revai, and
their likes displayed an anti-Semitism that was a kind of over-
compensation, intended to clear them in advance of charges
of treason—charges that were formulated by their own consciences.

In 1951 and 1952, tens of thousands of former bourgeois
were deported from Budapest to villages, where they often

lived in atrocious conditions. At least 30 per cent of these deportees were Jews. Then, late in 1952, when Stalin was planning a large-scale offensive against the Russian Jews, Rakosi hastened to effect a massive purge of Jews from the political police and other administrative departments. On receiving the news that a number of doctors, charged with a terrorist plot, had been arrested in Russia, Rakosi had several Jewish doctors thrown into prison. The anti-Semitism that this degenerated Jew indulged in at that time may be the most important reason for the absence of anti-Semitism during the insurrection. The spiritual fraternity between the young Jewish and non-Jewish fighters for freedom was a direct consequence of the fraternity born among the persecuted in the prisons and internment camps.

This absence of anti-Semitism in the insurrection is also accounted for by the important part Jewish writers and intellectuals played in the agitation which had preceded the uprising. According to some rumors, Imre Nagy himself is a descendant of Jewish artisans; but this is probably a legend invented by Stalinists. But it is true that among Nagy's most ardent supporters were many Jewish Communists, such as the writers Tibor Dery, Gyula Hay, Tibor Tardos, and Tamas Aczel, the main inspirers of the Petofi Society and the Writers' Union in 1956. These writers enjoyed ever-increasing authority in the country; intellectuals, workers, and peasants regarded them as the true spokesmen for the nation. Their patriotism was equal to their courage. It was the Jews Tibor Dery and Tardos who displayed the greatest boldness in formulating the national and liberal demands, defying the Rakosi police at a time when no one else dared to speak out. These Jewish intellectuals found Messianic, prophetic accents to express that idealistic cult of justice, which is the best heritage of their race and the religion of their ancestors. They communicated these accents to other writers, and raised the political debate to a moral plane, by condemning Stalinism in the name of Truth and Justice. Thanks to these Jewish writers, the conflict between Rakosi's party machine and the Petofi Society was transformed into a battle between good and evil—a theological and metaphysical dispute which the entire nation followed with baited breath. Never before in the history of Hungary had Jews and non-Jews been so closely united. They had a common enemy—the system embodied by the hated political police, the party machine, and the agents of Moscow. And the youth felt instinctively that any racist incident would play into the hands of the enemy and divert the struggle from its real goals.

The Jews who were killed by the insurgents were not killed because they were Jews but because they were Avos or party bureaucrats. The assertions spread by Communist propagandists that the insurgents had perpetrated anti-Semitic atrocities were proved false. On the other hand, it has been established that Jewish young people down to twelve-year-old children took part in the fighting. The revolutionary committees and workers' councils included many Jewish members, and in an appeal broadcast on November 2, the Rabbinical Council of Budapest and the revolutionary committee of the Jewish Budapest community "saluted with enthusiasm the achievements of the revolution," and asked foreign Jewish organizations to come to the assistance of the Hungarian people.[2]

Revolution and Counter-Revolution

The Hungarian youth, which repudiated anti-Semitism, also repudiated everything that might have given its revolt a reactionary or counter-revolutionary aspect. In this connection, the incident related by the journalist Sezso Kozak is particu-

[2] Cf. the statement made on November 16 by Mr. Zacharias Schuster, European director of the American Jewish Committee, and the communiqué printed in the November 15 issue of the *Bulletin of the Jewish World Congress*.

larly significant. At the Polytechnic School of Budapest there was a student whose parents had formerly been well to do and had the reputation of being reactionaries. When he asked to be given arms in order to join the fighters, he was told: "You will be our liaison agent with the Red Cross, but we shall not give you arms because we do not want to be charged with arming the reaction." It is in the same spirit that the insurgents were opposed to the return of *émigrés,* supporters of the old regime. They did everything they could to prevent the infiltration of *émigrés* at the Austrian border, and after the triumph of the insurrection, came out against the return of the old parties. The ideology of these partisans and guerrilla fighters was, if one may say so, anti-partisan. It was deeply influenced by a kind of idealistic, anti-materialistic, and patriotic socialism. After October 30, when many new parties were formed and old parties re-formed, there emerged a movement among the youth to form a youth party, gathering all those whose main concern was to preserve the marvelous solidarity born in the struggle.

What we have just said may seem to be contradicted by a number of lynchings perpetrated in Budapest and several provincial towns. The victims were not only AVO agents, but also several honest Communists. For instance, on October 30, the insurgents stormed the central offices of the Budapest party organization, which had been defended by about two hundred Avos, and slaughtered everyone they discovered in the building. It has been said that such incidents revealed a distinctly counter-revolutionary trend among the insurgents. It would, indeed, have been extraordinary if, in that Hungary which, before being controlled by the Soviets and Rakosi, had been subjected to twenty-five years of authoritarian rule by Horthy and anti-democratic indoctrination, elements influenced by that ideology had not attempted to divert the uprising into anti-democratic channels. But such attempts were only sporadic. In fact, the reactionaries, as was observed by several eyewitnesses, were no less surprised by the insurrection than were the Stalinists, and their influence on the young fighters was insignificant. As for the excesses perpetrated during the revolt, they were in most cases provoked by the Avos who opened fire on peaceful demonstrators. Incidents such as the terrible holocaust of October 25, when Soviet tanks after simulating fraternization decimated the defenseless crowd gathered on Parliament Square in Budapest, killing more than two hundred and wounding several thousand men, women, and children, exasperated the population. But despite the fury aroused by the cruelty of the repression, the masses of the insurgents refrained from acts of retaliation, and on several occasions intervened to rescue Avos threatened by the populace.

It must also be noted that in the general confusion attendant on the liberation of political prisoners, a large number of common criminals succeeded in making their escape. At a meeting of the revolutionary military committee held on November 2, the chief of the Budapest police estimated their number at about six thousand. It was established later that these criminals had been responsible for all the acts of banditry and individual murders perpetrated during the uprising. Most rumors ascribing a counter-revolutionary character to the uprising were refuted by observers on the spot, such as the English journalist Peter Fryer, Budapest correspondent of the London *Daily Worker,* who resigned from his newspaper in protest against the lies it was spreading about the Hungarian insurgents. Nor did the insurgents receive shipments of weapons from abroad. On this point we have the emphatic testimony of Marian Bielitzky, a Polish journalist. "The weapons used by the insurgents came from the armories of the Hungarian army," he wrote. "I saw the workers of the Budapest electrical-engine factory arm themselves in the barracks, and I saw them get guns from their soldier comrades."

Much the same can be said about the alleged intervention

of *émigrés* infiltrating across the Austrian border, or slipping in with foreign correspondents or Red Cross personnel. The fact is that the Austrian government, fearing to displease the Soviets, exercised great vigilance, supervising the Hungarian *émigrés* concentrated in Austria, and even barring the entry of former Premier Ferenc Nagy who had set out for Austria in the hope of getting in touch with his friends of the reorganized Smallholders party.

During the insurrection the Communist press made the most of the formation of a counter-revolutionary government at Gyor, under the leadership of the alleged Fascist Attila Szigethy. Actually, Attila Szigethy has never been a Fascist. He was a Communist sympathizer, a supporter of Imre Nagy, and was removed from office after Nagy had been condemned as a deviationist. An excellent speaker and organizer, Szigethy on October 26 was unanimously elected president of the Gyor revolutionary committee. He displayed courage and moderation in the exercise of his duties. Thanks to him a *modus vivendi* between the revolutionary authorities and the Soviet army command was quickly established. He leaned primarily on the workers' councils, and it is to them that he appealed on October 29 when a group of about 150 men seized the town hall and proclaimed a nationalist government. Szigethy went to the steel mill and came back with two thousand workers who, after a brief negotiation, disarmed the partisans of the would-be counter-revolutionary dictator, a certain Garamvolgyi, a mediocre poet whose main grievance was that his poems had been rejected by the editors of the insurgent radio.

After the second Soviet intervention, Szigethy went underground, and the Gyor workers proclaimed a general strike. The Soviet commander summoned the workers' representatives and asked them to return to the factories. The workers replied that they would not do so unless Szigethy came back. The Russian officer issued a safe-conduct to Szigethy, who resumed his duties at the town hall. He was there as late as February, 1957, despite the important part he had played in the uprising.

Kadar's official organ, the newspaper *Nepszabadsag,* in January, 1957, defined the meaning in which the terms "counter-revolutionary" and "reactionary" were used in reference to the insurrection. Since the dictatorship of the proletariat is exercised through the vanguard of the working class, it said, the Communist party is the sole guarantor of the building of socialism, and represents an advance over the bourgeois parliamentary system. Therefore, any attempt to restore bourgeois parliamentary democracy, however sincerely democratic, must be regarded as essentially counter-revolutionary, reactionary, and retrogressive.

It is in this sense only that the Hungarian insurgent youth can be described as counter-revolutionary. Most of the insurgents, particularly the politically educated workers, wanted to do away with the proletarian dictatorship as it had been practiced in Hungary, and in their press almost unanimously demanded a return to the parliamentary system that had been in effect between 1945 and 1948. This was undeniably a "return to the past"; but this return was accompanied by a notable progress in the Socialist organization of economic life, namely, the spread of the workers' councils, which is the first step toward industrial democratization, one of the great promises of socialism. The overwhelming majority of the members of the workers' councils was convinced that social democracy could not be realized without political democracy. Only the future will tell whether they were wrong. But the importance of the insurrection lies in the fact that it raised this question.

The Peasants and the New Agrarian Reform

The peasants, faithful to their tradition of distrust of everything that comes from the city, were slow to be aroused, but once in motion they clearly expressed their support of the insurgents. However, the main result of the uprising in the countryside was a new agrarian reform: 2,455 out of the 3,954 collective farms in Hungary were dissolved, and all over the country the peasants redistributed the collectivized lands. This new agrarian reform, which was carried out in a disorderly manner, without central leadership, strikingly illustrates the failure of collectivization in Hungary, which has been discussed in a previous chapter.

René Dumont, referring to collectivization as he had observed it in Romania, says: "The doctrinal purpose of transforming the structure of agriculture overshadows the purpose that should be given priority . . . namely, that of increasing production." [3] Much the same can be said about collectivization in Hungary. The Communist leadership had looked upon it as an end in itself. Most of the collective farms had been formed under constraint, and mechanization and collectivization resulted in a decrease instead of an increase in agricultural productivity. Between 1946 and 1955, the average output per acre dropped by 30 hundredweight for sugar beets, 9 hundredweight for fodder crops, 2 for tobacco, etc., as against prewar figures. The number of cows dropped by 70,000 as against that in 1938.

The Communist methods of collectivization aroused the hostility of the peasants. This hostility was further increased by the general redistribution of land which the government effected to round off the holdings of the state and collective farms. The government surveyors were escorted by AVO units, and many peasants received less land than had been taken away from them. Those who complained were told to join the co-operatives where they would not have such problems. And then, though they had been given less land, most of the peasants had to pay the same taxes as before. Some even had to

[3] René Dumont, *Révolution dans les campagnes chinoises* (Paris: Editions du Seuil, 1957).

make compulsory deliveries calculated on the basis of the holdings of which they had been deprived. And when they were bold enough to protest, they were summoned to the AVO and threatened with imprisonment. Under these circumstances, we can imagine how the peasants felt when Communist agitators spoke to them about "the alliance of the working class and the laboring peasants, the political basis of the proletarian dictatorship."

Nepszabadsag of January 24, 1957, contains an article by the Communist deputy Bela Szekely, which gives a detailed account of the events that had taken place at Kocsord, a typical large village of the Hungarian plain. The lands adjoining this village had formerly belonged to large estates; thus a considerable number of inhabitants had benefited from the agrarian reform of 1945. In 1949, they organized the first collective farm of the village, called Red Star. Two others were formed in 1952. In 1953, after the advent of the Nagy government, two thirds of the members of these collective farms withdrew. But later most of them were compelled to rejoin.

The news of the uprising reached the village on October 24. In the afternoon, the local organization of the Patriotic Popular Front, presided over by a Unitarian pastor, transformed itself into a revolutionary committee. Urged by the peasants gathered in the town-hall yard, the committee set about at once to draw up a plan for compensating the peasants who had lost land as a result of the redistributions. The village had about 680 acres in reserve; the committee distributed this land among 350 families. On the following day, October 25, the members of the three co-operatives met to discuss the future. Some of them demanded the immediate disbandment of the collective farms. Others opposed this measure out of fear of reprisals. The matter was decided by vote. The majority came out for disbandment, and the peasants immediately divided up the land, the livestock, the buildings, and the tools.

More or less the same thing took place all over Hungary, but not always so peacefully. Many Communist functionaries —party secretaries or chairmen of co-operatives—who had displayed excessive zeal for collectivization were maltreated. Their exact number is unknown—it may have been several hundred. As for the political aspect of the question, the peasants tended to regroup themselves around the local intelligentsia and the well-to-do peasants, or kulaks. The latter had for many years been the black sheep of the regime; and the persecutions to which they had been subjected had aroused the sympathy of even the poor peasants whom they had once exploited. Thus, as we have noted before, the Rakosi regime defeated its purpose: it unified the peasants instead of introducing the class struggle into the countryside. The political influence of the kulaks and the clergy is stronger there today than it was in 1945. On the other hand, the regime succeeded in allying the peasants with the workers—but against itself. In the course of October, and November, 1956, the peasants, while busy restoring or enlarging their "microfundia," frequently came to the assistance of the insurgents in the cities. It is a fact that Budapest and the other centers had never, since 1948, been as well supplied with foodstuffs as during the days of the insurrection. Thousands of peasants were seen at the approaches to the cities, distributing their produce or selling it at very low prices—this had never happened before. One of my informants told me that a peasant woman who had asked an exorbitant price for her eggs barely escaped being lynched by her fellow villagers.

Needless to say, the return to individual holdings, most often poorly equipped, and too small to be exploited on a rational basis, cannot be considered an economic advance. But the fact remains that the authoritarian Stalinist method of collectivization served only to strengthen the traditionalism of the peasants, and thus to delay rather than hasten the solution of the agricultural problems of Eastern Europe. In order to take root, co-operation will have to be practiced on an entirely new basis: it must be initiated by the peasants themselves, with the help of a government that the peasants will not in advance regard as an enemy.

Imre Nagy Between Two Fires

The first stage of the insurrection, which covers the period from October 23 to 28, was marked by immense confusion, a kind of national schizophrenia. The events unfolded on two separate levels. On one level, we see Imre Nagy trying desperately to rid himself of the Soviet agents who keep him under strict supervision, and at the same time to gain control of the insurrection and to get in touch with his supporters. On the other level, we see the insurrection spreading, organizing, creating a number of centers.

Imre Nagy, isolated from his followers and surrounded by enemies, wanted to persuade the Russians that their intervention had been a terrible mistake, that its continuation would compromise the chances of a solution satisfactory to all concerned. At the same time he wanted to assure the insurgents that if they laid down their arms democratization would continue. But did he believe this himself?

Even if Nagy had had the vision of Gomulka, it would have been difficult for him, if not impossible, to control the situation. Day after day, he issued appeals for calm, promising impunity to the insurgents. Some groups of insurgents complied, laid down their arms, and disbanded. But others ignored him, and their ranks were swelled by reinforcements coming from the workers' suburbs, the Officers' School, the police, and the army. Gabor Tanczos, secretary-general of the Petofi Society, and Gyula Hay came to Nagy's assistance, and endorsed his policies (radio appeals of October 24). But their appeals for caution were drowned in the din of battle, and the angry populace did not differentiate between them and the lying propaganda of Nagy's opponents, some of whom were members of his team. The Budapest radio repeatedly announced that order had been restored, and continued to brand the insurgents as counter-revolutionaries. Imre Nagy himself spoke of a counter-revolution, further confusing his followers, who suspected foul play. In the meantime, blood was flowing. As mentioned before, on October 25, Russian tanks fired point-blank at the demonstrators massed before the Parliament building. The infuriated demonstrators surged toward the tanks, which retreated to other points of the capital. Everywhere there were demonstrations—at Budapest, Szeged, Gyor, Nyiregyhaza, Miskolc. The dead and the wounded littered the streets, but there were plenty of loiterers even so, and women shopped for food despite the curfew. The people sang, prayed, hunted Avos, and continued to vent their rage on the statue of Stalin. All over Hungary, crowds smashed Soviet war memorials. The Soviet soldiers who had fallen in 1944 and 1945 were certainly not responsible for what was later done in their name, but everything Russian, everything that reminded the people of Russian domination, was execrated. Russian bookshops were ransacked, and Stalin's and Lenin's works were burned together with Tolstoy's and Pushkin's. A young insurgent told me that he was overcome by a strange emotion when he noticed that a record he was about to smash was an Oistrakh rendition of Beethoven's *Violin Concerto*. Beethoven! Oistrakh! He hesitated a moment, then decided that the record was Russian, and destroyed it.

On October 25, Imre Nagy, Kadar, Gero, Mikoyan, and the Soviet ambassador Andropov held a meeting in a cellar of the Parliament building. A few hours later the result of their talk became known. The Soviet delegates, perhaps realizing that the intervention had been a mistake, dismissed Gero who had misled them. It seemed that Nagy would now be able to form a new government including trade-unionists, left-wing Socialists, and non-party men. Kadar and Munnich were told to rally the elements loyal to the party, to appeal to the old militants, to the veterans of the Spanish Civil War, to all those who had suffered under Rakosi and then been shelved. Emissaries were sent out, but they came back empty-handed. No one trusted them. Attempts were made to mobilize the trade-unions. But the trade-unions, which the party had brought to heel, had disintegrated like the party itself. There remained only the workers' councils.

For out of the general confusion, a number of workers' councils had emerged as centers of authority, and on October 25 Nagy felt that a way out of the situation could be found if he negotiated with them, particularly with the most important of them, the workers' council of Borsod-Miskolc. On the morning of October 26, he announced that he was in agreement with that council's program which, among other things, demanded the evacuation of the Soviet troops before January, 1957. But this did not stop Nagy and Kadar: since they could no longer rely on the Communist party machine, they sought the support of the workers' councils, by taking them over, with all their demands, including the most extremist ones. On October 26, Kadar, acting in the name of the Central Committee, issued a manifesto approving the actions of the workers' councils. On the same day, the trade-union leadership (that is to say, Sandor Gaspar, a former Rakosist who had joined Kadar) broadcast a program recommending the creation of workers' councils in all factories, a radical revision of the economic plan, etc.

In itself, the idea of negotiating with the workers' councils was a sensible one. Just like Nagy and Kadar, these councils were opposed to any attempt to restore the pre-Communist regime. But even though the workers did not refuse to talk with Nagy, they were on their guard. There was no certainty as to Nagy's freedom of action or his ability to keep his promises, and before calling for resumption of work, the councils wanted to obtain guarantees. Miskolc, Szabolcs, Nyiregyhaza, and Gyor approved Nagy's intention of forming a new government, but they demanded that this government include new men, representatives of the youth, the proletariat, and the intelligentsia.

To meet the councils' demands, Imre Nagy sounded out several men who had not been compromised by collaborating with Rakosi. He knew that only a quick and bold decision, reflecting a radical change of policy, could produce a psychological shock capable of inducing the insurgents to stop fighting and the workers to resume work. But his hands were tied. He tried to obtain the co-operation of Socialists who enjoyed great popularity among the workers, such as Jozsef Kelemen and Anna Kethly. But the Socialists refused to consider participating in his government prior to an official authorization to restore their party. The Russians, the Geroists, and even Kadar found this condition unacceptable. They feared (and rightly so) that if the Socialist party were reconstituted, it would rapidly absorb the Communist militants who had lost all faith in their own party.

At 10 A.M., on October 27, the Budapest radio announced the formation of a new government. A result of compromise, it was doomed in advance. True enough, it did not include the most conspicuous Stalinists—Istvan Bata, Jozsef Darvas, minister of propaganda, who had long been boycotted by the writers and journalists, and Laszlo Piros, minister of the interior, who had been in command of the Avos during the fighting. But several ministers who had served under Rakosi were retained, such as Eric Molnar, a passive tool of Rakosi in the ministry of justice, who only a few days before had been violently attacked in the *Literary Gazette;* Imre Horvath, minister of foreign affairs; and the new minister of industry, Antal

Apro. Karoly Janza, a soldier politician who had no influence on the army, succeeded Bata as minister of defense. The new minister of the interior, Ferenc Munnich, was an opportunist who inspired little confidence in the country. Only one reformist Communist, the philosopher Gyorgy Lukacs, was included in the Cabinet as a sop to the intellectuals.

The only important non-Communist in the government, whose appointment aroused some hope, was Bela Kovacs, the new minister of agriculture. He had formerly served as secretary-general of the Smallholders party, had been imprisoned in 1947 under trumped-up charges of espionage, and released and rehabilitated in 1956. He enjoys great popularity among the peasants, and is held in high esteem for his integrity and courage. But his appointment, intended to appease the peasants who could interpret it as heralding the end of collectivization, had been somewhat precipitate. On October 26, he happened to be near Pecs, when he received a telephone call from Istvan Dobi, president of the Presidium (a former Smallholder whom no one took seriously), asking him to participate in the coalition government. Kovacs accepted on principle. But as he himself related several weeks later, on November 27, he was surprised when he discovered that the Cabinet included several former Communist leaders. "Next day, I wrote a letter of resignation expressing my objections to the composition of the new government, but my friends persuaded me not to send it. I did not know what were the intentions of the government."

On October 27, however, no one knew what this new government wanted. The country's reaction to it was perhaps best expressed by the free radio of Miskolc: "Imre Nagy has our confidence. But is this enough? The fighting in Budapest continues. And can we wish that the Soviet troops disarm the insurgents? Certainly not. No, the new government must not base itself on foreign arms. It should rather obtain the support of the people." This was the crux of the matter. The insurgents felt that victory was in their grasp, they saw that the Russians were in a state of confusion, and they regarded the new government only as a passing phenomenon. They were all the more intransigent because they counted on Western diplomatic assistance. In the afternoon of October 26, a group of fighters went to the British embassy asking that the question of the uprising be submitted to the United Nations. After all, had not all the Western radios been repeating that the Western powers would support the cause of an independent Hungary in the Security Council? Radio Free Europe in Munich was particularly emphatic on this point. In its broadcasts, which were subsequently much criticized, the announcers of this radio, Hungarian *émigrés* bitterly opposed to communism, exalted the insurrection, and probably going far beyond the American intentions, described Imre Nagy as a traitor, a "Communist like the others."

On October 28, even before the Security Council meeting on Hungary, Karoly Kos, Hungarian delegate to the United Nations, handed a note to Secretary-General Dag Hammarskjold protesting against any foreign intervention in Hungarian domestic affairs. It seems that Nagy knew nothing about this note. Two days later, the officials at the ministry of foreign affairs in Budapest formed a revolutionary committee presided over by Peter Mod, a friend of Rajk. The members of this committee discovered that Kos had been a Hungarian citizen for only a short time, that he was a Russian engineer whose true name was Leo Konduktorov, and that he had been given a post in the Hungarian ministry of foreign affairs by order of Moscow. When they informed Nagy about this, he was indignant, but he had to wait two days before recalling this Russian who spoke in the name of Hungary at the United Nations. The incident, by the way, is a striking illustration of the cavalier manner in which the Russians treated the sovereignty of their satellites.

On October 27, Mikoyan returned to Budapest. His attitude was conciliatory. He agreed that only a cease-fire would enable Nagy to find a solution of the crisis. Mikoyan's chief concern was to make it possible for the Soviet army to end its intervention without losing face, all the more so because the Russian troops stationed in Hungary were too "contaminated" to serve as an effective instrument of repression. It was necessary to replace them by fresh troops. At that moment, however, it seemed that the Kremlin leaders had decided to give Nagy a free hand, and at the same time to be ready to intervene if he could not persuade the Hungarians to accept a compromise. The Russians also kept an eye on the United Nations, and seemed to reckon with the possibility of an American intervention. Furthermore, before making up their minds as to what to do with Hungary, they probably wanted to consult their Chinese and Czechoslovak allies.

However that may be, at 1 P.M., on October 28, Imre Nagy ordered an immediate cease-fire. The troops loyal to the government, he said, would refrain from firing unless they were attacked. (But where were those troops? And what were their numbers?) Simultaneously, the Central Committee delegated its powers to a six-man directory consisting of Antal Apro, Karoly Kiss, Janos Kadar, Ferenc Munnich, Imre Nagy, and Zoltan Szanto. This directory in which Nagy was in a minority was nothing but another stage *décor*.

But there was still, there was always, Imre Nagy. Like Noah after the deluge, he emerged with his ark, from which he began to send out his doves of peace to the insurgents. Now that the Avos surrounding him had vanished, he spoke as though he himself had started the flood. In his radio address of October 28 he stated: "The government condemns the view according to which the formidable popular movement we have witnessed is a counter-revolution. To be sure, criminal, reactionary, and counter-revolutionary elements have attempted to use the movement for the purpose of overthrowing the regime of the people's democracy. But it is undeniable that on the whole we are faced with a great national and democratic movement which expresses the unanimous will of the nation." Nagy assured his listeners that the Soviet government had promised him to withdraw its troops, each withdrawn unit to be replaced by a unit of the new Hungarian army in formation. Negotiations for this purpose, he said, were in progress, and all this was being done "in the spirit of Soviet-Hungarian friendship and the principle of mutual equality and national independence of Socialist countries." Nagy also said that the AVO would be dissolved, that a general amnesty would be granted to the insurgents, that the old Kossuth emblem on the tricolor flag would be restored, and that March 15 would be observed as a national holiday.

This program failed to pacify the revolutionary authorities. They did not even try to conceal their distrust of the Russians. The committees demanded the immediate, unconditional withdrawal of the Soviet troops. Emboldened by their success, they also demanded the end of the one-party system, and free elections. And that was not all. On October 28, a national revolutionary committee was formed in Budapest, which claimed to represent all the revolutionary committees of Hungary (it took several days before it was realized that the claim was exaggerated). The head of the new committee, Jozsef Dudas, sent emissaries to Nagy, and then came to see him personally, asking him to broaden his Cabinet by appointing ministers representative of the insurgents, including himself; to denounce the Warsaw Pact; and to proclaim the neutrality of Hungary. Until October, 1956, hardly anyone had ever heard of this Dudas. Tall, florid, a Tyrolean hat on his black hair and a cloak thrown about his shoulders, a revolver in his belt, his legs encased in black puttees—such was the figure he cut before the surprised foreign correspondents. Some regarded him as a great patriot, others as a dangerous counter-revolutionary; most likely he was little more than an adventurer.

Dudas was an engineer, born in 1912. All that is known about his prewar activities is that he belonged to the illegal Communist movement, first in Transylvania, then in Hungary. In 1944, he was the representative of the Communist party in the military delegation sent by Horthy to negotiate an armistice in Moscow. (But later the Communists declared that they had not entrusted him with such a mission.) After the Liberation he emerged as a member of the Smallholders party, and it was on the list of that party that he was elected deputy in 1945. In 1946, he was arrested on the charge of participating in a counter-revolutionary plot. He was interned in various prisons, and then in the Recsk camp until 1954. In this camp Dudas met other political prisoners—Trotskyites, Rajkists, Socialists, trade-unionists, Catholics, reactionaries. When the insurrection broke out, these people rallied around him. I had occasion to speak with one of Dudas's lieutenants, a former Socialist with Trotskyite tendencies, who now lives as a refugee in France. He emphatically denied the rumors that branded Dudas as a Fascist. He was somewhat confused, ideologically, but a sincere patriot, an excellent organizer, and a courageous soldier; he was overflowing with vitality, and capable of communicating his enthusiasm to others. On October 27, after a stubborn fight against the Avos and the Russians, he seized the Szena Square, from which he controlled several quarters of Buda. On October 28, his troops crossed the Danube and occupied the building of *Szabad Nep,* where Dudas set up his national revolutionary committee. On October 29, he published the first issue of his newspaper, *Foggetlenseg* (Independence), which contained an appeal to the United Nations Security Council to support the Hungarian cause. His troops also occupied the Corvin department store, and for a few hours held the ministry of foreign affairs, no doubt to put pressure on Nagy to appoint

Dudas foreign minister. But Maleter, who, during those days of confusion, looked on Dudas as his most dangerous rival, dislodged and disarmed his gang. Imre Nagy, too, distrusted Dudas, preferring Maleter even though the latter refused to submit to the government as long as Russian troops stayed in Budapest.

Freedom on Reprieve

On October 30, the atmosphere cleared. It seemed that the triumph of the insurrection was certain. Yet there were still black clouds on the horizon. The invasion of the Sinai Peninsula by the Israelis diverted world public opinion from Hungary. The Anglo-French intervention in Egypt gave the Russians an unexpected opportunity: it seemed to justify their action in Hungary, and undermined the moral foundation of the Western protests. Brute force once again dominated the international scene. Many Hungarians were farsighted enough to realize the threat this change represented for their country. But the majority of the population, carried away by the *élan* of the struggle, rushed forward.

Titoism had by now been left behind. Bowing to the wishes formulated by the majority of the workers' councils and revolutionary committees, Nagy decided to replace his Cabinet of October 27 by a coalition government of the type that had ruled the country between 1945 and 1947. This implied the reconstitution of the old parties (the Smallholders, the National Peasants, the Social Democrats), but soon new parties emerged. Political passions, so long suppressed, burst forth in disorder. Three days later, Hungary had forty different parties!

Nagy and his friends negotiated with feverish haste: they knew they had little time to waste. The Russians were beginning to lose patience. Heirs of the most anarchistic revolution in history, they hated disorder; they liked only regimented, disciplined, docile populations.

On October 30, Nagy formed a provisional government, leaving some of the posts vacant and intending to fill them with Social Democrats. It included, in addition to Nagy and Kadar, Geza Losonczy, representing the Communists; Bela Kovacs and Zoltan Tildy, representing the Smallholders; and a leader of the old National Peasants party, Ferenc Erdei, whom Nagy had chosen by way of an expedient, for the other leaders of that party, like the Socialists, continued to bargain.

While Nagy's ministers negotiated with the other parties, he himself was busy receiving delegations of insurgents that streamed to Budapest from all over the country, filing into the Parliament building night and day. Foreign observers were struck by the infinite patience with which Nagy listened to the delegations' demands, which were often contradictory. He tried to appease everybody, by promising everything. His only concern was to stop the fighting, to induce the strikers to return to work, to restore order. In the meantime, the insurgents were busy demolishing the last bastions of the AVO. After storming the Budapest party offices, they set the AVO headquarters on fire. In the streets of the capital, frenzied bands of insurgents hunted Avos, killing and hanging them under the noses of the Russians. The panicked heads of the political police appealed to the Writers' Union to obtain from the insurgents an armistice which would guarantee their safety. The writers did their best to put an end to this manhunt, which the majority of the population condemned. On November 1, Maleter ordered the insurgents to prevent summary executions. But it took two more days before the popular fury was appeased and the regular troops and the new militias were in control of the situation.

The Role of Cardinal Mindszenty

During the very first days of the uprising, a number of Catholics demanded the release of Cardinal Mindszenty, who for the last year had been kept under house arrest at Felsope-

teny, in northern Hungary. He was guarded there by fourteen
Avos. On Tuesday, October 30, four officers from the military
camp of Retsag, near Felsopeteny, set out for the cardinal's
residence. They disarmed the guards—who, incidentally, put
up no resistance—and set the prelate free. According to the
account of his liberation published in the October 31 issue of
Magyar Honved, the new army newspaper, he was stunned
with joy and surprise. He expressed the wish to go to Budapest
at once, "in order to resume his work at the point he had left
it more than seven years ago." But in view of the danger of the
roads, the officers persuaded him to spend the night with them,
and took him to Budapest only the following morning, in an
armored car escorted by four tanks. In the interval, the news
of the release of the cardinal, whom the Catholics venerated
as a martyr, had spread throughout the country. The villages
through which he passed were decorated with flags and flowers.

The reappearance of the cardinal at the moment when the
withdrawal of the Soviet troops had been agreed upon, and the
political forces had begun to organize, changed the situation.
By throwing into the balance the immense prestige he enjoyed,
Mindszenty could tip the scales in favor of caution or rashness
—in favor of moderation or revenge. Mindszenty seems to
have been conscious of this responsibility and troubled by it.
Later, some of his critics said that, like the Bourbons, he had
learned nothing and forgotten nothing. I do not share this view.
Studying the cardinal's conduct and the statements he made
after his release, I have gained the impression that he attempted
to control his political passion, his ardent hatred of the Russians and of communism, which had characterized him before
his martyrdom, and which his sufferings had not diminished.
A great and worthy Christian, aspiring to sainthood, Mindszenty seems, during his few days of freedom, to have fought
the devil with all his strength. This effort is meritorious even
though it was not always successful. Actually, the situation

was too complicated for this man worn by imprisonment to find his way easily in the overexcited atmosphere of Budapest, where he arrived at 8 A.M. and was greeted by a kneeling crowd and the ringing of the church bells of the capital.

In his first statement issued to the press, the cardinal said prudently that before making up his mind he wished to inform himself about the situation. The same day he had long talks with Zoltan Tildy and Pal Maleter, who asked him in the name of Imre Nagy to support the efforts of the new government to restore order and to deprive the Russians of an excuse for a second intervention. On the other hand, he also got in touch with men who, speaking in his name, were working toward the formation of a National Christian Front. It may be argued that these politicians displayed too much haste, and that they would have acted more wisely if, like the Polish Catholics led by Wyszynski, they had refrained for the time being from forming a separate political party. It is true that in 1947 there had been three parties representing Christian denominations. But at that time, Rakosi had encouraged their formation in order to weaken the Smallholders party. Cardinal Mindszenty should have reminded his friends of this precedent. He doubtless had it in mind when, in his radio address of November 3, on the eve of the Russian aggression, he declared that he wished to remain aloof from party politics, adding that "at this moment Hungary needs many things, but as few parties and leaders as possible." But in his actual conduct Mindszenty seems to have been influenced by politicians who attempted to exploit his authority for purposes of their own.

It was at the request of the Nagy government that Mindszenty, after two days' reflection, delivered his radio address of November 3. This address contained many sensible ideas, which indicated the cardinal's sincere desire to contribute to public peace. "We must not think along the lines of the old nationalism," he said, among other things. "Even in the present tragic situation, we have no enemies. ... We, Hungarians, wish to live and act as the standard-bearers of true peace among the family of European nations. Being a small nation, we wish to live in a spirit of undisturbed friendship, of mutual and peaceful respect, with the great United States of America as well as with the powerful Russian empire. We wish to establish good-neighbor relations with Prague, Bucharest, Warsaw, and Belgrade." The cardinal also issued an appeal for the resumption of work. He was later accused of having taken a stand against socialism, for the return of capitalism, and the restitution of the nationalized domains of the Church. Under this form, the accusation is baseless. On the contrary, in a rather muddled passage of his speech—the cardinal has always written in an involved and confused style—he came out for "the classless society," and added: "We recognize a private property legally and fairly restricted by the public interest." Obviously, this sentence could be given the most various interpretations. But—and this is more serious—the cardinal, unlike his Polish counterpart Wyszynski, who was far more sensitive to the immediate interests of his country, rejected *en bloc* everything Hungary had done since 1945, not only since 1949 and the establishment of the dictatorship.

"In 1945, after a lost and pointless war," the cardinal said in the same speech, "brute force was used to set up in our country a regime all the details of which are now branded by its heirs themselves with the seal of contempt, disgust, and reprobation. It was the Hungarian people in its entirety that swept this regime out of office. This unprecedented struggle for freedom was waged because the nation wanted freely to determine its way of life, its fate, the administration of its state, and the use of the products of its work." This statement tended to discredit not only the Communist dictatorship but also the parliamentary democracy that emerged after the Liberation of 1945. Moreover, throughout his speech, Mindszenty expressed his distrust of the "heirs of the fallen regime," who "are today trying to escape from the consequences of their predecessors' actions." Cardinal Wyszynski, in order to save Poland, gave his blessing (even though under reservations) to Gomulka. Cardinal Mindszenty did not do as much for Nagy, despite his resolve to help him. He may have been influenced on this point by his chief collaborator during those eventful days, Msgr. Turcsanyi. But what really determined Mindszenty was, as always, his medieval conception of the primacy and political role of the Church. For this reason, the cries that were heard during a demonstration in Budapest, "Russians, go home! Mindszenty for President!" could only strengthen his reservations with regard to the Nagy team.

We must not exclude the possibility that later Mindszenty might have become the standard-bearer of the reactionaries, and that he might have attempted to set up a "moral order" dominated by the Church on the ruins of the people's democracy. But the Mindszenty-sponsored Christian Front would not have been automatically victorious. It would have had to win over the adherents of the Social Democratic party and the two great agrarian parties. Now, these parties had from the outset based their programs on the democratic reforms of the period between 1945 and 1948—the agrarian reform, the nationalization of large-scale industry, the democratization of the political institutions. By repudiating these reforms, Mindszenty and his followers would considerably have restricted their field of influence. By accepting them, they could have distinguished themselves from the other non-Communist parties only by their emphasis on Christian ideas and the intensity of their anti-communism. To say that Mindszenty was a priori sure to win, and to justify the second Russian intervention in the name of socialism and democracy, are at all events partisan arguments. If it is true that the appearance of Mindszenty raised the ghost of a possible return of clericalism in Hungary, it was incumbent on the Hungarian democrats, not on foreigners pursuing aims of their own, to counteract the clerical influence. After the cardinal was set free, the Communists used him as a Fascist bogyman. Even though the cardinal's conduct is not immune from criticism, the Communist version is nothing but a distortion of historical truth.

3

REVOLUTION DEFEATED

Mikoyan's Third Visit

ON October 31, the Soviet troops began to evacuate Budapest. In the afternoon a few tanks were still stationed in front of the ministry of defense, the ministry of the interior, and the Russian embassy, but it was announced that they would be withdrawn. Only isolated shots were heard.

The streets of the capital were filled with rubble, and strewn with improvised graves. There were crowds around the newsstands, buying various newspapers—each of the parties that had reopened its offices the day before now had its own organ. The Socialists published *Nepszava* (Voice of the People); the Petofi party, formerly the National Peasant party, *Uj Magyaroszag* (The New Hungary); the Smallholders, *Kis Ujsag* (Little Journal); the Communists, *Nepszabadsag* (The People's Freedom). The trade-union organization, which had thrown off its Communist shackles, issued *Nepakarat* (Will of the People); the ministry of defense, *Magyar Honved* (The Hungarian Army); Dudas's National Revolutionary Committee, *Fuggetlenseg* (Independence); and a group of revolutionary young journalists, *Igazsag* (Truth). Finally, independent organs that had been suspended for many years made their reappearance, such as *Magyar Nemzet* (Hungarian Nation), *Magyar Vilag* (Hungarian World), and the Catholic *Sziv* (The Heart). All these newspapers celebrated the victory of the insurrection; all

233

of them, including Dudas's, sharply condemned in one breath "the representatives of the pre-1945 regime and the Stalinists," Admiral Horthy and the dictator Rakosi. All of them approved Maleter, who had declared that "the national guard, the revolutionary committees, the workers' councils are firmly behind the freedom fighters who are waging a struggle on two fronts—against the Stalinists and against the reactionaries." No one admitted being a reactionary: the term was unfashionable. Nevertheless, differences began to appear behind the façade of national unanimity. While the young insurgents, those who had actually fought, were as though intoxicated with their victory and filled with patriotic enthusiasm, others, who had not taken part in the battle, were now out for their share of the spoils. A pre-electoral atmosphere prevailed in the country: the thunder of guns had yielded to the booming voices of public orators.

Imre Nagy found himself between two fires. On the one hand, there were the insurgents who continued to press forward. On the other, there were the Russians who were determined to uphold the prestige of their army.

Even after yielding to one of the major demands of the insurgents—the formation of several parties—and even after announcing that free elections would be held within the shortest possible time, Nagy found it difficult to assert his authority. On October 30, a regional national council representing all of Transdanubia had been formed at Gyor. This council sent delegates to Nagy, asking him not to content himself with the withdrawal of the Soviet troops, but to denounce the Warsaw Pact and to proclaim Hungary's neutrality. It was Dudas who had first formulated this bold demand, which was enthusiastically adopted by all workers' councils and revolutionary committees, including that of the army. The delegates argued that Andras Hegedus, the Rakosist premier who signed the Warsaw Pact, had deceived the Hungarians by asserting that it was in conformity with the United Nations Charter; and Russia, by intervening in Hungary on October 23, 1956, had violated the United Nations Charter and the Warsaw Pact, and Hungary was entitled to denounce the latter.

It may be asked whether those who had formulated this demand realized the danger of their position. But at that moment the Hungarians were swayed by the feeling that their country had a natural right to independence and neutrality, and did not stop to think of the consequences. Nagy could do nothing to alter that fact. The people demanded that Hungary enjoy an international status similar to that of Austria, Finland, or Yugoslavia. The demand was imprudent, but all the dams of prudence had been broken at the same time as those of servitude. Nagy was faced with a tragic choice. For despite everything he had remained a Communist loyal to the Soviet Union; at the same time he was a sincere patriot who had himself helped to touch off the uprising. But could a Socialist come out in favor of national oppression? Could a Communist devoted to his people put the Russians above his own country?

The insurgents urged him to make up his mind. Speaking at Pecs at a meeting of two hundred delegates of the Smallholders party, Bela Kovacs came out in favor of neutrality; so did Maleter; so did the Social Democrats. How could Nagy resist all those pressures? People were beginning to doubt his good faith. One of the Transdanubian delegates told him bluntly: "Many persons have no confidence in you. Don't you think, Comrade Nagy, that you should yield the premiership to Bela Kovacs?"

Nagy answered calmly: "I believe that the country has confidence in me. If I felt that I had lost this confidence, I should resign."

Nagy's friends, however, pressed him to stay. Finally he took the plunge: "Right or wrong, my country." In the afternoon of October 31, an immense crowd gathered in front of the Parliament building clamoring for Nagy. He appeared on the balcony, and declared that he would denounce the Warsaw Pact and proclaim Hungary's neutrality. He was applauded. A little later, Nagy confirmed his decision to an Austrian reporter, adding: "We have already begun negotiations on this matter."

He had actually begun to negotiate with the Kremlin envoys who had arrived in Budapest that morning. For the third time since the outbreak of the uprising, Mikoyan, the most liberal and Titoist of the Kremlin leaders, and Mikhail Suslov, a notorious Molotovist, had come to Hungary to find a solution to the crisis. This time they came with specific proposals. The day before, the Soviet government had issued a declaration intended to serve as a new basis for the relations between Russia and her satellites. The Russians for the first time recognized the need to revise the clauses of the Warsaw Pact dealing with the stationing of Russian troops in satellite countries. They also recognized that "serious inadequacies in the economic field and bureaucratic distortions" had contributed to the Hungarian uprising. Clearly, the Soviet government no longer held its original view, which had been criticized not only in Budapest but also in Belgrade, Warsaw, and Peiping, and according to which the uprising had been the work of counter-revolutionary elements and foreign agents. According to the Kremlin's new thesis, the popular movement was justified at the beginning; but "the forces of reaction and counter-revolution had soon joined this just and progressive movement of the workers in order to shake the foundations of the Hungarian people's democracy." It was at the request of the Hungarian government, the declaration said, that the Soviet government had sent military units to Budapest with a view to restoring order. But considering that "the presence of Soviet units in Hungary might lead to a worsening of the situation, the Soviet government has instructed its military command to withdraw these units from Budapest as soon as this will be found indispensable by the Hungarian government."

Mikoyan and Suslov told Irme Nagy, Janos Kadar, and Zoltan Tildy that the Soviet government was ready to open negotiations concerning the presence of Soviet troops in Hungarian territory. They said that Russia was willing immediately to withdraw all her troops except those stationed in Hungary on the basis of the Warsaw Pact. But they insisted on Hungary's continued adherence to the pact. Her withdrawal, they said, would change the balance of power in Europe, and the Soviet government would never permit this.

The Hungarian negotiators told Mikoyan and Suslov that considering the general atmosphere of the country, and the resentment aroused by the Soviet intervention, their government could not resist the people's demand for the denunciation of the pact, and that Soviet-Hungarian friendship and Socialist democracy in Hungary could be preserved only if the Soviets recognized Hungarian neutrality. The Hungarian negotiators pointed out that if Imre Nagy, Bela Kovacs, Tildy, the Socialists, Maleter, in short all those who more or less effectively controlled public opinion, adopted the Soviet point of view, they would be swept out of office. They also said that so far the uprising had remained within the framework of the democratic regime set up in 1945, and that the overwhelming majority of the population did not wish to restore capitalism and destroy the Socialist foundations of the regime. But this would no longer be the case if the present leaders of Hungary attempted to oppose the irresistible demand for neutrality.

These arguments were not unreasonable, but the Russian delegates were impervious to them. There is reason to believe that the Soviet line had been determined before Mikoyan and Suslov left for Budapest. The Russian leaders had realized that if they proved too weak to prevent the secession of Hungary, all satellite countries would rise against the alleged people's gov-

ernments. In the face of this danger, the chauvinism and national pride of the Soviet army leaders and the fears of the
party bureaucrats combined to overrule the so-called liberal
minority.

The Russian delegates' conciliatory but firm language foreshadowed the prospect of a second Soviet intervention. It
would seem, however, that the Hungarian leaders failed to
realize this, and that even after the suspension of the talks (a
suspension that was not definitive), they hoped for an ultimate
agreement. They did not believe, they refused to believe, that
the Russians, despite their scarcely veiled threats, would run
the risk of alienating world opinion by unleashing a war of
repression against Hungary. They also had confidence—and
the Hungarian nation shared this confidence—in the United
Nations. But the United Nations had no time for the Hungarian crisis: for the Anglo-French invasion of Egypt had
begun.

Strangling of Democracy

During the first three days of November, 1956, Hungary
offered a moving, unique spectacle. The country was taking
deep breaths of freedom, rejoicing over the departure of the
Russian troops, making plans for the future, burying the dead,
acclaiming the survivors, clearing the ruins of battle, and preparing for the resumption of work. But in the background a
continuous rumbling could be heard—that famous circular
movement of the Russians who had gone out by one door only
to come back by another in superior numbers. Never before
had joy and fear, freedom and anxiety, hope and the forebod-
ing of a national disaster, been intermingled to such a point.

Budapest, now completely evacuated by the Russians, came
back to life. Yet the damage was considerable. The city gave
the appearance of having undergone a prolonged and terrible
bombardment. But the streets were crowded. The restaurants,

the cafés, the famous *espressos,* had reopened, and were overflowing with patrons. The joyous cries of newsboys resounded
everywhere. The great factories, Ganz, Lang, Mavag, the
Csepel plants, one after the other, announced resumption of
work. At night occasional shots were still heard, but no one
knew who was firing at whom. The hunting of Avos—"a diver-
sion that took the place of the movies," as a French correspondent said—was becoming less intense. The *Literary Gazette*
reappeared on the stands; each article in the new issue was a
profession of faith in the future of democracy.

During the morning of November 1, Imre Nagy took over
the ministry of foreign affairs. At 7 P.M., he proclaimed Hungary's neutrality. "People of Hungary," he said in his radio
address, "the Hungarian national government, imbued with a
profound sense of its responsibility toward you and toward
history, declares the neutrality of the Hungarian People's Republic." Committees and councils held meetings everywhere.
Factories that had had no time to organize councils, did so
now. The peasants, too, were organizing. So were the parties,
and the administrative departments. Each of the ministries
now had its revolutionary committee, and each committee
formulated demands. The work of removing the Stalinists and
of rehabilitating the victims of the former regime was in full
swing. The president of the Rakosist trade-union organization
resigned after a stormy meeting of the executive board, which
decided to withdraw from the Communist-sponsored World
Federation of Trade-Unions. The Budapest revolutionary committee—the new municipal council—met at the former party
offices which the Csepel workers had taken by assault. General
Bela Kiraly, appointed commandant of the Budapest garrison,
organized the National Guard. "The army intends to safeguard the conquests of the revolution," he said to the Austrian
deputy Peter Strasser, "to defend the state against all attacks,

and to secure a period of transition until a new government is formed on the basis of free elections."

The formation of a new government on a broadened basis was making headway. Imre Nagy seemed resolved to rid himself of all those who did not enjoy the people's confidence, particularly Ferenc Munnich, whose removal had been demanded by many workers' councils and revolutionary committees. Nothing now seemed to stand in the way of an agreement with the Socialists.

For his part, Janos Kadar tried to reconstruct the Communist party by completely reshuffling its leadership. The party dropped its old name and was rebaptized the "Hungarian Socialist Workers' party." A provisional committee of seven men was appointed to organize and convoke a constituent national congress as soon as possible. The committee consisted of Ferenc Donath, Sandor Kopacsi (chief of the Budapest police who became very popular during the insurrection), Geza Losonczy, Gyorgy Lukacs, Zoltan Szanto, Kadar, and Imre Nagy—i.e., the majority of its members were Nagy partisans. The evening of November 1, Kadar delivered a radio address which shows him in a light very different from that in which he was to appear a few days later. "Hungarian workers, peasants, and intellectuals," he said. "In a glorious uprising our people succeeded in shaking off the Rakosi regime. We have conquered freedom for the people, and independence for the country, and without freedom and independence there can be no socialism. We can say that the best among those who prepared this insurrection were recruited from among our ranks. The writers, journalists, Communist students, the youth of the Petofi Society, the thousands of workers, peasants, and veteran Communists who had been persecuted by Rakosi fought in the front lines against political gangsterism and despotism. We are proud of our active participation in the armed uprising."

A few days later, Kadar was to be less proud of this; and

three months later he was to imprison the writers, journalists, and the youth of the Petofi Society whose heroism and patriotism he had praised. But on November 1, Kadar gave solemn assurances that the party would never return to its former criminal ways. The Hungarian democrats, he added, must fight on two fronts—against the threat of a counter-revolution, and against a foreign intervention that would transform Hungary into another Korea. "We must eliminate the nests of the counter-revolution," he exclaimed, appealing to all democratic parties, and particularly to the Social Democrats, to help consolidate the government.

After this address had been recorded, Kadar left the Parliament building for a meeting of the militants of the new party. Then, accompanied by Munnich, he drove in the direction of the Soviet embassy. Near the embassy the two men left their car for another one which had been waiting for them, and which drove off immediately. From that moment on, Kadar and Munnich were not to be found.

A few days earlier, Munnich, former Hungarian ambassador to Moscow, had said to the Polish journalist Wiktor Woroszylski: "The only thing left is to die with honor." He had apparently changed his mind.

The next day, Kadar's wife went to see Imre Nagy and asked him what had become of her husband. Nagy was surprised to learn of his disappearance, and sent out search patrols. It is not known whether Kadar had of his own accord gone over to the enemy camp with Kossa, Marosan, Apro, and a number of other Rakosists and Geroists, or whether he had been kidnaped. However that may be, Kadar soon reappeared in a new role, and there is some reason to believe that he did not do so of his own free will.

Parallel to the activities sketched above, the Soviet army's riposte to the failure of Mikoyan's mission began to loom threateningly on the horizon. At noon on October 31, the

Miskolc radio, once again ahead of the Budapest radio, had announced that several Russian anti-aircraft units, a large number of tanks, and several infantry units had entered Hungary. On November 1, alarming reports began to multiply. Soviet armored units had occupied strategic points during the night. The airfields of Budapest and Debrecen were surrounded by Soviet tanks.

The correspondent of the Yugoslav newspaper *Politika* happened to be with Nagy when the latter was informed by telephone from Cseroda (eastern Hungary) that the roads were literally flooded with Soviet troops. "These reports aroused all the more indignation in Hungary," the correspondent wrote, "because the Soviet government had promised not to send new troops."

Nagy protested in the sharpest possible terms. He summoned the Soviet ambassador, and demanded that the movements of the Russian forces be halted at once. At the same time, he told him of his intention to proclaim Hungary's neutrality and to appeal to the United Nations. The ambassador promised Nagy to transmit his note to his own government and to request a prompt reply. Later, at night, the Soviet embassy issued a communiqué recognizing that Hungarian airfields were surrounded and occupied by Soviet armored units, "in order to insure the evacuation of the families of Soviet army men stationed in Hungary." Actually, the Russians occupied the airfields in order to cripple the Hungarian air force.

By the morning of November 2, while Nagy and his friends were busy forming the new government, the encirclement of Budapest had been completed. Armored columns were converging on the capital from east and west. Nagy called a press conference for the afternoon. Numerous journalists gathered, but they waited in vain. Finally, a short statement was read, announcing that the Hungarian government had protested against the movements of the Soviet troops.

On November 2, Nagy sent the Russian ambassador, Andropov, three new notes. The first renewed the Hungarian protest concerning the entry of Soviet troops, and listed the names of the members of the Hungarian delegation appointed to negotiate Hungary's withdrawal from the Warsaw Pact. They were Geza Losonczy (Communist), Jozsef Kovago (new mayor of Budapest, leader of the Smallholders), Andras Marton (representative of the army), Ferenc Farkas (young and dynamic secretary of the Petofi Society), and the old Socialist economist, Vilmos Zentai.

In his second note, Nagy asked that the Soviet-Hungarian committee charged with arranging the details of the Russian withdrawal from Hungary meet immediately. The Hungarian members of this committee were Ferenc Erdei, Pal Maleter, General Istvan Kovacs, and Colonel Miklos Szucs.

In his third note, Nagy protested against the entry of the Soviet units that had been reported to him on November 1 and November 2.

Despite these protests the troop movements continued. This did not, however, prevent Sobolev, Russian delegate to the United Nations, from declaring at the Security Council meeting of November 2 that "Imre Nagy's statements according to which new Soviet forces have entered Hungary are absolutely baseless."

In the meantime, the Russians had seized control of the Austro-Hungarian border. Soviet officers declared that their purpose was merely to secure their lines rather than to carry out a military operation. Approaches to all important cities were controlled by Russian armor. Here and there delegates from workers' councils established contact with Russian soldiers who told them: "We have come here to fight against the Fascists, against those who want to restore the Fascist regime in Hungary." But the Hungarians replied: "There is no fascism here. The people are engaged in a struggle for freedom and prosperity."

The Hungarian leaders made a last-minute attempt to reassure the Russians as to their future plans. On November 2, Zoltan Tildy declared: "We have no intention, once our neutrality has been recognized, to join another bloc, and we shall never consider joining the NATO. We are surrounded by four Communist states, we must maintain good relations with them, and, needless to say, close economic relations. In speaking of neutrality, our premier mentioned Austria, but we must also think of Finland. . . . While politically we wish to become a parliamentary democracy on the Western model, economically and socially all the parties agree that the reforms carried out since 1945 should not be abrogated. The agrarian reform is an accomplished fact. The collective farms will of course be abolished, but the peasants will retain the land. The banks and the mines will not be de-nationalized, and the factories will continue to be owned by the workers. What we have achieved is not a restoration or a counter-revolution, but a revolution."

This statement was confirmed the following day by Geza Losonczy, after the new coalition government, which included agrarians, Socialists, and Communists, had been formed. Losonczy said that all the members of the government, whose authority was recognized by the insurgent army and by almost all revolutionary committees and workers' councils, were agreed that the social conquests of the Liberation must be maintained. Similarly, the newspaper of the university youth, which voiced the view of the vanguard of the insurrection, said that "Hungary has not achieved her independence in order to replace one occupant by another. Hungary does not want armed intervention by the United Nations." The Hungarians hoped that diplomatic pressure by the United Nations would be sufficient to stop the Soviets. But the United Nations did not intervene militarily, nor did it apply any serious diplomatic pressure. The afternoon of November 3, the Soviet delegate informed the Security Council, meeting for the second time to discuss the situation in Hungary, that Soviet and Hungarian military representatives were in the process of negotiating an agreement.

This time Sobolev was telling the truth. The Russians had agreed to meet the military delegates appointed by Nagy. A first talk took place in the morning, in a "cordial atmosphere"; then General Malinin and General Tolbaev asked Maleter and his companions to come to the Russian headquarters at 9 P.M. to continue the talks. Did it occur to Imre Nagy and Maleter that in March, 1945, Marshal Zhukov's delegates had addressed a similar invitation to fifteen leaders of the Polish anti-Nazi underground? Those leaders, headed by General Okulicki, had accepted a Russian invitation to a villa near Warsaw. Except for one or two of them, they were never seen again.

But Nagy and Maleter were confident. Throughout that day, despite the increasingly important movements of Russian troops which were encircling Budapest, the capital was calm. For the previous two days there had been no summary executions of Avos. The lynchers had been disarmed. Throughout the country administrative offices and factories had resumed work.

The political event of that day was the formation of the new Nagy government—the third since the beginning of the insurrection. It was a coalition government, in which the Communists were represented by Nagy, Kadar, and Geza Losonczy; the Social Democrats by Anna Kethly, Gyula Kelemen (former secretary of state for industries, sentenced to life imprisonment in 1948, and released on the eve of the October uprising), and Jozsef Fischer, an architect; the Smallholders by Bela Kovacs, Zoltan Tildy, and Istvan B. Szabo; the Petofi party by Professor Istvan Bibo, sociologist trained at Oxford, and Ferenc

Farkas, a dynamic and universally respected peasant intellectual; the army by Pal Maleter.

At 6 P.M., Tildy received the press in the Gobelins Hall of the Parliament building, decorated with the famous tapestry showing the Hungarian tribes gathered to elect their first chief, Prince Arpad. Former President Tildy was very optimistic: "The Russians have agreed to discuss the details of their evacuation of Hungary," he said. "This shows that the principle of the withdrawal is no longer in question. The negotiations will continue tonight and the next few days." Later, another minister, Losonczy, received the 250 special correspondents of foreign newspapers stationed in Budapest. "The atmosphere was very tense," wrote Thomas Schreiber, the young Hungarian-born correspondent of *Le Monde*. "The most alarming reports were coming in. We learned that Maleter's delegation had not given any sign of life. . . . I heard the telephone ring in Nagy's office. He was informed that new Soviet reinforcements were pouring in through Zahony. Losonczy, sweating profusely, gave us the latest scoops: armored units had been reported at Szolnok, they had occupied the road to Vienna. The capital was being encircled."

A night of anguish followed. Even so, the majority of Hungarians, who could not see the worried faces of Nagy and Losonczy, failed to realize the terrible acuteness of the danger. Hope persisted. But what if the Russians intervened after all? I telephoned from Paris to Mrs. Rajk, who was at Nagy's side during the ordeal, to ask her this question. "It's impossible," she said. "They won't do that. But if they do, everyone will fight to the last bullet, and beyond—the young and the old, the women and children." And this old Communist spoke of the Hungarians' hatred of the foreign occupant, which had reached an incredible intensity.

Sensing the danger, Professor Bibo and his friends thought of asking for the mediation of China, Yugoslavia, and Poland

—countries which had until then shown themselves favorably disposed toward the Hungarian patriots. They still hoped to find a compromise solution. But it was too late.

That night, in Paris, I listened to broadcasts from Communist countries. From hour to hour their tone grew harsher. It was like an artillery barrage before an attack. Zapotocky in Prague made a speech denouncing Hungarian "fascism," Imre Nagy's "weakness," and the counter-revolution. Then the radios of Sofia, Bucharest, Moscow, and even China joined in, repeating the insults and the accusations. Belgrade was silent. Warsaw was silent. Gomulka and Tito knew that the die had been cast. An island of calm in this crescendo of nervous excitement, Radio Budapest broadcast light music and reassuring news reports: the Hungarian-Soviet negotiations, it said, had begun under good auspices, an agreement on the withdrawal of the Russian troops was imminent, and the Russian embassy had described as absurd the rumors of a possible intervention.

I went to bed, hoping that Radio Budapest, and not Moscow and Prague, would prove to be right. In Budapest, too, the foreign correspondents returned to their hotels. One of them, the Pole Woroszylski, later wrote that before falling asleep he thought of the prospects of the Hungarian revolution as they appeared "in those days of stabilization": "I did not know what form the Hungarian republic would finally assume. But it seemed to me that we would be confronted with an interesting synthesis, combining the fundamental achievements of the people's democracy (all the land to the peasants, socialization of banks and factories) with a multi-party system, freedom of the press, and other freedoms characteristic of liberal democracy. Is not such a regime one of the possible roads—perhaps a very slow one—toward socialism? . . . As for the road along which men like Rakosi had led their country, I knew with certainty that it could end only in bankruptcy and servitude."

This testimony of a Polish Communist writer, which was confirmed by the ten other Polish witnesses of the Hungarian revolution and by almost all of the 250 foreign correspondents in Budapest, will be most valuable to future historians, for it exposes as a lie the pretexts invoked by Soviet propaganda to justify the intervention—the presence of foreign agents, the growing disorder, the victorious counter-revolution. The very next day, November 4, Sobolev declared at the Security Council, which had been convoked urgently at Nagy's request: "The Hungarian workers had formulated demands that were justified. But these demands were exploited by Western agents, particularly American agents. It was under those circumstances that Nagy formed his government. Nagy followed the Fascist path, he wanted to liquidate the people's regime. He based himself on elements recruited from among Horthy's officers, who had spread destruction, murder, and brutalities throughout the country in order to secure the return of a Fascist and capitalist dictatorship."

That was the keynote of the Soviet propaganda, of the background music accompanying the roar of the guns that were now soon to bombard the Budapest factories. But Woroszylski speaks of stabilization, democracy; he saw no fascism in Hungary, only the prospect of a Hungarian road to socialism.

Thus only nine months after Mikoyan and Khrushchev had denounced the macabre and bloody myths of Stalin, the Soviet Union returned to them, divorcing herself from the civilized world, and disavowing her own ideals and principles.

In 1949, Stalin had denounced Yugoslavia as a country that had fallen into the hands of Fascists and murderers. In 1956, eighteen months after their reconciliation with Tito, the Soviet leaders blandly declared that Hungary had fallen into the hands of Fascists and murderers. But in 1949 Stalin, while thundering against "Tito and his clique," had refrained from leading a punitive expedition against Yugoslavia. In 1956, the debonair successors of the bloody tyrant, the architects of liberalization, democratization, desatellization, the promoters of peace and coexistence, set out to destroy Hungarian sovereignty and democracy. And they acted with the vociferous approval of all the satellite leaders and the French Communists.

Nevertheless, there is also a tragic aspect in this sudden turn, this resort to brute force and cynical lies. The events in Hungary took the Russian leaders by surprise. The national uprising compelled them to disclose the imperialist and colonialist foundations of Soviet power at the very moment they were preparing gradually to correct the most glaring abuses of their rule.

At the Twentieth Party Congress—a congress characterized by those famous good intentions with which hell is paved—the Soviet leaders appeared in the role of reformists, comparable to the enlightened neo-colonialists of the West. Like the latter, Khrushchev, Mikoyan, and their partisans championed a humanization of the dictatorship. Their goals remained the same as Stalin's—preservation of the empire and strengthening of its international position; but they had made up their minds to use different methods. That was the meaning of their disavowal of their former master. But this disavowal was not sufficient to annul the consequences of Stalin's crimes: Khrushchev and Mikoyan now had to reap the national resentment that Stalin and Rakosi had sown. The uprising, the collapse of communism, and the awakening of the democratic forces in Hungary —forces that were Socialist and violently anti-Communist— confronted them with a tragic choice. They had either to give ground in Hungary at the risk of encouraging all the centrifugal forces of their empire, or set an example for all the satellites that might be tempted to break away from the Warsaw Pact and from the Soviet hegemony which was camouflaged by that pact.

The motives for which the Kremlin leaders chose the second

alternative have been indicated above. But the choice they
made inevitably threw them back to Stalinism, or, as they put
it, to "the heroic traditions of Bolshevism." Reformist paternalism yielded to terrorism. In the glow of the flames of Budapest,
Bolshevism resumed its primitive form—that of a military
dictatorship by a minority imbued with the belief in its historical mission to impose a bureaucratic paradise on nations that
do not want it. Next to the Budapest uprising itself, the new
Soviet intervention is the most crushing conceivable condemnation of the Soviet regime.

Let us return to Budapest. On November 4, the capital was
aroused at 5 A.M. by the roar of guns stationed behind the
mist-enveloped hills of Buda. Soviet tanks had opened fire on
the city. Jumping out of their beds, the foreign journalists at
the Duna Hotel could follow from their windows the luminous
trajectories of the tracer bullets. At 5:20 A.M., Imre Nagy, in
a voice broken by emotion, issued the following statement:
"This is Imre Nagy speaking. This morning at daybreak the
Soviet troops began an attack on our capital, with the obvious
intention of overthrowing the lawful and democratic government of Hungary. Our troops are engaged in battle. The government is in its place. I am informing the country and the
whole world of this."

The statement was then repeated in English, Russian, and
French.

At 6:08 A.M., Radio Budapest announced that Imre Nagy
had informed Dag Hammerskjold of the Soviet attack.

At 6:15 A.M., the first Soviet armored columns—TX-34's
—crossed the Danube bridges, followed by truckloads of infantry. MIG's were flying at a low altitude, but did not fire.

At 7:12 A.M., the government, which was still in the Parliament building, appealed to the Soviet officers and privates:
"Do not fire. Avoid bloodshed. The Russians are and will remain our friends."

At 7:56 A.M., Radio Budapest broadcast a statement issued by the Writers' Union: "This is the Writers' Union speaking. We appeal to all writers, scientists, to all unions of writers, to all scientific academies in the world, to the intellectuals the world over. We ask you to help us, to support us. Time is short. You know the facts. Help Hungary. HELP the writers, scientists, workers, intellectuals of our country. Help us, help us. . . ."

Never has a more moving appeal been broadcast. It remained unanswered. And yet, a few hours earlier, the United Nations General Assembly had showed itself very much concerned for the interests of another small country—Egypt. It had adopted a resolution calling for the formation of an international force to secure and supervise the cessation of the hostilities that had begun a few days before. A common Soviet-American-Arab front was improvised to defend Nasser's dictatorship in the name of the principle of non-intervention. Was this not a precedent that could and should have been applied to Hungary? But if the Soviets by their attack on Hungary had exposed the imperialist foundations of their power, the big and small non-Communist states assembled at the United Nations now revealed that the actual motives governing their conduct had nothing to do with international morality. Thus the Hungarian events taught the world a sobering lesson, if such a lesson was still needed. It revealed in a blinding flash all the hypocrisy of politicians who subordinate the most sacred principles to interests that are often sordid. Egypt benefited from the American-Russian competition for Arab friendship. Hungary was of little interest to the big powers. The Western nations used the Hungarian uprising only to add fuel to the anti-Soviet propaganda, and to divert attention from the Suez conflict. Similarly, the Communist propaganda used the Anglo-French intervention in Egypt to denounce capitalist imperialism at a moment when Soviet imperialism was intervening in Hungary.

This was a bitter lesson for those who believed in the progress of international morality, and a cruel disappointment for the Hungarians who had confidence in Western solidarity. The insurgents thought that they were fighting, as their ancestors had fought in the sixteenth and seventeenth centuries, for civilization, for world freedom. The indifference of the West crushed them.

At about 8 A.M. Imre Nagy received a Russian ultimatum demanding that the Hungarian forces capitulate before noon. Otherwise, the ultimatum said, Budapest would be bombarded.

At the same time, Sobolev told the Security Council in New York that the Soviet Union had intervened in Hungary under a clause of the Warsaw Treaty authorizing her to protect that country against subversion. At the same meeting the Hungarian delegate declared that "although he had been unable to establish direct contact with Budapest," he had been informed that Hungary had a new government. At 8:24 A.M., Radio Budapest broadcast a last SOS, which was repeated three times, and then fell silent. It resumed its broadcasts only at 9 P.M., under Soviet control.

The Kadar Government

The Soviet tanks and infantry moved down Revolutionary Youth Avenue, the main thoroughfare of downtown Budapest (the former Stalin Avenue, originally Andrassy Avenue). Systematically, they began to demolish the Hungarian bases of operation, concentrating on the defenses set up to protect the government buildings. Shell explosions and the rattle of machine guns reverberated throughout the city. This was obviously an uneven contest. The people of Budapest were attacking the Russian tanks with bottles of gasoline; the Russians used shells and phosphorus bullets. Workers began to build barricades to obstruct the tanks. The battle was particularly violent in Buda. At about noon the Russians took the Parliament building by storm. They found only one member of the Cabinet there—Zoltan Tildy. Imre Nagy and several of his partisans had taken refuge in the Yugoslav embassy.

Soviet military operations were simultaneously started in the provinces. At 10 A.M., Szombathely, a city in western Hungary, was in the hands of the Russians. Battles were raging in Pecs, Szekesfehervar, Dunafoldvar, and Veszprem. The Soviets had thrown into battle four thousand tanks, of which one thousand, or four armored divisions, operated in Budapest alone. By using such overwhelming strength, they no doubt hoped to crush Hungarian resistance in the shortest possible time.

The Hungarian patriots realized their weakness, but they accepted the uneven battle, and made a desperate effort to prolong it, because they hoped for a United Nations intervention. On November 4, the United Nations General Assembly had passed a resolution (50 votes for, 8 against, 15 abstentions) demanding that the Russians withdraw their troops. But this resolution was only a scrap of paper. The powers that a few months later were to consider sanctions against another David among nations—Israel—had no intention of applying the same standards against an international Goliath.

The Hungarian David worked miracles. In downtown Budapest resistance continued until November 7. And it was the workers who fought with the greatest stubbornness.

The evening of November 5, the Soviet high command issued a leaflet addressed to the workers, which said: "Hungarian workers, do not believe the slanders of those who would set you against us, your unselfish friends. We are soldiers of friendship among peoples. We fight for a just cause which is also your cause. We appeal to the soldiers and officers of the Hungarian army to fight on our side in order to restore freedom and democracy and crush the reactionary elements. We appeal to all Hungarians to take an active part in the defense of the people's democracy and to contribute to the victory of their country. This is the sacred cause of the people."

To this appeal, the fifty thousand Csepel workers who were barricaded in their workshops, many of them with their wives and older children, replied: "We are not reactionaries, but we do not want your people's democracy, nor the victory of our country that you offer us at the point of your guns."

The Csepel workers did not lay down their arms until November 14. The workers of Dunapentele, Borsod, Komlo, and Tatabanya also fought with desperate heroism. In the mountainous and wooded regions of Bakony, Peca, and Salgotarjan, groups of guerrillas continued to resist until Christmas Eve. At Miskolc, the insurgents succeeded in dislodging the Soviet troops, and held the city for several days. At Salgotarjan, they defeated the Russians, forcing them to retreat to Czechoslovak territory, whence they returned later with reinforcements.

To be sure, all these were partial exploits, very precarious victories. But if the Russians expected an easy triumph, their calculation proved false. They had not taken into account the stubbornness of the Hungarians and the intensity of their hatred. The Russians suffered considerable losses. Hungarian artillery destroyed about one hundred armored cars in Budapest. In reprisal, Soviet tanks fired point-blank at apartment houses. That behavior was scarcely in conformity with the Russian assurances of friendship. It must be said, however, that many Russian soldiers did not even know the name of the country in which they found themselves. Soldiers belonging to newly arrived units, many of them from Asia, thought that they were in Egypt and looked for the Suez Canal. Several were shocked on learning the truth. The Russian soldiers and officers were obviously unprepared to fight against workers and students. "Yesterday we were heroes. Today we are counter-revolutionaries. Who can understand this?" said the Csepel workers in a Russian-language leaflet addressed to the Soviet troops. These were embarrassing questions, but they did not prevent the Soviet army from crushing the insurrection.

The Soviet Union found it relatively easy, thanks to her material superiority, to carry out her military objectives in Hungary; but the realization of her political objectives proved a far more complicated task. The Soviet leaders wished to "shelve" the Hungarian business as soon as possible. The repression was not an end in itself, only a means. By intervening in Hungary, the Russians aimed primarily at making a show of force, in order to bring the Hungarians to their senses, to prove to them that they were isolated and at the mercy of the Soviet Union, and that they had to give up all ideas of neutrality and of setting up a democratic and parliamentary regime. The government of November 3 was inacceptable to the Russians, because Imre Nagy and his Cabinet were in a sense the prisoners of the insurgents who pressed for Hungarian independence.

No Soviet leader could condone the secession of Hungary from the Eastern bloc. Both the army and the party were emphatically opposed to such a move, and Soviet strategy, national pride, and doctrinal considerations demanded that the Hungarian rebellion be quelled. The only way out of the impasse, as the Russians saw it, was to apply force, to oust Imre Nagy, and to disarm the insurgents. In imperialist language, that is called "pacification." Now, this pacification was to pave the way for a compromise along the lines of the Soviet statement of October 30, which included a number of concessions to national communism. That is why the Russians chose as their puppet Janos Kadar rather than Gero, who had been definitively discredited. They thought that Kadar would reassure the Hungarians, and convince them that the Soviet

Union did not intend to set up a Rakosi-Gero regime after order was restored, but a regime similar to Gomulka's in Poland.

Various hypotheses have been advanced to account for Kadar's willingness to collaborate with the Soviets and to serve as a Hungarian Pétain. Many of his fellow countrymen compared his position to that of Rajk in 1949. Kadar, too, knew Rakosi's prisons and torturers; according to some reports, he had been emasculated by Vladimir Farkas. It is not impossible that the Russians forced him to become the premier of an anti-Nagyist, pseudo-Gomulkist government, just as they had forced Rajk to confess that he was a spy.

I have questioned many Hungarian refugees who saw much of Kadar during the insurrection. All of them have described him as a stern but sincere Communist, incapable of duplicity. His sudden about-face, they said, was proof that the Russians had broken his spirit.

But it must be kept in mind that a man faced with a confused and unforeseen situation sometimes undergoes a complete inner transformation. A law-abiding citizen can become a criminal, a physician a murderer, and a prostitute a Joan of Arc. In the case of Kadar, it is certainly possible that at the eleventh hour the party man's instinct of self-preservation won the upper hand over the authentic patriot. In the last analysis, it is the stiffening of the party bureaucrats in the Soviet Union as well as in all the satellite countries—their almost animal reflex in the face of the common danger represented by the insurrection, the democratic movement, and the dislocation of the Communist empire—that accounts historically, sociologically, and psychologically for the Soviet intervention, and for all the well-orchestrated cries of rage, hysterical applause, justifications, exhortations, and oaths of loyalty to Leninism, that accompanied it.

At the moment of supreme danger, when the insurgents

were summarily executing Avos and even some Communists whose hands were not bloodstained, the bureaucratic machine recovered its unity—a unity of policemen, of oppressors obsessed with the fear that the class consciousness of the workers whom they had alienated, expropriated, and neutralized might be aroused.

It is possible that, as many Hungarians believe, Kadar was abducted by the Russians on November 1, and that he consented to turn against Nagy, to dissociate himself from the insurrection, and to condone the intervention only after being "worked over" for several days. It was not until November 9 that he returned to Budapest, and even then he stayed out of the limelight for several days. Later, when he appeared publicly, his eyes were those of a man tormented by uncertainty. But I think that the pressure applied to him was chiefly psychological and that he yielded easily to it, for it is difficult to conceive that he was not frightened by the turn the events had taken after October 30. It was much harder for Kadar than for Nagy to resign himself to the disintegration of the party, the overthrow of the people's democracy, and the return to parliamentary government. And since he was charged with the mission of reorganizing the party, he realized more clearly than Nagy could how difficult it was to make a new start. For communism in Hungary, as the insurrection demonstrated, was a Russian import. Without Russian support, it could rely only on a few thousand idealistic intellectuals, who were politically useless, and a few tens of thousands of "workers' cadres" who benefited from the regime. The Hungarian national character was impervious to communism in its Soviet form; Hungary had more in common with Finland than with neighboring Czechoslovakia. Nagy seems to have concluded from his predecessors' failures that communism must be brought into conformity with Hungarian traditions. Kadar apparently decided that the Hungarians must be re-educated by force, for he shared the Communist distrust of all popular spontaneity; for him (and in this he was like Gero) man is something to be organized. The excesses committed by extremists during the uprising further increased his distrust.

At the very moment the Soviet artillery began the bombardment of Budapest, at 5 A.M. on November 4, the Szolnok radio broadcast an appeal signed by four former members of the Nagy government—Kadar, Munnich, Apro, and Kossa. In this appeal the turncoats explained why they had decided to break with Nagy and to form a "revolutionary worker-peasant government." "We have taken this decision," they said, "because we realized that the Imre Nagy government had become paralyzed under the pressure of the reaction, and that by staying with this government we would be unable to fight against the counter-revolutionary danger threatening our People's Republic, our worker-peasant regime, and our Socialist achievements." And Kadar and his companions went on to say:

"Respected champions of the working-class movement have been murdered, among them Imre Mezo, secretary of the greater Budapest party committee; Comrade Kalmar, old Communist militant of Csepel; and Sandor Sziklai, director of the Museum of War History. Worthy sons of the working class and of the peasantry have been exterminated. As members of the government, we could not stand by idle while, under cover of democracy, terrorists and bandits were murdering our brothers, workers and peasants, terrorizing our peaceful citizens, and dragging the country into anarchy. . . ."

An hour later, the same radio announced that the new government, "acting in the interest of our people, of our working class, of our country, has requested the command of the Soviet army to help our nation to crush the black forces of reaction and to restore order and peace in the country."

Most Hungarians looked upon these declarations as an act of treachery and a provocation. The Russians needed a legal excuse for their intervention; Kadar and his friends supplied it, for this second intervention had begun at a time when order had been restored, when the extremist insurgents had been disarmed, and when the summary executions of Rakosists had been stopped. But Kadar may have suspected that the lull was only temporary, and that the insurgents were merely controlling themselves in order not to offer targets to Soviet propaganda. The other members of the new government had even better reasons than Kadar to feel unsafe. A few days earlier, Budapest crowds had demonstrated their hostility for Munnich. As for Antal Apro, he had been dismissed from the Nagy government; and the former Socialists Istvan Kossa, Gyorgy Marosan, and Sandor Ronai were repudiated by their former comrades. For these people the advent of democracy meant the end of their political careers. Kadar alone could hope to find a place in a democratized regime, because he enjoyed respect even among non-Communists. Bela Kovacs himself had recently referred to him as a friend of the Resistance. That is why Munnich and the others could not do without him.

However that may be, the overwhelming majority of the people regarded the eight members of the revolutionary worker-peasant government as mercenaries, Quislings, who, except for Kadar, deserved only contempt.[1] And with the grim irony characteristic of the populations of Eastern Europe, which have so often been maltreated by history, the citizens of Budapest were saying: "At least the Russians have found eight genuine Hungarians to defend the country against nine million counter-revolutionaries and agents of foreign imperialism."

[1] The composition of the new government was as follows: premier, Janos Kadar; deputy premier and minister of defense and public security forces, Ferenc Munnich; minister of state, Gyorgy Marosan; minister of finance, Istvan Kossa; minister of heavy industry, Antal Apro; minister of agriculture, Imre Dogei; minister of commerce, Sandor Ronai. According to a broadcast by the Moscow radio of November 4, several ministerial posts had not been filled, and "the other parties" had been asked to designate their representatives in the new government.

This estimate was somewhat optimistic. As the new intervention began, the Russians actually found several hundred Hungarians who were ready to collaborate with them and who even looked upon them as liberators. They were the former AVO and army officers who had survived the uprising. In the city quarters occupied by the Soviet troops, and in the deserted streets where only Russian tanks and cars circulated because of the curfew, the foreign journalists emerging from their cellars saw the sinister units of repression, consisting of two or three tanks, an armored car, and a half-track with Russian soldiers. Under their protection there marched AVO agents, whose notorious leather coats will always remain for the Hungarians the symbols of the Stalin-Rakosi people's democracy. These mixed units were busy rounding up young patriots, who then were loaded onto trucks and sent in the direction of the Russian border. Such activities were in singular contrast with the fatherly appeals of the Kadar government, which promised impunity to those who would lay down their arms. It is probable that Kadar accepted the bargain offered him by the Russians in the sincere belief that he would succeed in pacifying the population. But, once again, resort to force designed as a temporary measure resulted in the rule of force pure and simple.

And yet, the program outlined by Kadar in his appeal of November 4, which was broadcast by the Moscow radio, was seductive enough. Kadar had taken over Nagy's program, except for free elections and neutrality. The overwhelming majority of the Hungarians would have enthusiastically accepted this program if the Russians, on the night of October 23, instead of joining with Gero had helped the people to rid themselves of him and his police. Kadar's program, if we set aside his justification of the Soviet intervention, was formulated in the spirit of national and democratic communism, and was designed to please everyone. It sharply denounced the crimes of "the Rakosi-Gero clique," promised full pardon to the insurgents, the liquidation of the bureaucracy, freedom of speech for the intellectuals, revision of the economic plans, higher standards of living, democratization of local government, assistance to small businessmen and craftsmen, industrial democracy and workers' councils, and even the withdrawal of the Soviet troops after restoration of order.

Unfortunately, all this was announced and promised at the very moment the Soviet troops were demolishing Budapest, executing Csepel workers, rounding up students, and arousing such a fear of deportation that the youth began to flee westward en masse. Nearly 180,000 Hungarians, or 2 per cent of the total population, chose self-exile: this figure is eloquent of the state of mind of the Hungarians in the face of the Soviet intervention.

Under such circumstances, Kadar's promises and concessions sounded like provocations. This would not have happened if the Communist party had retained any influence in the country, if the Soviet intervention had been supported by the organized efforts of revolutionary Communists. But except for a few groups of policemen, there were no Communists. It is because of this national unanimity, which Rakosi himself had created against his dictatorship and against the Russians, that the Hungarians, even after they had been crushed, disarmed, and deserted by the world, refused to acknowledge their defeat. This was an unprecedented fact: the revolution continued even after it had been defeated. It is not surprising that the Russians were bewildered. As mentioned above, the Hungarians during the insurrection had become impervious to fear. They were no longer afraid of prison or of death. Later, they were to relearn fear, for there are limits to human endurance, but they relearned it much more slowly than the Russians had expected. For the time being the Hungarians stubbornly refused to be bullied. In the face of the victorious

Russians they sported their tricolor cockades. They continued to hope, they waited for the arrival of United Nations observers. They refused to believe that the West would capitulate. Therefore they were determined to resist and to sabotage the government's efforts to restore order, which they knew was necessary for the nation's survival. And it is precisely this necessity to live, to eat, to keep warm, to work, that was one of Kadar's principal trump cards. Every streetcar or bus restored to circulation, every street cleared of rubble, meant a political victory for Kadar. The Hungarians refused to grant him such victories. They chose to follow the path of large-scale passive resistance, in the tradition of 1848 and 1849, which continuously haunted the Hungarians.

In 1849, the Czar intervened in Hungary, at the request of the Hapsburgs, in order to crush, in the name of the sacred principles of order and public peace, "the anarchy and Red terror" embodied by Kossuth—though Kossuth actually was a very moderate liberal infatuated with constitutional government. There are striking analogies between 1849 and 1956. In 1849, the Russian command trapped the thirteen best Hungarian generals. In 1956, the Russians kidnaped Maleter. In 1849, Kossuth issued a last-minute appeal to world liberal opinion, which met with no response. In 1956, Nagy issued a similar appeal, with similar results. And after the insurrection of 1848–1849, the overwhelming majority of the Hungarians refused to collaborate with the victors and adopted an attitude of passive resistance. As a result, the Hapsburgs, unable to bring over to their side the administration that had emerged from the revolution, ended up by imposing an almost completely Austrian administration on the Hungarians. This administration, consisting of Austrian, Czech, and Croatian functionaries, ruled Hungary for eighteen years. Only then, after the Austrian armies had suffered defeats in Italy, did the imperial government negotiate with the chief of the resistance,

Ferenc Deak, the Imre Nagy of that time, whose physical characteristics and stubborn character Imre Nagy, a native of the same region, seems to have inherited. Ferenc Deak, one of the few survivors of the Kossuth government, whom the Hungarians nicknamed "the Sage of the Fatherland," demanded that Austria recognize Hungarian independence. The Austro-Hungarian accord of 1867 was the result of a stubborn resistance of eighteen years.

It was this historical precedent that inspired the Hungarians in their determination to resist even after the insurrection had been defeated. When the din of battle ceased, a dreary silence spread all over the country—that of the general strike, which was proclaimed on November 4. The first appeals of the Kadar government ran into this wall of silence. "No government has ever found itself in such a difficult situation," Radio Budapest admitted on November 9. "The factories are closed. Traffic is still crippled. Armed gangs are rampant. The population of the capital is threatened with starvation."

On November 10, Janos Kadar made his first official broadcast as head of the new government. He said in an imploring voice that he could understand the people's distrust of him: all he wanted was to end the bloodshed, to get the Russians to withdraw their troops, and to put into effect his democratic and national program.

Kadar had returned to Budapest on November 9, and installed his government in the Parliament building. Polish journalists tried to see him there. They found Parliament Square filled with Russian tanks. The adjoining public gardens had been converted into artillery parks. Soldiers had built fires on the lawns, and were cooking kasha and soup. The Parliament lobby was crawling with guards—Avos and Soviet soldiers. At the top of the stairs stood a machine gun with its barrel aimed at the visitors. A Soviet officer politely showed them to the door. "The Hungarian government is very busy

and cannot receive you," he said. "You will understand that it
has many important matters to deal with. It's a most unfortunate situation."

It was indeed unfortunate: Kadar's task was not an enviable
one. He was facing a completely new political setup. At the
head of each ministry, each prefecture, each municipality,
there was a revolutionary committee, which, defying the Soviet
intervention, continued the work of cleansing the administration by dismissing Rakosists, Geroists, or even Communists
pure and simple. The committees did not recognize Kadar,
and the government officials were staging a sit-down strike.

After a few days, however, Kadar succeeded in establishing
contact with his subordinates. To be sure, everyone distrusted
him. But the promises that Kadar multiplied between November 10 and 20, whether or not he knew that he would
never keep them, did not sound unreasonable. For Kadar was
not alone in desiring a compromise. The moderate intellectuals
and leaders of the workers' councils thought that it was in the
interests of both the Russians and the Hungarians to reach a
modus vivendi, pending a fuller agreement. Even while considering Kadar a spokesman for the Russians, many Hungarians believed that it was possible to talk with him, were it only
in order to clarify the situation. They knew that the strike
could not continue indefinitely. Only very few workers could
afford the luxury of sacrificing their wages; and to be paid,
they had at least to report to work. Thus while Kadar was in
a difficult situation in the face of the country, the leaders of
the workers were in an equally difficult situation in the face
of the workers whose interests they represented. Kadar adroitly
exploited these difficulties. His plan, providing for an alternation of promises and threats, had been prepared during Mikoyan's and Suslov's fourth visit to Budapest.

The purpose was to demoralize the country, to neutralize
resistance, and to restore the party dictatorship in a somewhat

milder form. The tactic suggested to Kadar was that he should at first make common cause—as Imre Nagy had done after October 28—with the revolutionary committees and the workers' councils. Instead of denouncing the insurrection, Kadar's radio propaganda astutely divided the uprising into two stages, describing the first, which took place between October 23 and 28, as a "just and glorious battle," and the second as a counter-revolutionary and Fascist coup, which made the Soviet intervention inevitable. Only three months later, after consolidating his position, did the Kadar government adopt the Soviet version of the events according to which the uprising had from the outset been inspired by counter-revolutionary elements.

But that was still a long way off. While disavowing Rakosi,[2] Kadar applied the latter's so-called *salami* tactics, and did not shrink from any measure susceptible to confuse and divide the country. Thus, on November 9, Kadar's entourage spread rumors that Kadar was willing to negotiate the return of Imre Nagy, who, it was just then learned, had taken refuge with a number of his followers in the Yugoslav embassy.[3] On November 10, Kadar proclaimed the restoration of the Kossuth emblem. On November 11, he announced a series of important concessions, including the impending opening of talks for the withdrawal of the Russian troops (three months later he admitted frankly that no withdrawal was in question), the liquidation of the political police (he reinstated it in February, 1957), the introduction of new army uniforms with the Kossuth emblem (the Red star reappeared in 1957), the abolition of the compulsory teaching of Russian, and of com-

[2] "The terrorism of the Rakosi and Gero governments, the lies, the demagogy, the cruelty, and the stupidity of their policies have been justly rejected by the working class," Kadar said on November 10 in a radio appeal to the workers.

[3] On November 14, Nagy sent a message to the foreign correspondents stationed in Budapest and to the workers' councils, emphatically denying these rumors which were intended to deceive the opposition.

pulsory deliveries of agricultural products, the inclusion of democratic elements in the government, etc. On November 14, Sandor Gaspar, whom Kadar tried to use as his liaison agent with the workers' councils (which, however, refused to have anything to do with this former Stalinist), declared that the one-party system was definitely a thing of the past.

Having thus paved the way for negotiations, on November 14, Kadar got in touch with the central workers' council in Budapest.

A few words about this council may be in order. It had been formed on October 28, the day following the withdrawal of the Soviet troops from Budapest, in the course of a meeting attended by about two thousand delegates of workers' councils from all over the country. These councils continued to be created throughout Hungary even after the second Soviet intervention. The factory councils elected departmental and regional councils, which in turn elected the central workers' council, whose membership consisted largely of Social Democrats and Nagyist Communists.

A spontaneous creation, the central workers' council emerged after the crushing of the insurrection as the only national force that held its own against the Kadar government, which was regarded as a foreign agency. It was a kind of national council of the resistance movement, which the whole country recognized as its representative, though it was composed exclusively of workers.

The existence of this central workers' council seemed to offer Kadar an unexpected opportunity to consolidate his power, to acquire a popular and proletarian basis, and to achieve a reconciliation between the party and the proletariat. That was the opinion of the Yugoslav leaders, who, however, disapproved the workers' councils when these demanded the calling of general elections. "The workers' councils were the only truly Socialist force in Hungary," Eduard Kardelj declared at the Yugoslav national assembly on December 7, 1956. "They would probably have eliminated anti-Socialist influences if the government had used them as its chief organs in the factories, in the autonomous municipalities, and in the administrative departments. But the Hungarian Communists had a different conception of the role of the workers' councils. They kept repeating that work must be resumed, and did not breathe a word about government functions."

Kardelj's criticism seems justified. When we study the negotiations between Kadar and the councils, we cannot help thinking that Kadar looked upon them as enemies. He treated them just as Rakosi and Gero had treated the trade-unions. He assumed that no agreement was possible with them in the long run, and that they had to be infiltrated, corrupted, divided, and humbled at all costs. It is, however, likely that even if Kadar had wanted to associate the central workers' council with his government, the Russians would have prevented him from doing so, for they could not forgive the councils their violent anti-Sovietism. Once again the Russians proved that national and imperialist strategic considerations were more important to them than revolutionary and proletarian solidarity. A revolutionary and proletarian power, such as the central workers' council, was of interest to Lenin's and Stalin's disciples only in so far as they could exploit it for their own immediate purposes. When this proved impossible, the revolutionaries were quickly denounced as counter-revolutionaries, bourgeois nationalists, or anarchists.

But on November 14 Kadar still tried to ingratiate himself with the councils. He wanted them to stop the strike. To achieve this aim, he was ready to promise anything.

To the workers' delegates who expressed their wish to see Nagy return to the government, Kadar replied in an almost conciliatory tone: "Nagy is at present at the Yugoslav embassy, that is, in foreign territory," he said. "Under these circumstances we cannot get in touch with him to offer him the premiership. But as soon as he returns to Hungarian territory, we are ready to negotiate with him."

It is hard to believe that Kadar was speaking in good faith. We know, from disclosures made later by the Yugoslavs, that on November 14 he was already negotiating with them concerning the fate of Nagy and that he had decided to deport him to a satellite country. Kadar was scarcely more sincere when he assured the workers of his desire to hold "clean and honest" elections, with the participation of several parties. "It is probable that our party will be defeated in such elections," he said. "But the Communists are strong enough to reconquer the workers' confidence."

He also promised to publish without delay all the trade agreements that Hungary had concluded with the Russians. He assured the councils that he had obtained from the Russians a pledge to stop the deportations. He showed himself intransigent only on the point of neutrality. But on the whole his statements seemed to promise a satisfactory solution of the crisis, and on November 16 the central workers' council ordered general resumption of work.

As though to seal this agreement and to give a supplementary token of its good will, the Kadar government published a list of Stalinists and Rakosists who had been definitely removed from office. The list included Gero, Hegedus, Andor Berei (former chief planner) and his wife Elisabeth Andics, who had long been one of the pillars of the censorship, Laszlo Piros, former minister of the interior, Chief Prosecutor Gyorgy Non, Istvan Bata.

Tension relaxed somewhat. Encouraged by Kadar's concessions, one of the most remarkable members of the Kadar team, Istvan Bibo, leader of the Petofi party, wrote a memorandum of which he sent copies, on November 20, to Kadar, to the Russians, to the revolutionary committees, and to the

workers' councils. The document outlined the conditions of a
modus vivendi between the Hungarians and the Russians. Bibo
explained, to begin with, that the Kadar government could not
remain in power if the Russians withdrew, for it was obvious
that this government would be swept out of office the moment
the Russians left. Moreover, he went on to say, the Communist
party had fallen into disrepute because of the Russian intervention, and hence the one-party system could no longer be
maintained. On the other hand, Russia feared that free elections would unleash a tidal wave of anti-communism and anti-
Sovietism, which would create a permanent tension between
Hungary and Russia, something nobody could wish for. In
order to break this vicious circle, Bibo made the following
suggestions:

1. The Nagy government was to be restored and the
sixteen-point program of October 23 put into effect.

2. Hungary was to proclaim her independence rather than
her neutrality. Her government would choose between two
solutions: Either it would continue to adhere to the Warsaw
Pact, on condition that it be no longer a military alliance but
a consultative body, to which Yugoslavia would be admitted;
or Hungary would denounce the Warsaw Pact, and sign a non-
aggression treaty with Russia.

3. A general amnesty was to be granted to all political
offenders who had acted in good faith. The administrative
departments were to be reorganized, and appointments made
on the basis of real competence. Communists were not to be
excluded.

4. The Soviet troops were to evacuate Hungary by stages
within six weeks. After the evacuation of Budapest and the
southern regions (first stage), the Nagy government would be
reinstated and the revolutionary committees would be given
legal recognition. After the evacuation of western Hungary
(second stage), the Hungarian army would occupy the Aus-

trian border and prevent emigration. After the evacuation of eastern Hungary (third and fourth stages), a new provisional Parliament elected by the committees would determine the internal and international status of Hungary.

5. Hungary was to remain a republic. It would be ruled by a democratic and parliamentarian government. The agrarian reform and the nationalization measures would remain in force. The workers would share in the management and the profits of enterprises. There would be religious freedom. The electoral system would be determined later.

6. The United Nations was not to be asked to send troops to Hungary, unless the withdrawal of the Russian troops provoked serious incidents.

Bibo's proposals were favorably received by the writers' and the workers' councils. But neither Kadar nor the Russians replied to them. The Russians distrusted the Hungarians, even the most moderate.

Moreover, the lull did not last long. While Kadar and his ministers continued to receive numerous workers' delegations and to make the most alluring promises to them, the arrests and deportation of young people continued all over the country. Under these circumstances many workers criticized the order to resume work, arguing that it should have been issued only after the government had begun to carry out its promises. Partisans of moderation and those of intransigence clashed within the central workers' council. Kadar had achieved his first objective—to break the unanimity of the resistance.

However that may be, on November 19, work in the factories was resumed only partially; but from that moment on Kadar's attitude stiffened. Marosan, his minister of culture, who had been given this post probably because of his extraordinary lack of culture—a former baker, he had always distinguished himself by his brutality and unbridled demagogy— violently denounced the "counter-revolutionaries," charging them with instigating the strikes. At the same time the government threatened to dismiss all strikers. This change of attitude coincided with the arrival of Soviet reinforcements. Moreover, the new Hungarian police began to take shape. It was organized by the greatest Soviet police expert, General Serov, head of the Soviet security department.

Serov's tactics can be described as a war of nerves. His victims were harassed without respite. He aroused their hopes, then hit them on the head. The moment they came to, he spoke to them gently, reassured them, only to deliver another well-aimed blow at the right moment. These police methods, which are characteristic of brain washing, were now applied to an entire nation.

On November 19, a government spokesman congratulated the central workers' council. Two days later, on November 21, Kadar issued a decree endorsing the workers' councils in all the factories, but confining their functions to supervision of working conditions. The councils were not to interfere with the activities of the trade-union committees or the state-appointed managers. The decree was an immense disappointment for the workers' councils, which had assumed actual management of the factories and representation of the workers' interests. The central workers' councils called an important meeting at the People's Stadium in Budapest, to discuss the new decree. The meeting was to be attended by five hundred delegates representing Budapest and most provincial centers, as well as delegations of students and intellectuals. But when the delegates, at the appointed hour, arrived at the stadium, Soviet soldiers and Hungarian policemen manning tanks and armored cars turned them back. The delegates decided to hold their meeting at the central streetcar depot. The police followed them there. Then an officer ordered them to disperse on the ground that they intended to set up a new government and start a new uprising. The delegates denied the charge, and after long bargaining persuaded the police to withdraw.

In protest against this vexation, the workers' assembly decided unanimously to issue a call for a forty-eight-hour general strike, beginning at midnight November 23. It also demanded that the central workers' council be immediately recognized as the representative body of all Hungarian workers. If the government acceded to this demand, the council would stop the strike on November 24. Otherwise the strike would continue. Furthermore, the delegates asked the government to resume negotiations with the central workers' council on the basis of the program of November 15, which, as we have seen, provided for the return of Imre Nagy, the evacuation of the country by the Russians, and the liberation of all prisoners captured by the Russians.

In the face of this display of firmness, Kadar immediately beat a retreat and renewed his promises. On November 22, the trade-union newspaper *Nepakarat* printed an editorial endorsing one of the workers' major objectives—the independence of the trade-unions. "The Hungarian trade-unions want to rid themselves, and they *will* rid themselves, of state control. . . . The trade-unions must be independent, and neither the state nor the party will be permitted to interfere in their internal affairs. It would be absurd for tens of thousands of workers to be subjected to party control, when the majority of these workers do not belong to the party. . . . We must see to it that the election of new trade-union leaders takes place on a strictly democratic basis," the editorial concluded. "Henceforth the choice of the leaders will be determined by the confidence of the workers and not by party membership." That was sweet music to the workers.

Furthermore, on November 22, Kadar promised a delegation of the central workers' council that he would recognize the workers' councils as consultative bodies and that the factory managers would be elected by the workers. Kadar stipulated only that the councils must be elected by secret ballot, and command a majority of at least two thirds of the workers of a given factory. The delegation accepted this condition, all the more willingly because Kadar hinted that the Nagy affair would soon be settled. Kadar also said that he had opened negotiations with Bela Kovacs and other parties with a view to forming "a left Socialist government of national unity." (*Sic.* Cf. a report from the Budapest correspondent of the Yugoslav newspaper *Politika.*)

It seemed that all difficulties had now been cleared away. The workers' delegates and Kadar signed an agreement under which the central workers' council was to order resumption of work on November 23, instead of November 24, although the overwhelming majority of the workers had followed the council's call for a general strike.

At the time this agreement was signed, Imre Nagy and his friends had already left the Yugoslav embassy. At 1 A.M. on November 23, the embassy issued a communiqué to this effect, mentioning a letter addressed by Nagy to the Belgrade government, expressing thanks for his eighteen-day asylum.

This report was confirmed in a broadcast by Radio Budapest at 12 A.M. But at 3 P.M. it was learned in Belgrade that the Yugoslav government had asked Kadar to inform it at once why Imre Nagy, Geza Losonczy, Ferenc Donath, and the other refugees had not returned to their homes after leaving the Yugoslav embassy. "If these persons fail to return to their homes," the note said, "the Yugoslav government will consider this a flagrant violation of the friendly relations between the two countries."

The Abduction of Imre Nagy

The abduction of Imre Nagy will no doubt be remembered as one of the most cynical provocations of contemporary history. Those responsible for this act were obviously determined to demonstrate to the Hungarian people that their hope for Nagy's return to the government was vain, to Kadar that he amounted to nothing without the Russians, and to the Yugoslavs that the Soviet Union was not concerned with their prestige, and that it would deal harshly with all manifestations of national communism.

Late in the afternoon of November 23, the Hungarian radio broadcast an official communiqué which said: "On November 4, former Premier Nagy and several of his friends went to the Yugoslav embassy asking for asylum. The asylum expired on November 22. More than two weeks ago, Imre Nagy and his friends asked the government's permission to leave Hungarian territory for another Socialist country. With the consent of the government of the Romanian People's Republic, Imre Nagy and his friends left for Romania on November 23."

By the time this communiqué was issued the Hungarians had learned from foreign broadcasts that the Yugoslav government had protested against the disappearance of Imre Nagy. But even without such a protest, no one in Budapest would have believed that Nagy and his companions had consented to leave their refuge for Romania. From the outset it was surmised that they had been kidnaped by the Russians. This hypothesis was confirmed a few days later in the light of the disclosures published by the Belgrade *Borba*. Once again the Russians had shown themselves faithful to certain traditions of Oriental cunning of the crudest kind. The group that had sought refuge in the Yugoslav embassy included Nagy's closest associates. Among them were Geza Losonczy; Ferenc Donath; Gabor Tanczos, secretary-general of the Petofi Society; Sandor Haraszti, an old Communist militant who during the insurrection had been elected president of the Journalists' Union, and who had become famous in 1955 when he slapped the chief of police, Vladimir Farkas; Ferenc Janosi, Imre Nagy's son-in-law, former secretary-general of the Patriotic Front, whom Rakosi had dismissed in 1955; Laszlo Rajk's widow; Zoltan Szanto, former ambassador to Belgrade and Paris; Zoltan Vas, former president of the planning commission and commissar of supplies in Nagy's government of November 3; and the philosopher Gyorgy Lukacs. Szanto, Vas, and Lukacs had left the embassy a few days before Nagy; they had been arrested, then released, only to vanish again.

As we have said, the negotiations between Belgrade and Budapest concerning the fate of these refugees had begun immediately after Kadar's return to Budapest. From the outset the Yugoslavs had insisted on the fact that Nagy wished to stay in Hungary, "in the interest of normalizing the situation," and that he wished to go to Yugoslavia only if he were not permitted to stay. But he and all his companions had explicitly refused to go to Romania.

After long bargaining, a basic agreement was reached on November 16. Kadar told the Yugoslav ambassador, Soldatic, that he was ready to give the written guarantees requested by Tito. Nagy and his companions, he declared, would be in a position to leave the embassy the next day, that is, November 17. It was agreed that there would be an exchange of letters confirming the agreement.

The Yugoslavs had begun to draw up the document, when Kadar's representatives declared to Soldatic that Nagy and Losonczy must publicly renounce their ministerial posts, express their support of Kadar's struggle against the counter-revolution, admit their past errors, and pledge themselves not to oppose the policies of the Hungarian government. Moreover, the sixteen refugees were to go to another Socialist country and stay there until the situation in Hungary became normal.

Imre Nagy and his companions informed the Yugoslavs that they rejected these proposals.

On November 18, the Belgrade government sent a new note to Kadar, reiterating its earlier requests, and asking for a written guarantee of the personal safety of the refugees. On November 21, Kadar finally acquiesced. In a note handed to Soldatic, he stated: "In order to settle this affair, the Hungarian government, in conformity with the proposal stated in the letter that the Yugoslav government addressed to me on November 18, 1956, hereby confirms the declaration made orally on several occasions, according to which it wishes to inflict no punishment on Nagy and the members of his group for their past activities."

On the strength of this note, which did not grant the refugees explicit permission to stay in Hungary or to go to Yugoslavia, Nagy and his companions left the embassy. They were escorted by two Yugoslav diplomats. At the door the party was invited to board a motor coach, where a Soviet officer joined it. Then the motor coach, preceded and followed by Russian cars, drove to the Soviet military headquarters. The Yugoslav diplomats protested against this unexpected procedure. They were unceremoniously ejected. "But this is a violation of the agreement signed by the Hungarian government," one of the diplomats exclaimed.

The Soviet officer in charge of the operation shrugged his shoulders: "This is none of our concern. I was ordered to take care of these people."

Then two armored cars replaced the cars that had escorted the motor coach, and drove off with the latter for an unknown destination.

This was an obvious snub to Tito, who had up until that moment displayed extreme eagerness not to dissatisfy the Soviet Union. At this point it may be interesting to review the fluctuations of Yugoslav policy in the face of the Hungarian insurrection, which had badly shaken Eastern Europe, and had profound repercussions in Yugoslavia.

Three stages are discernible in Belgrade's attitude toward the insurrection. During the first stage, between October 23 and November 1, the Belgrade press and government spokesmen voiced both anxious surprise at the uprising and sympathy for Nagy and Kadar. On October 26, for instance, *Borba* voiced Yugoslav satisfaction with Kadar's election as first party secretary, replacing Gero, and pointed out that "the tendencies expressed in Kadar's and Nagy's speeches are in harmony with the demands of the Hungarian masses." Like all other Yugoslav newspapers, *Borba* compared the Hungarian situation to the Polish one, saying that in both countries "all resistance to the progress of democratization . . . is futile." The appearance of Soviet troops, "whose intervention should have been averted above everything else," was judged severely. As for the uprising, it was blamed on the Stalinists, particularly Rakosi, "the most hated man in Hungary," and his "right hand, Gero." At the same time, *Borba* referred to Imre Nagy as "the man who enjoys the country's full confidence and who is believed capable of carrying out far-reaching reforms in the political and economic life of Hungary."

Clearly, at that time the Yugoslav leaders were still hoping that their liberal friends would gain the upper hand in the Kremlin and impose a Gomulkist solution in Hungary. This hope was reflected in Tito's letter addressed to the Presidium of the Hungarian Communist party and dated October 29, which said: "The Yugoslav working class fully understands the bitterness of the Hungarian people after the errors and crimes of the past. It would, however, be extremely harmful for the interests of the laboring masses of Hungary, for socialism in general, and for international peace, if this legitimate dissatisfaction undermined the workers' faith in socialism and in the indispensable development of Socialist democracy." It was also reflected in the attitude taken by the Yugoslav delegate Brillej at the United Nations Security Council, who ab-

stained from voting on the Western proposal to include the
Hungarian situation in the agenda. While reiterating his government's opposition "to the participation of foreign troops in
a national action," Brillej spoke against "the political exploitation of a tragic situation."

The Yugoslav correspondents in Hungary gave much place
in their reports to the emergence of revolutionary workers'
councils, observing that "the Hungarian government's attitude
toward them varied." *Politika* of October 29 said that the government "does not encourage their creation but does not condemn it either. It recognizes them where they are in existence,
but regards them as political groups and not as government
organs. . . . The majority of the members of these councils are
capable men who up until now have been kept out of public
life."

During the second period, from November 1 to November
10, the Yugoslav leaders were bewildered by the evolution of
the political situation in Hungary (proclamation of neutrality,
renascence of the old parties of the 1945 coalition, Nagy's
support of free elections). Their perplexity was further increased as the threat of a second Soviet intervention began to
take shape, all the more so because, as the *Borba* correspondent wrote on November 1, "the Hungarian Communist party
gives the impression of no longer being in existence." Belgrade
was worried by the strong shift to the right, reflected in the
growing influence of the Social Democrats, the Smallholders,
and the men around Mindszenty. "Every concession to the
forces of the old regime in Hungary automatically leads to
concessions to anti-Socialist ideas and reactionary tendencies,"
said *Borba* on November 2. Belgrade was obviously disappointed with Nagy, who "had let things get out of hand," and
worried by the prospect of a westernization of Hungary and
the return of liberal parliamentarianism in a neighboring country. Therefore the second Soviet intervention was regarded by

the Yugoslav leaders as a lesser evil, although in theory they opposed "the use of foreign troops for the purpose of clarifying the internal situation." A communiqué of the Tanyug press agency of November 4 said that "peace, progress, and independence in East European countries can exist only on the basis of socialism." Belgrade shared the Soviet view, according to which the abolition of the one-party system in Hungary would endanger socialism and pave the way for an "inevitable" restoration of capitalism. Under these circumstances, a well-timed intervention was judged to be preferable to a return to the old regime. Belgrade seemed to take at its face value the Soviet "declaration of intent" of October 30. Tito apparently thought that the Soviet intervention would remove the "counter-revolutionary" threat and would be followed by a democratization of Hungary *à la Gomulka.* The Yugoslav leaders knew Janos Kadar; and they approved his programmatic speech of November 4. Expecting that Hungary would be given as much independence as Poland, they instructed their delegate at the United Nations to vote against the resolution condemning the Russian intervention, which had been introduced by the Western powers.

The third stage of the Yugoslav evolution began on November 10. On that day the seven Yugoslav journalists who had witnessed the Hungarian events returned to Belgrade. One of them, the correspondent of *Politika,* summed up his impressions as follows: "The Hungarian masses are in a state of unrest. The Communists are compromised as a result of the Rakosi policies; the people are disillusioned, and extremely discontented by the Soviet intervention. While Nagy failed, Kadar's task seems even more difficult. No one believes anything. The people are irritated, and that is why many of them refuse to lay down their arms. The reactionary forces are more active than ever, and the conditions are favorable to their activities."

The malaise that is reflected in these statements is accounted for by the reaction of Yugoslav public opinion, which clearly condemned the Soviet intervention, and by the attacks which the Stalinists in Russia and in the satellite countries had launched against Yugoslavia. On November 8, the Moscow *Pravda* had printed an article by Enver Hodja, Tito's enemy Number One, in which he charged Belgrade with having confused the Communists by grotesque ideas of national communism and democratization. As the Russian attacks grew more violent, Belgrade replied in kind. On November 11, in a speech delivered at Pula, Tito blamed the Kremlin Stalinists for the tragic events in Hungary. He still referred to the second Soviet intervention as "a lesser evil," but at the same time he condemned the view that "military strength can settle everything." It was as though, before the poignant spectacle of Hungarian resistance, the former rebel had won the upper hand over the party dictator. "A people, barehanded or almost, can oppose a formidable resistance when it pursues a goal . . . when it seeks liberty and independence!" he exclaimed.

During all that time the Yugoslav government continued negotiations with Kadar concerning the status of Imre Nagy and his companions. Tito, who had declared that Khrushchev, Mikoyan, and Shepilov were men of good will, had not doubted their word; and the abduction of Nagy unleashed a storm of indignation in Belgrade. This "felonious deed," perpetrated three days after Tito's speech at Pula had been denounced by the Tass agency, convinced the Yugoslavs that they had overestimated Moscow's good will and perhaps also the intelligence of the Russian rulers.

Several weeks later, on December 7, Kardelj expounded the Yugoslav view on Hungary in a speech delivered at the national assembly. His arguments were as subtle as they were embarrassed. He recognized that despite the presence of "reactionary elements, it was more than likely that the Socialist forces would have succeeded in preserving the Socialist basis of Hungarian society." How then could the second Soviet intervention be justified, even from a purely "Socialist" point of view? It was doubtless in order not to disavow the attitude adopted by Yugoslavia after November 4 that Kardelj advanced the thesis that Soviet intervention would have been justified only if Kadar had subsequently adopted a policy enabling the workers to exert real influence through their councils. At the same time, Kardelj reproached Kadar for "fearing the workers' councils." According to him, the Hungarian uprising had proved the correctness of the "democratic Socialist" policy that the Yugoslav Communists had pursued since 1949, and it encouraged them to continue on this path, which Gomulka's Poland was now also entering. But the deterioration of the Hungarian situation continued to worry the Yugoslav leaders, who disliked having next door a Communist regime that was upheld by foreign troops and spurned by the entire nation.

Kadar Against the Workers' Councils

The abduction of Imre Nagy gave the signal for a decisive test of strength between the Kadar government and the workers' councils. The Russians had made it unmistakably clear that they would not negotiate; that they had decided to ignore Imre Nagy and his group; that they were looking for lackeys rather than partners; and that they would not consider any compromise solution before breaking the backbone of the opposition.

At that moment the Russians had barely scratched the surface of Hungarian resistance. The morning of November 30, an appeal had been posted in Budapest calling on the population to show its disapproval of Kadar by stopping all work for an hour. From 2 to 3 P.M. Budapest had the appearance of a dead city. The streets were completely deserted. No one could mistake the meaning of this demonstration.

Later in the day, the central workers' council met to discuss Kadar's embarrassed account of the abduction of Nagy, which violated all his previously made promises. The members of the council were appalled. Even before they had reached any decision, the Csepel council had issued an appeal for a general strike in protest against the abduction. But the members of the central workers' council hesitated to extend the appeal to the country as a whole; the partisans of moderation and negotiation were beginning to gain the upper hand. It was not certain, they argued, that Kadar had been responsible for the abduction; more likely, the Russians had forced his hand. And they concluded that in the interests of the workers the council represented, it should display the utmost patience. Finally, the council decided to ask Kadar to reveal Nagy's whereabouts. Moreover, it demanded that the negotiations with Nagy be conducted jointly by the Kadar government and the council, "such negotiations being urgent and indispensable for the realization of national unity and the normalization of production."

Kadar did not fail to realize that the council had begun to waver. On Sunday, November 25, he received the workers' delegates in the Parliament building. He began by telling them that the government would accept the council's demands as a basis for negotiations—and Nagy's participation in the government was one of those demands! But Kadar immediately contradicted his own statement, telling the bewildered workers that the Nagy affair had become "a thing of the past." And the premier, who only a few days before had declared his willingness to include Nagy in his Cabinet, went on to draw up a full-fledged indictment against his former friend: "Nagy committed an impardonable sin against his people, since he took the side of the White Terror," he said. "He also sinned against communism, since he condoned, instead of exposing them, the counter-revolutionary massacres, and the manhunts organized against party members. On November 4, he called on the people to fight the Soviet troops, whose intervention had been requested in order to put an end to the White terrorists' murders. And when he saw that his position was hopeless, he packed his trunks, left the Parliament building by a secret staircase, and asked for asylum in the Yugoslav embassy."

He concluded this fantastic story with the assertion that Nagy had actually informed him of his wish to leave the country. "We had no longer anything to do with him, and since the Russian government was willing to give him asylum . . ."

The workers were skeptical. Kadar went on to say that he had promised Nagy and his friends that he would not start any judicial proceedings against them, "even though they were heavily responsible for the events."

"All these are lies," one of the delegates muttered. "They were deported, pure and simple."

"Not at all," Kadar retorted calmly, and he repeated that Nagy had left the country of his own accord, adding that this was preferable in any case. "Just imagine what would have happened if a counter-revolutionary gang, for the sole purpose of embarrassing us, had attacked Nagy or any of his group in their home? If they had been murdered, we would have protested in vain, no one would have believed us."

"But you said that you were planning to broaden your government by admitting Nagy, leaders of other parties, and independent experts."

"This is still my intention," Kadar said. "But I cannot carry it out before this insane strike is stopped, and order is restored." He added that workers who failed to report on Monday, November 26, at the latest would not be paid their November wages and would be dismissed.

"And how about higher wages?"

"Don't forget that I myself was once a worker. I understand

your worries. But you must understand for your part that any raise in wages might cause an inflation."

The delegates left to report their conversation with Kadar to the council. The next day they visited him again, and presented three immediate demands:

1.   That contact with Imre Nagy be established at once with the consent of the Romanian authorities.

2.   That the workers' councils be authorized to publish their own newspaper: they were dissatisfied with the trade-union organ *Nepakarat,* which distorted their views and reflected solely those of the government.

3.   That the decree concerning the organization of workers' councils be revised.

Kadar declared that he would be unable to consider the first demand before two or three weeks, and that he would discuss the others with his Cabinet. The delegates, to show their good will, pledged themselves to hasten the end of the strike; at the same time they voiced their dissatisfaction with Kadar's account of the situation.

As the negotiations dragged on, it became every day more obvious that Kadar's aim was to demoralize the council and discredit it in the eyes of the workers. He displayed a certain skill in this war of nerves. In the meantime, the deportations and arrests had resumed. Schools were searched, workers' delegates were imprisoned; some were released, only to be arrested again.

Then suddenly Kadar—this inconsistent, tormented, hated, sincere, and hypocritical Kadar—took a sterner tone. "Free elections? You're joking!" he declared to a delegation of workers, adding that his party, numbering 900,000 members, had nothing to fear from free elections. The workers were amazed: where had he got that figure? Didn't everyone know that if free elections were held Kadar would gather a few thousand votes at the most?

On November 27, the government began an offensive against the central workers' council. There was no longer question of Imre Nagy's return; the workers themselves, discouraged, had dropped this demand. Kadar also refused to authorize the council to publish its own newspaper. The council riposted by appealing to the workers to stop buying and reading the official party and trade-union organs: "We demand freedom of the press." But by now Kadar ignored the council; he had reorganized the trade-union federation on a "democratic basis," having appointed, among its leaders, a number of Social Democrats who had once been popular but who were now old and harmless. Most of these, incidentally, learned of their appointments only from newspapers.

On December 4, the government decreed the dissolution of the revolutionary committees that had been created in the administrative departments. On December 5, several hundred demonstrators gathered in front of the British and United States embassies to protest against the government policies. On the same day, fifteen thousand women carrying flags demonstrated before the Parliament building. They were dispersed by the Soviet police. On December 5, the Hungarian police forced several hundred officials to organize a pro-government demonstration which was staged under the surveillance of the AVO and a few Soviet armored cars. The parade of the pro-Kadarists who shouted, "Peace! Order! Calm! Long live the worker-peasant government! The strikers are counter-revolutionaries!" ran into a group of counter-demonstrators. According to an eyewitness, "The cortege was pelted with stones at several places, and a shot was fired at the pro-government demonstrators in Octagonal Square. Then the police opened fire." There were casualties. On December 7, the central workers' council handed Kadar a protest against the arrest of a large number of members of workers' councils in the capital and in the provinces.

On December 9, Kadar struck his great blow. The government proclaimed martial law, and decreed the dissolution of the central workers' council and of all other workers' councils, except the factory councils. In a statement justifying these measures, the government charged the central workers' council with having encouraged and organized counter-revolutionary provocations, and having permitted its ranks to be infiltrated by reactionary elements. On the same day, Munnich's agents tried to disarm the workers' militias, and arrested several workers' delegates.

The central workers' council riposted to this new provocation by ordering a forty-eight-hour general strike, beginning December 12. The workers demonstrated in the streets; traffic was stopped once again; fighting was resumed in several provincial industrial centers, particularly in the mining regions.

On December 13, the police arrested two leaders of the central workers' council, Sandor Bali and Sandor Racz. The workers of the Beloyannis plant, where the two young leaders had been employed, took the initiative of extending the strike twenty-four hours and even longer. Their example was followed. On December 14, no smoke rose from the chimneys of the Budapest factories. The Beloyannis factory, occupied by six thousand strikers demanding the release of their comrades, was surrounded by Soviet troops and the Hungarian militia. The Csepel workers also went on strike, defying Munnich's militiamen and the Soviet tanks stationed in front of the workshops.

This much must be said for Kadar: he was not a bit discouraged by all these signs of resistance, which might have moved a softer heart. Once again he tried to influence the members of the central workers' council, though this council was now illegal, by means of new promises. He proposed to organize elections for the workers' councils on "a truly democratic" basis; the government, he said, would recognize such councils once they had been endorsed by the working class, and grant them wide powers. Then, he added, Christmas was around the corner, a truce was necessary in any case. Once again Kadar spread rumors that he was about to broaden his Cabinet. He beat all records of political mendacity, combining threats, promises, concessions, conciliatory appeals, and brutality in a bewildering cacophony. He released Sandor Bali, one of the leaders of the central workers' council, who had been arrested on December 13, but kept the other in prison; some deportees returned, but a new wave of arrests swept the provinces; and the Soviet tanks withdrew from the factories, only to return a few days later.

Christmas marked a period of meditation: Hungary remembered her dead, and hoped against hope. Both the government and the people respected the truce of God. India sent a special ambassador to Budapest, he saw a number of influential people, and collected data for his report to Nehru; his visit strengthened the current of hope that spread in the country. Kadar hinted that he was preparing a program that would rally all sincere patriots. The curfew hour was moved ahead.

On January 1, when Khrushchev and Malenkov came to Budapest to preside over a meeting of Communist leaders of the Soviet Union, Bulgaria, Czechoslovakia, Romania, and Hungary, the capital had sobered down and was fit to receive the illustrious guests. The purpose of the meeting, which was held from January 1 to 4, was to consolidate Kadar's position and discourage his opponents by a show of strength, and to tighten the bonds uniting the orthodox members of the bloc. Yugoslavia and Poland, which had voiced heretical views on the Hungarian uprising, were significantly absent.

The communiqué on this meeting was published on January 6, 1957, simultaneously with Kadar's program, which had been so anxiously awaited, but which failed to clarify the situation. The program was couched in very general terms, and it laid particular stress on the need to strengthen the state. The only important concessions to public opinion it contained related to agriculture and the Church. Farmers were permitted to buy land. "Ceilings for family-owned farms will be 10 to 12 hectares. Fields may be leased for participation or money. Free sales of produce will be secured, with the exception of produce of state monopolies. A reserve of land will be constituted with a view to meeting the demands of the peasants who had suffered losses as a result of the foundation of co-operatives." As for the Church, the statement "guaranteed religious classes in the schools." A few weeks later, however, Kadar was compelled to go back on this promise, which touched off a real stampede of children to Sunday schools. Whereas before the uprising only 4 to 5 per cent of the parents had dared to register their children for religious classes (most parents, in order to avoid trouble, taught their children the catechism at home), now everybody was rushing to church; and children whose parents had forbidden them to attend religious classes were persecuted by their schoolmates. Thus seven years of anti-religious propaganda had resulted in an unprecedented strengthening of religion. Adherence to the Church was a method of protesting against the totalitarian regime. The young, down to the smallest children, abhorred communism, and three months after the insurrection, on January 23, most Hungarian schoolchildren demonstrated against the regime by sporting tricolor cockades and lighting bonfires in the school yards and the streets with their Russian textbooks.

Kadar's program completely ignored the demands of the working class. After January 6, the government reinstated in a number of factories the managers and chief engineers who had been dismissed by the workers' councils. In protest against these measures, the central council of Csepel and several other councils resigned collectively. Then Kadar made new promises, and some minor concessions. The councils stayed on, but their powers were progressively abridged. The government first induced them to consent to the reopening of party offices in the factories, then to co-operate with the party, and finally to expel undesirables.

Day after day, the government organ, *Nepszabadsag,* and the trade-union newspaper, *Nepakarat,* printed articles attacking one or another workers' council, which was accused of including suspicious, bourgeois, Social Democratic, or even criminal members. The councils could fight against such charges only by calling strikes. But the workers could not go on strike every day, especially since the government had a formidable weapon against them. As a result of the shortage of fuel and raw materials, economic experts had foreseen that a certain number of factories would have to be closed completely or partly as early as December. This meant that the government could lay off workers at will. It is true that in the meantime Kadar had offered the workers' councils the ambiguous privilege of designating the workers to be dismissed. In many instances, the councils used the opportunity to rid themselves of Kadar's agents. This was an episode in the daily skirmishes between Kadar and the workers. The government for its part was on the lookout and often forced the councils to rehire the expelled Communists. Another cause for friction between the government and the workers was the government's effort to reinstate the factory committees, which it planned to use as a counterpoise to the councils.

By the end of February the workers' councils had been largely neutralized. It was no doubt to celebrate its victory over the workers that the government at that time ordered that the Red star, which the insurgents had replaced by the national emblem, be restored on the roofs of the factories. This operation led to a large number of violent clashes between the police and the workers. It would be difficult to find a more poignant illustration of the paradoxical results of the Hungarian tragedy.

The Red star, once the symbol of internationalism and freedom, had become in the eyes of the overwhelming majority of the Hungarian workers a sign of servitude and foreign domination.

The Kadar government's efforts to void the achievements of the October uprising and to deprive, piecemeal, the working class of all the attributes of its political and economic power were marked by such methodological skill that they will no doubt be studied by all the anti-proletarian dictatorships in the world. If the October uprising was a revolution—and it was one in the eyes of the Hungarians—the restoration of the old order as carried out by Kadar could only be a counter-revolution. The Hungarian workers regard it as such. They say that Kadar practices Rakosism without Rakosi, just as Khrushchev practices Stalinism without Stalin.

It is true that under the circumstances he could not have acted otherwise. His predicament was best summed up by one of his supporters, who wrote: "In October, 1956, the Hungarian masses strove for a higher standard of living, national independence, and democratization. But after November 4, what could the government do, even if it had the best intentions? After the insurrection, the national income dropped by 12 billion florins; the course of the events had led to a foreign intervention; and democracy was hampered for reasons of state. How can this threefold vicious circle be broken? Perhaps by patient, stubborn work, in an atmosphere of confidence. But for several years the country has been steadily losing confidence in its leaders, and the events of October proved that the people's patience had been exhausted. . . ."

In the face of such general distrust, Kadar could assert his authority and obtain support only by means of intimidation and repression. On January 9, the Karhatalom (the new name of the political police whose effectives are estimated at ten thousand men) began a systematic drive against the former insurgents in the workers' suburbs of Budapest, in the universities, and in various provincial towns. The party press assumed a harsh tone: it no longer spoke of patriots, but of counter-revolutionaries, and the chiefs of the National Guard, which had been created in October, were branded as gangsters.

The new chief prosecutor, Geza Szenasi, formerly of the AVO, epitomized the government's view in a statement made to the Hungarian Telegraphic Agency. Referring to the measures he was taking to stop the exodus of Hungarians fleeing the regime, he said: "Humanity is out of place. Whether by means of summary procedures or by regular trials, we must show the Fascists that it is futile to resist the Karhatalom."

On January 10, Jozsef Dudas and his aide-de-camp Szabo were sentenced to death and executed. This was the first of a series of trials the purpose of which was not merely to avenge the Avos who had fallen defending the regime and to intimidate the enemies of Kadar, but also to defame the insurrection. Thus, the defendants in a trial held by the special court of Budapest late in February included both genuine revolutionaries, such as Obersovszky, editor in chief of one of the most popular newspapers during the insurrection, *Igazsag* (Truth), and his collaborator, Jozsef Gali, author of a poignant play about Rajk, and common criminals who had infiltrated the ranks of the freedom fighters.

Kadar Against the Intellectuals

After the crushing of the insurrection its spirit survived in a number of organizations which, like the central workers' council, had been created during the uprising. One of these was the revolutionary intellectuals' council, which included the Writers' Union, the revolutionary students' committee, the Radio Workers' Union, the Journalists' Union, organizations of motion-picture actors, artists, architects, professors, etc.

The intellectuals' council was led by the Communist econo-

mist, Gyorgy Marko. On November 14, it called a general
strike of the intellectuals to continue until the six points of its
program, which it had posted on the walls of the Russian-occu-
pied capital, were carried out. This program was similar to
that of the central workers' council: it demanded Nagy's return
to the government, the evacuation of Hungary by the Russians,
neutrality, the implementation of the United Nations resolution on Hungary, and official recognition of the fact that the
uprising had not been a counter-revolution but a struggle for
national independence. Thus began this "strike of pens and
brains," which has no precedent in history, and which has continued to this day, despite the fact that early in December,
1956, the government dissolved the intellectuals' council at the
same time as the central workers' council. The various unions
which belonged to it have kept up the fight. The government's
efforts to obtain their co-operation have been of no avail. They
have yielded neither to blandishments nor to threats.

To be sure, Kadar could have ordered the arrest of the ring-
leaders as early as mid-November—they expected this—and
deported them to Romania at the same time as Nagy and his
group. But realizing their moral authority both at home and
abroad, Kadar avoided a headlong clash with the intellectuals;
he hoped to use them for his own purposes, to coax them into
co-operation, assuring them that their participation in the uprising would not be held against them, and that the government would continue, in the intellectual field, the policy of
liberalization of which the principal champions had been the
writers Hay and Dery. Kadar doubtless counted on the opportunism of some of the intellectuals, and the disillusionment of
others. But the intellectuals stood their ground, and all attempts
to divide them failed. Each of their meetings, held under the
noses of the Russian occupant and Kadar's militiamen, was a
new manifestation of national resistance.

In the meantime, a number of journalists had been authorized by their union to resume work at the radio, at the press agency, and on Kadar's newspaper, but on condition that they were never to be forced to say or write anything against their convictions. Thus it came about that one day an editorial in Kadar's newspaper was followed by this amazing note: "The Hungarian people's desire for independence is so powerful that there is no force in the world capable of destroying it. To be independent or to die, that is the choice of the Hungarians."

Defying the government, the writers and journalists developed their own diplomatic service: they kept in touch with Western writers' organizations, and missed no opportunity to bring their struggle to the attention of world public opinion. At the same time they gave an icy reception to the Soviet writers and journalists who came to Budapest to persuade them of the counter-revolutionary character of their activities.

On December 6, the government became impatient, and ordered the arrest of a number of young writers and journalists, among them the poet Etienne Forsy, the playwrights Jozsef Gali and Gyula Fekete, the historian Etienne Gaal, and the novelist Zoltan Molnar, who were charged with writing illegal pamphlets and editing illegal newspapers. They had also committed the crime of being rude to Soviet visitors. One of the most cultivated Communist journalists, Miklos Gimes, was imprisoned following a conversation he had had with the Indian ambassador. These arrests were meant as a stern warning. Kadar also tried to reduce the intellectuals by starvation: he banned the collections of foodstuffs and money that had been organized in their behalf in factories, administrative offices, and villages.

But the writers and journalists continued to hold out. When Gyorgy Marosan, Kadar's chief propagandist, denounced them as enemies of the people, they contemptuously rejected the charge. Then Marosan tried to infiltrate the Writers' Union, to intimidate its weaker members, and to mobilize its five or six

Stalinist members. Two of the latter, the colonel of the Russian army, Bela Illes, a mediocre novelist, and Gyorgy Boloni, an undistinguished Communist, published, in a French Communist newspaper, articles justifying the Soviet intervention. The Writers' Union sent a protest to Paris, declaring that Illes and Boloni "expressed the opinion of only an insignificant minority of Hungarian writers."

On December 25, the voluminous Christmas issue of Kadar's newspaper appeared without a single article, poem, or short story by a known writer.

Three days later, the Writers' Union held a plenary meeting to discuss—once again—its attitude toward the government. Tibor Dery, hero of the Petofi Society meeting of June 27, 1956, took the floor to reply to a letter addressed to the Union by the Soviet novelist Sholokhov, who had no doubt acted under government pressure. The text of this letter, which was immensely publicized in the world Communist press, said in substance: "As long as you fought against the Rakosi clique, I was with you. But then you went too far. You unwittingly opened the gate to the counter-revolution." Dery's answer, which his audience received with acclaim, was: "I do not question Sholokhov's good faith, but he knows nothing about our struggle. We invite him to come to Hungary and learn about the situation at firsthand."

At this last free meeting in Hungary, which was held on December 28, the pro-government minority chose as its spokesman Professor Trenchenyi Waldapfel, formerly a distinguished humanist who had become a Rakosist, and later a fanatic Kadarist. He was given full opportunity to express his views, but he convinced no one. By 270 votes to 8 and three abstentions, the writers adopted a resolution condemning the Soviet intervention and reasserting the demands of October.

The text of this resolution had been drafted jointly by Tibor Dery, Communist novelist; Peter Veres, peasant novelist, who had for some time been a fervent Rakosist; Gyula Illyes, peasant poet; and Aron Tamasi, nationalist novelist and playwright who had taken no part in politics since 1949. This shows the unity that persisted among writers of various tendencies. Edited by Tamasi and couched in moving terms, the resolution of December 28, the swan song of the Hungarian uprising, celebrated the revolution of October 23 as a "living spring originating in the Hungarian people's sufferings and striving for freedom." "It is with bitterness that we say that the Soviet government committed a historical error in staining the water of our spring with blood," the manifesto continued. "We venture to assert that a time will come when the misguided power will repent its mistake. . . . We warn the world against the erroneous belief that the revolution would have destroyed the conquests of socialism, had it not been for Soviet armies. We know this is not so. The working class, the peasants, and the intellectuals of our country were and still are partisans of the conquests of democracy and socialism. They did not want to suppress them but rather to bring them to life, by adjusting them to the structure and the national traditions of Hungary. . . . That is why we declare, individually and collectively, that we support the agrarian reform of 1945, as well as the nationalization of mines, factories, and banks. . . . But can the land yield enough produce if the peasant does not enjoy cultivating it? Can socialized property be fruitful in a society that is not healthy?"

The writers concluded by saying that unless their country is independent, the peasants, workers, and intellectuals can have no enthusiasm, and that prosperity is impossible without a healthy social structure. "It is precisely for the sake of social progress that we must secure national independence."

That was more than the government could bear. It resorted to drastic measures. On January 17, 1957, the Presidium of the people's republic, on a motion of Ferenc Munnich, minis-

ter of the interior, issued a decree suspending the activities of
the Writers' Union. On the same day Kadar summoned Peter
Veres, president of the Union, to inform him of the decree.
While Veres was absent the police occupied the Union's offices
and searched them minutely. Thus Kadar showed that he no
longer hesitated to make a frontal attack on a group that was
more sacred in the eyes of the Hungarians than the Church itself—the writers.

He went further. On January 20, Tibor Tardos, Zoltan Zelk,
and two young writers, officials of the Union, Balaza Lengyel
and Domokos Varga, and Sandor Novobacki, former editor of
Szabad Nep, were arrested. The Kadarist newspaper, which
reported these arrests a few days later, justified them on the
ground that the writers in question had engaged in subversive
and illegal activities. But it was clear that the government was
planning to use the imprisoned writers as hostages: Kadar declared that he would release them if their eminent colleagues
made due apologies and resumed work. The government also
applied other forms of pressure. There were violent denuncia-
tions and threats, such as those uttered on January 22 by
Karoly Kiss: "The dictatorship of the proletariat will not hesi-
tate to crush its enemies even if these are well-known writers."
Writers were put under strict police surveillance—for instance,
Tibor Dery was followed by two police cars wherever he went.
At the same time, non-Communist writers such as Milan Fust,
Jeno Heltai, and Laszlo Nemeth were suddenly the objects of
tributes and flatteries; to everyone's surprise, the National The-
ater was ordered to include in its repertory a play by Nemeth,
Galileo, which had been banned under Rakosi.

Then the government organized a kind of counter-union, in
which twenty or so second-rank writers were grouped around
a few moderate Stalinists (the most virulent Stalinist, Sandor
Gergely, whom everyone despised, was not included). The result of all these maneuvers was rather disappointing: a few

timorous individuals, such as Adras Ronas Mihaly, and some opportunists, such as Erno Urban or Lajos Mesterhazi, joined the government camp—and that was all. But even if Kadar's government, with all its various means of pressure, should eventually win this uneven battle against a handful of writers armed only with their consciences, the loyalty, perseverance, and courage of the overwhelming majority of Hungarian writers will inscribe a glorious page in the history of their people.

The journalists, too, displayed exceptional courage in defending the honor of their profession. For instance, on November 23, when the editor in chief of *Nepszabadsag,* Denes Polgar, resigned in protest against censorship, all the other editors resigned with him. (The government had forbidden Polgar to publish a comment in which he sided with the Yugoslav *Borba* against the Moscow *Pravda.*) For several months following this collective resignation, the newspaper was edited by a few party officials supervised by the Rakosist economist, Istvan Priss. Later, a few journalists threatened with starvation agreed to resume work, but on condition that their names did not appear in the newspaper. The fact that they imposed this condition and that it was accepted strikingly illustrates the unpopularity of the Kadar government at that time.

Kadar met with no more success among the students. Late in November, in order to regain a foothold among the university youth, who had participated en masse in the uprising, and 10 per cent of whom had emigrated to the West, Kadar reached a compromise with the revolutionary students' committee. Under this compromise, the committee, which had been democratically elected by students of twenty-two establishments of higher learning, was permitted to maintain its demands of October 23 concerning national independence and the withdrawal of the Soviet troops, but pledged itself to struggle against "all attempts, whether rightist or leftist, at a restoration," and expressed its willingness to co-operate with the government in the work of rehabilitation. At the same time, the committee accepted the creation of a large-scale organization grouping all the university unions (known as the MEFESZ).

The agreement was published on November 30. From that moment on, the government concentrated its efforts on the executive board of the MEFESZ, seeking to obtain its unconditional submission to party directives. But the students resisted fiercely. As a result, on January 8, the police raided the MEFESZ offices and arrested eight leaders of the organization, charging them with conspiracy. Day after day, the police raided the universities and students' homes, where it confiscated large quantities of weapons.

One of the most interesting episodes in this struggle between the government and the students was the rebellion of Sarospatak, an old university town and one of the strongholds of Protestantism in Hungary. Early in December, about three thousand students seized the town hall, disarmed the police, and for several days controlled the municipal administration. They were finally dislodged by Soviet troops.

Early in February most universities reopened. But the students took every opportunity to manifest their disapproval of the government policies; and the agitation was not appeased, even though hundreds, perhaps thousands, of students were arrested.

On February 26, Kadar's ministry of education announced that henceforth admission to universities would be governed by stricter standards, that the number of first-year students would be reduced from ten thousand to six thousand, and that only sons of peasants and workers would be eligible. Actually, in October, 1956, the overwhelming majority of students had been of proletarian extraction. By brandishing the threat of a new *numerus clausus* directed against the bourgeoisie, Kadar merely tried to conceal the fact that the students of popular

origin had displayed much more determination than their
petty-bourgeois comrades to destroy a regime which promised
them privileged posts but flouted their deepest aspirations—
their will to truth and justice, and their sense of national
dignity.

Reconstitution of the Party and the Police

One of Kadar's most arduous tasks was the reconstitution
of the party. As we have seen, the party collapsed completely
under the first blows of the insurrection: with nearly 900,000
members and governed by about 30,000 officials, it turned
out to be nothing but a clay giant. After November 4, Kadar
had to start from scratch. During the first days of his regime,
the party was the police, and its true chief was Munnich. But
this was merely one of the paradoxes that characterize Kadar's
entire experiment: this Titoist, this irreconcilable anti-Ra-
kosist, who had solemnly pledged himself never to return to
"the crimes of the past," to eliminate the Rakosi-Gero clique
from public life, and to build socialism "on a democratic basis
in conformity with the Hungarian national character and tradition," could not take one step without resorting to the help
of Rakosists, of the AVO, of the most sectarian party elements
who owed everything to Rakosi and whose authority was based
solely on terror.

At the beginning of his rule Kadar posed as a liberal Communist; his propaganda invoked the examples of China, Yugoslavia, and Poland rather than the example of Soviet Russia.
He addressed his appeals primarily to the "patriotic" militants
of the old party, those who had been influenced by the Petofi
Society and the Writers' Union. But these militants remained
faithful to Imre Nagy and refused to have anything to do with
a Communist party that denounced the uprising and justified
the Soviet intervention.

Under these circumstances, Kadar, who did not wish to ally

himself with prominent Rakosists and who could not count on the Nagyists, fell back on second-rate Rakosists. Thus he was compelled to put in charge of his organ, which he had hoped to build up as an attractive, popular, and liberal newspaper, a particularly harsh Rakosist, Istvan Friss. The only "democratic and national Communist" of note he could recruit was the journalist Gyula Kallai, former minister of information, who was appointed minister of culture on February 28, 1957. His other associates in the government and in the party were either fanatics devoted to Russia or so-called leftist opportunists like Gyorgy Marosan, a cynical sectarian who criticized Rakosi, not for his regime of terror, but for his failure to crush all the "counter-revolutionary" elements and to exterminate them physically.

In their recruiting campaign for the Socialist Workers' party, Kadar's agents first of all approached high party and government officials who had been dismissed during the uprising. Only after a nucleus of these had been formed did the campaign extend to the intellectuals and workers. But the workers showed themselves most impervious to the arguments of Kadar's propagandists. The majority of the workers' councils, as has been noted above, not only did not admit Kadarist members, but stubbornly resisted the recruiting agents, and in many cases drove them out of the factories. On December 1, only 360 out of a total of 30,000 workers at the Csepel plants were registered as party members, and most of these were office employees. "It is painful to acknowledge," Kadar's newspaper said, "that as a result of the crimes and errors perpetrated by the Rakosi-Gero clique, the people distrust the Communists. It will be very difficult to regain their confidence."

As for the intellectuals' reaction to Kadar's campaign of recruitment, we are informed about it thanks to the above-mentioned document drawn up by a group of Nagy partisans. This is, in effect, what Kadar's agents said to the Communist intellectuals: "Whether you like it or not, the party will for some time be the only legal political force in the country. If you boycott the party, you will sentence yourselves to a kind of exile within the country and complete intellectual paralysis. Your place will be taken by all sorts of opportunists, by non-Communists, nationalists, and peasants willing to co-operate with us. On the other hand, how can you forget that Kadar has always bitterly opposed Rakosi and Gero, and that he has adopted some of Nagy's reforms, including the abolition of compulsory deliveries and the setting up of workers' councils?" They could also point to the fact that under Kadar many more Western motion pictures were shown than under Rakosi; that the theaters were producing plays by Anouilh, Giraudoux, Priestley; that works by Hemingway, Faulkner, and Freud had been announced for publication; that the press was far less narrow-minded, and even printed pictures of lightly dressed beauty queens, portraits of Gina Lollobrigida and the new princess of Monaco. And then, had not Kadar dismissed Rakosi's chief collaborators? By joining Kadar's party, the intellectuals would have a chance to help the partisans of de-Stalinization and democratization.

According to our document, the intellectuals turned a deaf ear to these siren voices. Their reply was: "Under Kadar, we see that Rakosists blacklist other Rakosists. Moreover, the men who have been dismissed keep themselves in readiness: they are sure to return to the gravy pots, and then they will boast of having always been Stalinists, even at a time when Kadar did not dare admit being a Stalinist himself. What Kadar calls the specifically Hungarian path to socialism is the leadership of a Presidium inspired by Rakosi and Gero and taking its orders from the Russian ambassador, Andropov, and the chief of the Russian army command, General Lashchenko."

The majority of the Nagyist intellectuals did not join the party. As for those who let themselves be inveigled by Kadar's promises that the party regime would be a democratic one, they were bound to be disillusioned. For, as the party effectives increased, the leadership stiffened ideologically. In November, it had spoken of freedom of discussion within the party; in February, it insisted on the need for discipline. In November, new members had been admitted unconditionally—the party had been only too happy to receive them; after December 8, the party program demanded that all members repudiate Nagy's and Losonczy's deviations, recognize the counter-revolutionary character of the uprising, etc. In November, *Nepszabadsag* had defended the principle of free trade-unions; on February 28, the Central Committee branded this principle as a reactionary heresy, and *Nepszabadsag* said that "the duty of the trade-unions is to strengthen the authority of the state," and that strikes "are not a working-class weapon under the dictatorship of the proletariat." In November, the propaganda had been nationalistic; in February, it condemned national communism, and on the occasion of the thirty-ninth anniversary of the Red army, the Stalinist Bela Illes wrote: "The Soviet army is invincible, for the people's desire for freedom is invincible."

These shifts certainly unmasked the duplicity and inconsistency of the Kadar team, and they scarcely contributed to increasing the prestige of the party and to dispelling the mistrust about which its leaders had complained. And yet the party effectives continued to increase. By the end of 1956, its membership amounted to 90,000; early in February, it was 170,000; and on February 28, 190,000. On the other hand, few people adhered to the party of their own accord: the recruiting agents' strongest weapon was the threat of dismissal. Under these circumstances it is not surprising that many of these agents showed little enthusiasm for their work. This may be illustrated by the following incident which was reported to me. An AVO agent searching the premises of the Writers'

Union was asked by the Union's secretary whether he was proud of his job. The agent made sure that no one was eavesdropping, and said: "No, I'm not, but what can you do—a man has to make a living."

This reply is indicative of the state of mind of many of Kadar's agents and perhaps of Kadar himself. The majority of these people adhered to the party only under pressure, and they well know that other men, more courageous, look upon them as collaborationists. Indeed, to join the Hungarian Communist party in January, or February, 1957, was to make common cause with those who had kidnaped Nagy, imprisoned Maleter, executed Dudas, and deported thousands of insurgents.

But it is precisely human cowardice, weakness, and despair that the party uses to set people against each other, to compromise and intimidate them, and to bind them to each other by ties of complicity. The party is now composed of traitors despite themselves, collaborationists who abhor what they are doing. What mattered for the party was to put the machinery in gear, to impose its domination at all costs. As for beliefs and convictions, they would come later. Communist propaganda has always exploited with particular effectiveness one psychological truth: that most people end up by liking what they are doing, because they need to believe that they are good, and because they are only too happy when they are provided with excuses for their weakness and cowardice.

It is thanks to such methods, unsavory but effective, that by the end of February, 1957, the Kadar regime seemed well on the way to consolidation. To be sure, this consolidation can only be precarious so long as the Soviets refuse a true compromise. But no nation deprived of weapons, and of outside help, can live permanently in a state of insurrection. Late in February, the Central Committee could draw a partially satisfactory balance sheet of its achievements since November 4.

The country was still recalcitrant, but the party was back in the saddle.

Economic Prospects

One of Kadar's strongest cards in his striving to restore the totalitarian regime is the people's need for order and work. Similarly, one of his strongest arguments is that the uprising had caused considerable damage to the economic life of the nation. One of its results (but due chiefly to Russian bombardment) was to worsen the housing shortage. According to the report of the United Nations mission headed by Philippe de Seynes, published on January 18, 1957, about 40,000 dwellings had been destroyed or damaged during the uprising. Transportation services had also suffered heavily: after October 23, 1956, 1,500 to 2,000 trucks were destroyed or left the country with refugees. Finally, according to official estimates, the almost complete stoppage of work for ten weeks reduced the national income by about 25 per cent, or 10 billion florins.

The principal difficulty facing the government in its task of rehabilitation is a shortage of raw materials and fuel, which was acutely felt even before the insurrection, particularly in transportation. The drop in oil production (1,600,000 tons in 1956; estimate for 1957—1,700,000 tons) is due to the forced methods of exploitation applied in previous years by the Soviet supervisors of this industry. Coal production (22,300,000 tons in 1955, and an estimated 24,000,000 tons in 1956) dropped considerably as a result of prolonged strikes and the desertion of the mines by a large number of workers. In December, 1956, the labor force in the mines dropped from 100,-000 to 50,000. In January, however, a certain number of them returned to work, and the government recruited several thousand additional miners from among workers and employees who had been laid off in other industries. But the productivity of the miners dropped considerably. The government expected to be 3,000,000 tons short during the first half of 1957 and 2,000,000 tons short during the second half. This deficit will be partly covered by the Soviet Union, which undertook to supply about 700,000 tons of coal before March, 1957. But Hungary cannot count on any notable contribution from Poland, which is beset by her own difficulties. As for the power plants, in January, 1957, they produced only three quarters of their normal output of current.

Under these circumstances, the government, after compelling the workers to resume work under penalty of nonpayment of wages, on December 30 decided to reduce the production of industries consuming coal and current. One third of the labor force of the Pecs uranium mines was dismissed. In February, 1957, the food industry operated at only about 60 per cent of its former capacity; light industry at half or less; heavy industry at 20 to 25 per cent; and chemicals were down to 10 per cent.

According to official estimates, the number of the unemployed will reach from 100,000 to 200,000 in 1957 (*Nepszabadsag*, December 23, 1956). To this number one may add that of the partially unemployed, which is estimated at 700,-000 to 800,000, or about 30 per cent of the total number of workers, who will receive for a limited period allocations of from 300 to 600 florins. The government made an effort to return to agriculture a large part of the 300,000 to 400,000 peasants who had been drafted for industrial work in the course of the last seven years.

The food situation during the winter 1956–1957 was not critical despite the bad harvest and the reconstitution of stocks. But the peasants lacked fodder and were compelled to slaughter livestock. Early in March, 1957, Budapest began to suffer from a shortage of bread and flour.

At the beginning of his tenure, Kadar, for demagogic reasons in order to compensate the workers for their lost freedom, decreed considerable increases in wages (from 8 to 10 per cent for wages lower than 1,200 florins). In January, 1957, the value of the industrial output was estimated at 3,000,800,000 florins, while production costs rose to 4,000,600,000 florins.

On the other hand, according to the estimates of the Seynes mission, Hungary needed to import 60,000 dollars' worth of consumer goods during the first half of 1957. The value of the exports for the same period is estimated at 600,000 florins, or 10 per cent of the normal figure. Hungary was virtually compelled to suspend the execution of her trade agreements; the deficit of her trade balance will amount to 140,000,000 dollars for the last two years.

"To relieve the country of its economic troubles," *Nepszabadsag* said on December 29, 1956, "we need, among other things, foreign loans." But Kadar's Hungary was badly placed to obtain loans from the West—this fact served to increase Kadar's unpopularity. To resort to the International Bank was impossible, because Hungary is not a member of that institution. Aid could come only from the East. The Soviet Union undertook to grant to the satellite she had crushed credits amounting to 1,000,000,000 rubles—20 per cent of this sum in free currencies, and the rest in goods. The total assistance promised to Hungary by the Socialist camp amounts to about 50,000,000 dollars, a sum that falls far short of the country's needs.

Measures were enacted to put the handicraftsmen back on their feet (their number had dropped to 58,000 in 1953 from 300,000 in 1948), and to encourage individual peasants. But whereas in 1945, after the ravages of the war, the Hungarians had set to work with enthusiasm and hope, the resumption of work in 1957 took place in a frightful psychological climate. The people had to earn a living, but they were cheerless, filled with a kind of helpless rage and despair. This inevitably affects productivity. The population feels that it is being gradually deprived of all the gains of the uprising, and that by working it serves the cause of its oppressors. The resulting discouragement is all the greater because Hungarians like work well done. One of the major grievances of the workers under Rakosi was that they could not do a good, careful job, because work was badly organized. The workers' councils, to which the government appealed (while subjecting them to all sorts of vexations) to stimulate the workers' interest in the task of rehabilitation, seemed themselves torn between the wish to produce and the will to resist. Thus the Hungarian example proves that a degree of freedom, democracy, human faith, and hope is indispensable for the workers of a modern industrialized nation. But in 1957 the Hungarians felt that they had been reduced to slavery.

CONCLUSION

NEVER has a revolution been the object of so many controversies and slanders as the Hungarian insurrection. Some writers describe it as reactionary, counter-revolutionary, and foreign-inspired. Others refer to it is a Titoist or national-Communist movement. Still others underline its proletarian features, such as the part played by the workers' councils. It has also been called an anti-Communist rebellion par excellence, which may mark the beginning of the end of world communism. Finally, it has been described as an accident that marked only a temporary setback to communism and that has no intrinsic importance.

The heated disputes, almost theological in character, to which the uprising has given rise among ideologists of all schools, are no doubt to be accounted for by the novelty of this uprising—by the fact that it does not fit the various patterns evolved by theorists of revolution. The Hungarian insurrection was the first large-scale revolution under a Communist regime, the first anti-totalitarian revolution. For Communist ideologists, the very idea of such a revolution is a contradiction in terms; genuine revolutions, they believe, can be made only against capitalism, or at least against capitalist imperialism, and can be led or at least inspired only by the Communist party. But the Hungarian revolution was directed against the Soviets and the Communist party; its goal was Hungary's secession from the Socialist camp and the replacement of the one-party totalitarian regime by a parliamentary and democratic government. It is not surprising, then, that the powerful

Communist propaganda machine has been bent on proving that the uprising was "objectively" counter-revolutionary despite the well-established fact that the majority of the insurgents, particularly the workers, had no intention whatever of restoring the former feudal and capitalist regime, of joining the North Atlantic Pact camp, or of giving up certain fundamental conquests of socialism. Even independent, nonconformist writers, who are not controlled by Soviet propaganda, have been disturbed by some unexpected features of the uprising, namely, by the presence among the insurgents, along with Communists and Socialists, of purely nationalist, and even reactionary and clerical, elements.

Now, one of the most important contributions of the Hungarian revolution to contemporary thought lies in the circumstance that it compels us to revise our ideas of the nature of revolutionary movements. More particularly, for Marxists of all shades, or for non-Marxist Socialists and liberals, the Hungarian revolution is a solemn warning, a summons to serious self-criticism. They must ask themselves: Are not our theories, our understanding of the world in which we live, lagging behind actual developments? Has not the stagnation of Soviet thought spread beyond the boundaries of communism; has it not infected non- and anti-Communists, and the entire European left?

And yet, a close examination of the events in Hungary reveals that they do not contradict the classical concept of revolution. According to Marx, a revolutionary situation arises when "the social forces of production at a certain stage of their development come into conflict with the existing conditions of production, or with the juridical forms of these, i.e., the property relations within which they have hitherto evolved, and which fetter, instead of furthering, the development of the productive forces. At that moment there opens an era of social revolutions." (Marx, *Contribution to the Critique of Political Economy*.)

If we set aside the nineteenth-century economists' jargon in which this definition is formulated, we find that it fully applies to the Hungarian uprising. This uprising was the result of an acute conflict between the majority of the Hungarian producers and the political, economic, and social conditions in which they were forced to live. The majority of the population felt that the Rakosist regime was an obstacle to both individual and national prosperity. The writers and artists were hampered by censorship; the workers were fettered by a form of planning which ignored their legitimate aspirations and deprived them of the defensive weapons that they had formerly used against capitalist exploitation. The technicians were obstructed in their work by incompetent party agents. The peasants rebelled against forcible collectivization. The entire population felt that its productive energies were being crippled in the name of the most progressive ideas and of a religion of productivity; and that the Communist leaders had set up, in the name of rational planning, an essentially anarchistic and irrational regime.

The malaise produced by the Rakosist lies, by the contrast between official optimism and nauseating reality, is at the very source of the Hungarian revolt. It was a revolt of a people nauseated by the regime's lies, by the total incongruity between the regime's theories and practices. The insurgents condemned the "system" in the name of its own principles. The Hungarian Communists had behaved as if their faith in collectivism was sufficient to prove its superiority over all other systems. But it is not enough to have faith in the virtues of planning; it is also necessary to know how to plan. The value of a system must be measured not by the ideas it champions, but by the creative intelligence of the men who apply these ideas. It would, of course, be false to infer from the Hungarian events that communism or Socialist planning is a total failure. But these events did reveal the total failure of a specific Communist experiment, that which was conducted between 1948 and 1956; and they cast a lurid light on the errors, weaknesses, and crimes that marked the various Communist experiments conducted outside Hungary.

The possibility of a popular revolution against a Communist regime has not always been denied by Soviet theorists. Even Stalin acknowledged in his last work that "a revolutionary explosion is not entirely impossible in the Soviet Union." Everything depends, he said with surprising common sense, on the policy pursued by the leaders: "If the leaders pursue a correct policy, the contradictions cannot degenerate into antagonisms, and will not result in a conflict. But not so if our policies are unsound. Then a conflict will be inevitable, and our conditions of production may become a serious obstacle to the development of the productive forces." After Stalin's death, however, the party leaders dropped the thesis that an explosion was possible under the Soviet regime; they decided that it was safer not to speak of the devil. They adopted another thesis, according to which the Communist system develops slowly and harmoniously. Is not the party endowed, by definition so to speak, they argued, with the ability to recognize its defects and to correct them before it is too late? But the assumption that a popular revolution is impossible under a Communist regime is an act of faith rather than a scientific insight. No system is a priori safe from explosions. Soviet society is characterized by antagonisms that are more and more difficult to conceal; and the Hungarian revolution was precisely one of those explosions which Stalin had foreseen. Like all revolutions in history, the Hungarian revolution took place at a moment when the popular forces were pressing for a structural reform of the system, and when the representatives of the regime proved incapable of controlling and channelizing the popular movement, when they resisted it without possessing the moral and material resources needed to master it.

Every revolution—the Hungarian revolution merely reminds us of this truth—is a complicated, contradictory affair. It is an eruption of a people's unconscious, with all of its infantile, reactionary, progressive elements. The longing for a return to the past asserts itself side by side with the yearning for change and progress. Everything is pell-mell, sympathetic and antipathetic, reassuring and dangerous, beautiful and violent. Every revolution is a return to the state of nature—that is what makes it both frightening and sublime.

The Communists, however, had come to identify every revolution with a *coup d'état,* to conceive of revolutions as events prefabricated in the Kremlin offices. That is why they have so consistently attacked an event which proves that revolutions are not the monopoly of the Russian Communist party, and that under given circumstances they can even aim at overthrowing that party. That is the first lesson that the Hungarian revolution teaches us.

The second lesson is this, that one must not trifle with the soul of a nation, with national sentiment. Our philosophers of history have underestimated its importance. In fact, the founders of Marxism recognized the importance of nationalism, and even made it the cornerstone of their philosophy of history; but their Soviet disciples, even though Lenin and Stalin theorized about nationalism, flouted it in practice as they did other important elements of Marxism. Referring to the revolution of 1848, Engels wrote to Kautsky: "For a great nation it is a historical impossibility to be concerned with any internal question so long as it has not achieved national independence. Before 1859 there could be no question in Italy of socialism, nor even of a republic, and yet the republicans of this country were the most energetic." And he added: "No international cooperation is possible unless it is between equals. . . . So long as

Poland remains divided and subjugated, no genuine Socialist movement can develop there. . . . Every Polish peasant and worker, once aroused from his apathy and made conscious of public affairs, is first of all confronted with the fact of national oppression. . . . To do away with that oppression is the condition *sine qua non* of all sound and free development."

These words were true in 1882; would their truth have vanished in 1956? Lajos Mesterhazi, a writer who jumped on Kadar's bandwagon in January, 1957, has maintained that the struggle for national independence, which was justified in countries subjugated by the Hapsburgs or the Czars in the nineteenth century, has now become obsolete because today the major conflict is that between the Socialist and the imperialist camp, and because the Socialist camp is by definition the champion of the independence of small nations. This is proved, according to this writer, by the fact that Soviet Russia supports the anti-imperialist struggle of the colonial nations. But aside from the fact that no party doctrinaires can decide whether or not the feelings or resentments of a nation are legitimate, one thing the Hungarian revolution has proved is the imperialist, and even colonialist, nature of the Soviet regime.

To be sure, the Soviet Union has always posed as the guardian of the national interests of her satellites. To some extent, the Soviet Union actually did defend these interests, particularly if they were identical with her own strategic interests, as was the case in Czechoslovakia, Bulgaria, and to some extent in Poland (the Oder-Neisse line). It is also true that Communist propaganda has tended to integrate the patriotism and national traditions of her satellites into Socialist internationalism. It was out of this practice that was generated the Hungarian paradox: thanks to the Communist teachings, which made use of Hungary's national revolutionary traditions, those nineteenth-century romantic, liberal, and democratic ideas, as reflected in the writings of Petofi and Vorosmarthy, found a far wider response after 1945 than ever before. It may even be said that thanks to the Communists those traditions for the first time reached the entire population, which immediately turned them against its oppressors and educators. Thus it was the Communists who really taught the Hungarians the meaning of their history; it is they who gave or restored a liberal and democratic orientation to Hungarian nationalism. In this sense, they actually played the part of apprentice sorcerers. For in Hungary, as elsewhere, patriotism—to which the Soviets appealed for reasons of doctrine—was scarcely compatible with recognition of Soviet superiority.

Russian imperialism, by reason of the specific nature of Russia's economic and strategic needs, differs in many respects from the imperialism practiced by the old colonial powers and from American economic and ideological expansion. Nevertheless, the Hungarian revolution proves irrefutably that the nations belonging to the Eastern bloc did not join it of their own accord. The Soviet Union forced Hungary to join it by gradually depriving her, with the help of the Communist party machine, of the last vestiges of her national independence, and by breaking the democratic *élan* of the period between 1945 and 1948. Despite Stalin's solemn promise not to export the revolution to other countries, the overwhelming majority of the Hungarians knew that the Communist regime had been imposed by foreigners. Moreover, the Soviet Union implanted the myth of her ubiquitous superiority in Hungary by such crude methods that she defeated her own purpose. As I have shown in my book, *Histoire des Démocraties Populaires,* Soviet Russia in persecuting what she called "bourgeois chauvinism" actually persecuted the patriotic instincts of the Eastern nations. Instead of eliminating patriotism, she only repressed it. Chauvinism and anti-Semitism re-emerged under new forms, as could be seen in Poland after October, 1956.

By preventing the Eastern countries from forming one or more federations in 1945, the Soviet Union acted against their interests and aspirations. Furthermore, it has been established beyond all doubt, after the revelations made by Gomulka in Poland and by several economists in Hungary, that the Soviet Union derived considerable unilateral advantages from her economic relations with her satellites. It has only recently been learned that in Soviet-Hungarian commercial transactions the ruble was calculated as equal to 2.93 florins, while the actual rate of exchange was 1.50. The Hungarians were more than right in speaking of the Soviet spoliation of their country.

As we have said, early in 1956 the Soviet leaders made an effort to change this state of affairs; they displayed a willingness to make concessions to Hungarian national sentiment, and after the Twentieth Congress they dangled the prospect of a socialism in conformity with each country's traditions. But they never went beyond promises or formal concessions. In actual fact, the Russians had never ceased intervening in internal Hungarian policies. They authorized the party to rid itself of Rakosi only to impose Gero. Then they intervened militarily at Gero's request. And finally, when the Hungarian people were struggling to recover their freedom, the Soviet Union intervened a second time, and Khrushchev justified this second intervention, in a reply to a letter from British Labor leaders, by saying cynically that the Hungarian people had chosen to adhere to the Warsaw Pact and could not change their mind. Thus, according to the Russians, Hungary was tied to Russia by "indissoluble bonds." It may be recalled here that the "choice" referred to by Khrushchev had been made by Rakosi, Hegedus, and Gero, whose "monstrous errors" were recognized even by Moscow, and who had not consulted the Hungarian people before adhering to the pact.

Thus the October insurrection unveiled the falsity of a propaganda which portrays the Soviet Union as the natural

guardian of peoples who strive for independence. The French
Communists, who are the most zealous champions of Algerian
nationalism, were compelled by their faith in the party and by
party discipline to deny the legitimacy of Hungarian or Polish
nationalism. But the facts are there. The Polish and Hungarian
nations have existed for more than a thousand years whether
or not this fact is in conformity with the Communist theory of
history.

The popular and national revolution in Hungary exploded
the Stalinist myth, the big lie of the "happiness" of the oppressed nations, on which Sovietism had been imposed to
camouflage colonial robbery and the defense of certain strategic conceptions, which are, incidentally, misguided. "From
now on we shall no longer be the playthings of a colonialism
camouflaged as socialism, and we shall no longer serve as
pawns on a chessboard to carry out a conqueror's plans," we
read in the first issue of the newspaper of the liberated trade-
unions, *Nepakarat* of November 2, 1956. Hungarian freedom
lasted only five days; but those five days were enough to give
a new meaning to the phrase "national independence."

This is not to say that national independence is the supreme
value. Genuine international solidarity must certainly be
prized more highly than national independence. But when a
nation has been oppressed, exploited, or subjected to coercion,
achievement of independence is a progress. The Socialist
camp, despite the attempts at reform made in 1955–1956, cannot be regarded as a free union of nations, but rather as a Holy
Alliance of Communist party machines aiming at securing
Soviet hegemony. That is why the Yugoslavs, despite their desire for a rapprochement with the Soviet Union, rejected the
Soviet thesis according to which a nation's adherence to socialism must inevitably be followed by its adherence to the Socialist
camp (cf. the speech of Popović, February 2, 1957). After
their reconciliation with Yugoslavia, the Soviet leaders seemed

to disavow this arbitrary thesis, and to grant the possibility that a Socialist country may be effectively independent and stay outside the Soviet bloc. It was this shift of the line that gave new impetus to the national Communist movement in various satellite countries, where it had been repressed since 1948.

However, following the Polish and Hungarian October revolutions, Soviet policy has stiffened on this point, and resumed the Stalinist tradition demanding obligatory adherence. But these revolutions dealt a mortal blow to another myth, that of "inevitable unity." The common ideology can no longer be regarded as a sufficient foundation for the Eastern bloc. Gomulka justified Poland's continued adherence to this bloc by "reasons of state" as much as by ideological solidarity. Now, a Communist who invokes "reasons of state," i.e., the national interest, is a national Communist. On the other hand, the Hungarian revolution demonstrated the precariousness of national communism, at least in satellite countries. In actual fact, national communism, that is, a regime independent of foreign control, exists only in Russia, China, and Yugoslavia. In these three countries the present regime was brought into being by revolutions and authentic civil wars from which the Communist parties emerged victorious. To these three countries one might add Czechoslovakia and Bulgaria, in which the Communist parties represent important forces; their submission to Moscow is more or less voluntary, and at all events is not accounted for by the presence of Soviet occupation forces.

In the other satellites, communism, whether national or not, depends on the Kremlin's good will. Thus, in Hungary, national communism, i.e., a reformed Stalinist system, could have been set up by Imre Nagy only if the Russians had encouraged him or at least if they had not sabotaged his experiment. By intervening against it, they compelled the national Communists to appeal to the masses which were not Communist. As a result, the movement touched off by the national Communists developed into a movement for democratization, in which national communism was merely one current among several. In countries where a Communist regime can be maintained only with the help of Soviet tanks, national communism is conceivable only as a compromise, with the national Communists serving as mediators between the Soviet leaders and the anti-Communist nation. If the Communist leaders refuse to run the risk of being ousted by the right, a risk which is implied in the setting up of a national Communist regime, the national Communists have the choice only between surrendering national sovereignty and a revolutionary struggle (peaceful or not) in alliance with non-Communist democrats and nationalists. In this sense, the Czechoslovak newspaper, *Rude Pravo,* is perfectly right in establishing an intimate connection between national communism and what it calls "revisionism," that is to say, rejection of the dogmas proclaiming the need for a dictatorship of the proletariat and the leadership of the Communist party. "National communism," said *Rude Pravo* in an editorial of February 25, 1957, "tends to replace Marxism-Leninism by revisionism, and champions revisionism as a specific national path leading to communism." The truth concealed behind this partisan terminology is that wherever the Communists strive to take root without the help and protection of the Soviet army and refuse to doom themselves to inefficiency for the sake of pleasing the Moscow doctrinaires, they must revise their ideas and resume the revolutionary democratic traditions of the working-class movement. But the Soviets cannot recognize this necessity to revise the doctrine without undermining the ideological foundations of their power. This accounts for their ruthlessness, even after Stalin's death, in combating heresy.

The revisionism of the Hungarians (and of the Poles) attacked one of the fundamental ideas of Stalinism—the myth that a one-party regime is indispensable for the advancement

of socialism. Even the Yugoslavs are still firmly attached to
this myth, as proved by the shocking imprisonment of Djilas.
It is true that Khrushchev, in his report to the Twentieth Congress, recognized that socialism can be achieved by various
methods, all of them equally legitimate. He even admitted that
a parliamentary regime could lead to socialism. But the Moscow exegetes emasculated this view, and suggested that the
parliamentary method was for them that of Prague or Budapest, where the Stalinists, taking advantage of a democratic
and parliamentary prelude, infiltrated and overthrew the regime to set up a one-party system.

It has not occurred to any of these exegetes that the dictatorship of the proletariat, that is to say, government by the laboring classes (workers, peasants, intellectuals), could be exercised under a multi-party system. Now, it might be granted
that the one-party system was provisionally necessary to defeat
the bourgeoisie, to lay the foundations of socialism, to free the
productive forces, to emancipate the minds, and to remove
the capitalist and feudal fetters from the productivity of labor.
But once the bourgeoisie had been destroyed, nothing justified
the maintenance of the one-party dictatorship with the police
terror it implied.

In 1937, Stalin advanced the absurd theory according to
which the class struggle increases rather than decreases in
violence after the revolution. This theory served to justify the
great purges, and the show trials, and to transform Soviet justice, with the help of the diabolical Vishinsky, into a handmaiden of the political police. Recently, an article published
in the organ of the Central Committee of the Russian party
(issue of November, 1956) asserted that this theory, which is
the very essence of Stalinism, was still valid for Hungary and
the other people's democracies, if not for Soviet Russia. The
passage in question deserves to be quoted: "The events in
Hungary are nothing but a phenomenon reflecting a sharpen-

ing of the class struggle. . . . The experience of Soviet Russia
has proved that the resistance of the defeated exploiting classes
gains in intensity at the most crucial moments of the revolution
and the building of socialism. These events have once again
proved that the building of socialism is impossible without
class struggle, without pitiless repression of the defeated
classes, which, supported by outside imperialist resistance,
seek to enslave the workers and the peasants. . . . That is why
we must condemn the opportunistic theses according to which
the transition to socialism can be effected on the basis of harmony between the class interests and the complete reconciliation between the exploiters and the exploited, which would
exclude the class struggle. Obviously, the Hungarian workers
advanced just demands in criticizing the errors actually committed in the building of socialism. But this was exploited by
the counter-revolutionary gangs which unleashed the Fascist
terror."

This article in the official party organ reflected a tendency
to return to orthodox Stalinism which had appeared since the
early days of October and heralded a radical shift in policy.

The fact that the Soviets must resort to "pitiless repression"
as their only defense against nations that they both despise and
fear discredits once and for all the one-party system, under
which this repression is inevitable. For socialism is above all
an expression of the legitimate aspirations of the popular
masses; and even the Kadar government imposed by the Russians did not at first dare to come out openly in favor of the
one-party system. This is another great lesson to be learned
from the uprising: The system created by Stalin stands revealed as a parasitic and reactionary force, as a regime of terror that decimates the elites, demoralizes the technicians and
economists, emasculates political life, and silences the best
writers and artists.

In fact, even Communists who cannot be charged with revisionism realized that it was impossible to continue the one-party system in the form inherited from Stalin. Gomulka, who, after the January elections, did everything to put a brake on the revolutionary *élan* of the Polish people, decided to grant some scope and freedom of action to the former coalition parties. The Chinese, too, quickly drew the necessary theoretical conclusions from the Hungarian situation. Thus *Yen Minh Yeh Pao* (People's Daily) of November 21, 1956, said: "A political system admitting several political parties is possible in a Socialist democracy like China, and is perhaps preferable to the one-party system if it is properly understood." The article from which the above quotation is taken was written by Shan Shih Yuan, member of the permanent committee of the Chinese Democratic League.

In Hungary, incidentally, the foundations of socialism (the agrarian reform and the nationalization of industry) were not laid by one party, but by a democratically elected coalition government—a fact that is often overlooked. Rakosi and Gero merely appropriated these reforms and made the world believe that they had carried them out at the cost of immense sacrifices —but those sacrifices were actually made by the Hungarian people impoverished and tortured by the Horthy regime, the German occupation, and finally by the Russian occupation. For the Hungarians, as for most other people who had had a taste of the Stalinist methods, the one-party system was absolutely incompatible with socialism. An ever-increasing number of people realized that the revolutionary achievements could be preserved only if political life was organized on a democratic basis, if every form of dictatorship was rejected, and if freedom of conscience and speech was respected.

To be sure, a totalitarian country that returns to democracy runs the risk of a civil war. But risk is inseparable from life as such! Democracy implies a continual struggle for a better society, against oppression, against exploitation of one class by another, and against the enslavement of peoples by capitalists or empires. A political democracy based on the collective ownership of the means of industrial production has never been tried; it is difficult to set up such a regime in underdeveloped countries where the populations would have to be persuaded (but not compelled) to "tighten their belts" for some time in order to develop industry, and where the peasants would have to be induced (without being persecuted) to co-operate with a view to applying modern technology to agriculture. But no one has the right to underestimate and to despise the people's intelligence, and it is certain that the Stalinist methods of industrialization and collectivization failed lamentably outside the Soviet Union.

Finally, the Western Communist parties' adherence to the Stalinist doctrine of the one-party system has hampered the efforts to rebuild popular fronts, to revive a political left, and to lay the foundations of a socialism which in the West can only be democratic.

That is why the lessons of the Hungarian uprising must be meditated on by all those who remain devoted to Marxism and the Socialist ideals. An alliance of the proletariat, the peasants, and the intellectuals—this alliance which Stalinism champions in theory but sabotages in practice—will be possible only on a democratic basis.

Another problem raised by the Hungarian revolution concerns the monolithic character of the Communist party. This revolution strengthened most Communist parties, including the Soviet party, in their conviction that freedom of discussion within the party must be very restricted in order to prevent dissensions and the ultimate liquidation of the Communist movement. "If the Hungarian party had not been deeply divided," it is said, "the uprising could never have broken out." This is no doubt true; but it shows only one side of the medal. For the question is: What *caused* the division of the party? In

Hungary's disastrous situation, this division seems to have been inevitable. It would doubtless never have assumed such proportions if during the preceding years the party leadership had not demanded blind obedience on the part of the members, imposing a climate of suspicion and terror within the party itself.

Later, the Stalinists made it impossible for the Nagyists to express their views and to organize an open debate of proposed solutions; and their persistent efforts to preserve the dictatorship led to the disintegration of the party. As we have seen, the party members joined the insurgents; the party organizations did not exist, for they had been emptied of meaning as a result of Stalinist stubbornness and stupidity.

To be sure, the organizational problems of a workers' party are complex, and there can be no workers' party without a minimum of discipline. But the Hungarian uprising has disclosed the boundaries beyond which discipline becomes tyranny, the party machine becomes divorced from the mass of the militants, and the party is transformed into an army whose officers can no longer count on the obedience of their soldiers in the event of battle.

The Hungarian revolution compels us to reflect on the meaning of the dictatorship of the proletariat. Here again the actual facts have singularly contradicted Marx's theory according to which "the proletariat will use its political domination to wrest gradually all capital from the bourgeoisie, in order to concentrate all means of production in the hands of the proletariat organized as a ruling class, and to achieve a rapid increase of the productive forces."

To the Hungarian proletarians who rose in arms against the police regime, the theory that described them as the ruling class of the people's democracy could only seem a bad joke. To them, the alleged dictatorship of the proletariat was a dictatorship over the proletariat—a totalitarian dictatorship under which the proletariat as a social class disposed of no means of defense against exploitation.

That is why the Hungarian revolution was marked by a tendency to abolish central state control: it gave rise to autonomous government bodies (revolutionary committees, workers' councils) that took the place of the administration whose authority had collapsed. The Communists have described this tendency as anarchistic, and accounted for it by bourgeois, anti-Communist, and anti-Socialist influences. They point out that the Hungarian working class had undergone considerable transformation during the recent years. The number of workers almost doubled as against 1938 because several hundred thousand peasants and a large number of handicraftsmen, shopkeepers, and even members of the former bourgeoisie have been integrated into industry. These new elements brought new blood to the industrial proletariat, but also traditionalistic ideas; and the regime had neither the time nor the means to re-educate them. One reason for this was that the regime had appointed several thousand Communist workers to posts in the political and economic administration. These workers' cadres became the most zealous defenders of the regime; but at the same time they moved away from the working class, and acquired the mentality of employers or foremen. During the insurrection the workers treated them as class enemies; on the other hand, the same workers often elected proletarized bourgeois elements to the workers' councils.

There is little doubt that the altered composition of the proletariat played a part in giving an anti-Communist accent to certain spontaneous actions of the workers during the uprising. Nevertheless, those who reject *en bloc* all the expressions of this spontaneity evidence a singular aberration of mind. Such a distrust of the proletariat often characterizes ideologists who (usually out of a bourgeois sense of guilt) flaunt a naïve faith in the proletariat's mission and consider this class the chosen people of history. Such ideologists see the proletarian as a stereotype character; they do not know, they are not interested in, the real proletarians; the proletarian in the name of whom they speak is an abstraction, a prefabricated being who lends himself without resistance (precisely because he does not exist) to be used as cannon fodder for the great strategic plans of the ideologists.

To be sure, the workers' spontaneity must not be made into a new idol, the demiurge of history. To overestimate the importance of spontaneity in modern history, particularly in the history of revolutions, would be no less erroneous than to overestimate the importance of ideas and organization. But it must be recalled that from its beginnings the international workers' movement has been characterized by the alliance and interpenetration of intellectuals and manual workers, philosophers of action and militant workers. Such an interpenetration also preceded the events of Hungary: for instance, the idea of forming workers' councils came from intellectuals who had followed the Yugoslav experiment. But this idea found a fertile soil, and could mobilize the workers' spontaneity, precisely because it expressed major aspirations of the proletariat.

This leads us to a crucial development that the Hungarian revolution has fully confirmed: The totalitarian state which reduces all political organizations to impotence, which actually atomizes society, has itself become no less alien to the social body than the absolutist, anti-national dynasties of the past. When this state was overthrown, nothing was left; and since the entire administrative armature, down to the factory committees and municipal councils, was regarded as the instrument of the fallen government, everything had to be rebuilt from scratch.

This was of course an exceptional case, which may not recur in this form anywhere, and we should not draw rash conclusions from it. But basic historical trends are always best seen in the light of exceptional cases. Thus the French Revolution had been unique in history until the Russian Revolution; yet it was the French Revolution that disclosed most eloquently the depths of the popular mind at the moment of breaking traditional bonds. Similarly, the Hungarian revolution has disclosed to us the deep aspirations of the people under a regime in which the bourgeoisie had been expropriated and private enterprise replaced by state capitalism.

Now, the first of these aspirations manifested by the workers is for a freely elected professional representation, and for the recovery of the means of struggle against the state employer (the right to strike), whether this employer is Socialist or not. With a rare unanimity, the Hungarian proletariat rejected totalitarianism as a system of government. This is a serious warning to ideologists. Those who put their faith in the supreme effectiveness of total planning may continue to do so, but they can no longer speak in the name of the proletariat. For the proletariat, when it recovers freedom of speech, demands freedom and democracy; and it insists on being distinguished, as a productive class, from the administrators, even if these administrators are elected.

Another workers' aspiration is for active participation in factory management. The workers' councils formed during the insurrection not only took over the functions of the trade-unions in representing the workers' interests; they also demanded the right to appoint and dismiss managers, and to perform the functions of boards of directors.

All this, of course, does not prejudge the future: the manner in which the principle of workers' management should be applied will be discussed a great deal, and will have to be subjected to the test of reality. But the principle itself has now been firmly established and has become inseparable from socialism. The Yugoslavs must be credited with reviving the idea of "direct workers' management," which Lenin dropped reluctantly because of the Russian people's political and economic immaturity. But the world proletariat has developed since 1921, and so have the methods of scientific management. Science and the workers' interests converge to give a new meaning to workers' participation in management and profits, to the principle of centralization by way of decentralization.

From the first days of the uprising, the various workers' councils began to form regional and national federations, just like the local revolutionary committees that had taken over the functions of the municipal councils. Similar organizations were formed by the students, intellectuals, teachers, and technicians. Thus, on the ruins of the totalitarian state, there began to take shape a new state of workers, peasants, intellectuals, and the youth—a state that was no longer to be an instrument of oppression in the hands of a privileged clique, let alone of a Red aristocracy based on a police force and foreign troops.

As mentioned before, the central workers' council in Budapest enjoyed great authority, and assumed the status of a second government which opposed the occupant and its agents. There is good reason to believe that if the Nagy Cabinet had not been ousted and deported, and if the Soviets had respected the explicit will of the Hungarian people, a useful co-operation might have developed between the national government and the central workers' council, representing the working class. This central workers' council was about to become a consultative body attached to the planning office and the economic ministries. Nagy would probably have put those ministries in the hands of men designated by the central workers' council. We know that he appointed one of the chiefs of the military revolutionary committee his minister of defense.

Thus a Socialist democracy of a new kind, "a government of the people, by the people, and for the people," was taking shape. In my introduction to the special Hungarian issue of

Les Temps Modernes (January, 1957), I said that some of the features of this Hungarian revolutionary democracy brought to mind "the peaceful, federalist, and productive anarchy that Proudhon, Bakunin, and Kropotkin once dreamed of." Jean-Paul Sartre criticized this remark as "more Proudhonian than Marxist." Indeed, we are attracted to Proudhon's anti-authoritarian socialism, for the simple reason that people are closer to us than gigantic but inhuman state machineries. This is not to say that we completely reject state control, even though we somewhat distrust it. And the Hungarian insurgents themselves, whose motives we have tried to elucidate, were far from that primitive anarchism which rejects not only the totalitarian state but the state pure and simple. All the workers' councils acknowledged the need for a central government, but they wanted this government to reflect the national interests and the long-repressed social aspirations of the people. That was not anarchism, it was a democracy in process of being born—a democracy which was not given the time to define itself and to choose between traditional parliamentarianism and a new type of popular representation based on trades and professions.

The Hungarian revolution has also revealed the artificiality of the totalitarian solution of the peasant question. The moment the central government began to lose its grip, the peasants dissolved most of the collective farms (70 per cent) and reconstituted the old peasant parties, but did not turn against the city proletariat. On the contrary, they often displayed a moving sense of brotherhood with the workers. For their part, the workers through their councils solemnly recognized the peasants' right to determine their fate, and repudiated the Communist authoritarian paternalism, which treated the peasants as minors, depriving them of any opportunity to express their own ideas and to organize themselves in accordance with their own wishes.

Needless to say, the problem of modernization of East European agriculture will not be solved merely by granting the peasants freedom of action. But after the Hungarian revolution it is difficult to conceive of a solution of this problem which would not imply peasant democracy, for the Soviet type of agricultural collectivization has been completely discredited by the Communists. Collectivization by force defeats its purpose, and dooms agriculture to stagnation. Peasant cooperation must be the work of the peasants themselves. Some indications toward such a development appeared during the uprising: those collective farms which had decided to continue formed an agricultural revolutionary committee and rid themselves of the incompetent Stalinist policemen who had previously ruled them. Sandor Meszaros, vice-chairman of this committee, listed the demands of the peasants in a radio address. These were: substantial state subsidies with a view to mechanizing agriculture; rehabilitation of peasant leaders who had been unjustly eliminated; a statute governing an independent co-operative movement; adherence of this movement to the national federation of co-operatives.

We may note in this context that the Hungarian revolution has also exposed one of the most grotesque errors of the Communist regime, the suppression of handicrafts and retail trade, without putting anything in their place. This was a quite useless sacrifice on the altar of total planning.

The crucial part played by the intellectuals in arousing the national, political, and social awareness of the Hungarians could set an example to all revolutionary intellectuals in whom Stalinism has fostered a sense of inferiority with regard to the working class. Stalinism has also cleverly exploited the intellectuals' sense of responsibility (or guilt), by posing as an indispensable intermediary between the intelligentsia and the proletariat.

The Hungarian example—and so many other examples—proves that the Stalinist machine, far from being a valuable intermediary, is an obstacle to fruitful contacts between intellectuals and proletarians. The Hungarian example, moreover, confirms that the essential function of the intellectuals is to seek the truth, to speak this truth (even at the risk of losing social privileges or of being treated as were Hay, Tardos, and Gali), to express the people's aspirations, and to create works dictated by a free inspiration.

The Hungarian writers' congress of September, 1956, will no doubt stand as a landmark in the history of the human mind. The resolutions of this congress add up to a declaration of the rights of the man of letters, the rights of the intellectual and writer. Even before the uprising, the Hungarian writers and journalists had taken an oath never to lie again, never to practice intellectual diplomacy, and always to speak the truth. They took this oath after realizing that the *sacrificium intellectus* they had made for the sake of the party, by silencing their doubts, closing their eyes to embarrassing facts, and forcing themselves to have faith in the absurd, was a useless sacrifice. The party itself had not profited from it; on the contrary, the lying propaganda had helped to separate it from the people, to make it the victim of a kind of collective paranoia.

The writers and journalists made the important discovery that lies cannot contribute to progress. They discovered that the workers' Socialist movement needs the truth that can be achieved by means of discussion and the free confrontation of ideas. They also discovered that the right to speak freely and to criticize, which seemed to them indispensable if they were to perform their function, was inseparable from the right of the people to struggle against exploitation and oppression.

The independent republic of the Hungarian writers, which was proclaimed in September, 1956, and which two Soviet interventions failed to subjugate, was the first breach opened in the totalitarian system. It foreshadowed the revolutionary committees and the workers' councils: for the autonomy of the intellectuals is inconceivable without the democratization of other areas of public life. The struggle against censorship logically led the writers and journalists to the struggle against all oppressive features of the regime.

It may be asked whether the right to criticize everything, to put everything in question, does not lead necessarily to anarchy. Had not Dery, Tardos, Hay, and their companions touched off a movement that they later proved unable to control? It must be granted that the Hungarian intellectuals, although they enjoyed a tremendous prestige, did not reveal themselves as leaders and organizers at the moment of crisis. The revolution with its excesses bewildered them. But can this fact be used as an argument against intellectual freedom? The truth that writers and journalists formulate, the ideas that they launch, are explosive only if the situation itself is explosive. This contention is not novel, but it bears repeating from time to time.

Most Communist leaders interpreted the Hungarian events as proof that intellectuals must be kept in check. But the campaigns against intellectuals launched by the various Communist parties only served to underline their own terrorist and retrograde nature. The arrests and convictions of writers and journalists in satellite countries will serve at the same time as a warning to those intellectuals who still believe that communism advances culture. The truth is that totalitarianism is incompatible with intellectual freedom, and that it reduces the intellectual to the role of propagandist.

The intellectual is nothing if he cannot say what he thinks. An intellectual who serves totalitarianism is a traitor to his calling. He betrays the young whom it is his duty to guide. One of the most moving aspects of the Hungarian uprising was precisely the meeting of the youth with the intellectual elite, their communion in the idea of freedom. Who will ever forget the nobility, purity, boldness of the Budapest students, who were the vanguard of the uprising? The Kadar government later tried to explain the students' hostility to the party dictatorship and Soviet control by the fact that "class standards" for admission to the universities had not been strictly applied. According to a statement made by Magda Joboru, deputy minister of public education, only 40 per cent of the students were of worker or peasant extraction. But this statement is contradicted by previously published statistics, and, as we have said, the students would have even more violently anti-Soviet if more of them had been of proletarian extraction.

The Hungarian revolution has cast a crude light on the internal contradictions of the Communist regimes. It has revealed the basic unpopularity of these regimes, and for this reason it is undeniable that it has dealt a severe blow to the international prestige of the Soviet Union, and compelled her leaders to revise their entire strategy in Eastern Europe. After November, 1956, the Kremlin took a number of measures to consolidate the Communist bloc, to strengthen the unity of the party machines, and to check the spread of national-Communist and revisionist ideas. The Communist world has lost a great deal of its self-assurance, and has been put on the defensive.

Must we conclude that the October uprising marks a victory for the West? I do not think so. There can be no question, in particular, of a victory of capitalism over socialism. While rejecting the totalitarian Communist system, the Hungarian people displayed no desire to return to the bosom of capitalism. The path of the uprising did not lead backward; it led forward, toward the democratization of socialism.

But even apart from the question of the social regime, the West lost a battle in Hungary by its failure to give effective assistance to the Hungarians, by making it possible for the

Russians to prove to all their satellites that revolution does not pay.

Some persons think that under the prevailing circumstances the West could not help the Hungarians without running the risk of war. I am not convinced that this is so, although such a hypothesis cannot be summarily dismissed. Others accounted for the obvious caution of American diplomacy by the fact that the United States still recognizes the Yalta agreements, which assigned Eastern Europe to the Russian zone of influence.

However that may be, in November, 1956, the Hungarian people, who are traditionally oriented toward the West, were no less disappointed than the Czechoslovak people had been in 1938. They, too, had their Munich; they, too, were deserted by the West; and Soviet propaganda did not fail to exploit this fact.

However, a revolt is never calculated in advance; and the Hungarians, though they see themselves surrendered to the mercy of the Russians, have not resigned themselves to servitude. Hungarian resistance continues; it has only changed in form. The inner deterioration of the situation in Hungary has inevitable repercussions in other Communist countries; Hungary is a seedbed of crises and of a malaise that threatens to spread beyond her borders and prevents the Soviets from clothing their totalitarian paternalism in that debonair and relaxed garb that Khrushchev has tried to give it since 1955. The Polish crisis, too, is far from resolved. East Germany is laden with dynamite. Under these circumstances the day is perhaps close when the Soviets will show themselves willing to accept a general settlement of the problems of Eastern Europe.

For it is certain that the Hungarian question can be solved only within the framework of a general European settlement. "Germany remains the key to the situation of Western and

Eastern Europe," I said in the conclusion of my *Histoire des Démocraties Populaires*. Now, the integration of all of Germany into the Soviet orbit is a prospect as intolerable for Western Europe as it is for the security of the United States. On the other hand, the military strengthening of West Germany is one of the bogeys that Russia uses to frighten the Poles and Czechoslovaks into submission.

It is also clear that while the present balance of forces prevails, the Soviet Union will not let go of the territories she holds without some compensation. Thus, if the East European nations are to recover their independence, the West must be ready to contribute something toward the cost. It remains to be seen whether the West can pay a price acceptable to the Russians without weakening itself. More specifically, the question is whether the West will consent to the neutralization of Germany as the Western contribution to the reorganization of Europe, and as the price paid for the withdrawal of Soviet troops from Hungary and the other East European countries that are under Soviet domination.

At all events, the Hungarians know that their fate depends on the answer to this question.